THE LIFE OF CHARLES DICKENS

VOL. I

John Dickens.

from an Oil Painting by John Jackson. R.A.

THE LIFE

OF

CHARLES DICKENS

AS REVEALED IN HIS WRITINGS

BY

M.A., F.S.A.

'. . . A merrier man,
Within the limit of becoming mirth,
I never spent an hour's talk withal :
His eye begets occasion for his wit ;
For every object that the one doth catch,
The other turns to a mirth-moving jest,
Which his fair tongue—conceit's expositor—
Delivers in such apt and gracious words.'
LOVE'S LABOUR'S LOST

IN TWO VOLUMES—VOL. I

WITH A PORTRAIT AND FACSIMILE

HASKELL HOUSE PUBLISHERS LTD.

Publishers of Scarce Scholarly Books

NEW YORK. N. Y. 10012
1973

HASKELL HOUSE PUBLISHERS LTD.

Publishers of Scarce Scholarly Books

280 LAFAYETTE STREET

NEW YORK. N. Y. 10012

Library of Congress Cataloging in Publication Data

Fitzgerald, Percy Hetherington, 1834-1925.
    The life of Charles Dickens as revealed in his
writings.

    Reprint of the 1905 ed.
    1. Dickens, Charles, 1812-1870. I. Title.
PR4581.F59 1973   823'.8   72-4115
ISBN 0-8383-1607-7

MARCUS STONE, R.A.

DEAR MARCUS STONE,

I cannot deny myself the pleasure of associating you with myself in this volume, which tells so much of the genial Boz whom we both knew so well.

You and I were of the old Gadshill times, and heard the chimes at midnight in its cosy chambers. Did not these ring back to us on that night in the early time of the Boz Club, at its first meeting, when each stood up and rehearsed his recollections?—A strangely interesting meeting it was: it seemed to bring back the spirit of the amiable Boz himself.

This work will, I hope, remind you of many a pleasant incident, and sometimes of your old friend,

PERCY FITZGERALD.

PREFACE

'YOU have everything in Dickens,' wrote the late Jules Verne: 'imagination, humour, love, charity for the poor and oppressed—in fact, everything.' And I lately heard Lord James of Hereford make this statement: 'Dickens was one of the best public servants England ever had.' Here are two very novel and striking utterances, which really furnish the text for these volumes.

The popular idea is that Dickens was merely a great story-teller, with vast tragic and humorous gifts. But the Frenchman's utterance goes far deeper, and might be greatly developed. 'You have everything in Dickens.' That is, you have qualities which he united with a unique and original form of story. This story forms a picture of his time, owing to the minuteness of the observation—enforced by an elaborate system of pictorial illustration, and so continued for over thirty years.

Here we find characters innumerable—nearly two

vii

thousand, as some have reckoned ; lessons of religion —so far as they go ; sermons and prayers ; the broadest fun and refined satire ; grief of the most poignant and real kind, so that it seemed to be felt for a living person. His own friends and other personages walk through his stories. Everything that he felt, suffered, did, or observed, is there. All the attractions of his native land—its cities, streets, buildings—are shown in the most poetical fashion. He made his figures so vivid that they now seem as though they had lived ; and their abodes have become just as interesting and important as those of historical personages. So that the things he sets forth are not tales, but narratives or chronicles ; his own life and experiences are retold with entrancing effect. He had learned by cruel apprenticeship something of every trade and profession. He knew what the depth of misery was, and also the height of prosperity and success. What wonder, then, that we find ' everything in Dickens.' And this novel and interesting inquiry is what has been attempted in these volumes.

Of this having ' everything in Dickens,' a striking illustration is furnished by a work of my own on ' Pickwick '—an elaborate dictionary or cyclopædia of some hundred closely printed pages—which,

without undue exaggeration, supplies alphabetically
a complete *tableau* of the world as it was in the
thirties. It might, indeed, be called the 'life and
times of Mr. Pickwick and of his friends'; indeed,
there is little reference to the story.

During the past thirty years or so, Charles
Dickens's image has been so vividly and so un-
interruptedly in my memory that at this moment
I see him as clearly, and hear the cadences of his
flexible voice as distinctly, as though he were standing before me 'in his habit as he lived.' No one left
so deep an impression; it was as indelible as that of
some great performer whom we remember in our
youth. There are survivors who have known him
as well; but not having the training, the power of
observation, the catching of fleeting expression, in
which all of his 'school' were disciplined, they
might naturally fail to convey what they saw and
felt. Therefore it is that I come to this grateful task
well equipped as a 'literary man' and observer,
and also as one who enjoyed rare opportunities of
intimacy with him.

It will be noted that I have spoken with great—
perhaps undue—freedom of my own affairs, introducing details of private matters connected with
myself and my family. The sole reason for these

confidences was the desire to exhibit Boz's truly engaging sympathy and interest in his friends, and the hearty fashion in which he entered into their plans. I fancy the reader may be inclined to welcome these trivialities, though I know I run some risk in putting them forward. And I may add : that I seem to myself to have known him as thoroughly as I did the oldest of friends, to have understood his feelings and all he was aiming at — he always spoke so freely and so gaily, and without the least restraint. It is nearly thirty-five years since his death, and yet I recall distinctly the amazingly expressive eyes ; even the tint of his cheeks, the very *crimpled* wrinkles of enjoyment about his mouth.

I cannot but think that this free personal element in the character of the narrator will furnish a better idea of the subject than would the correct orthodox form. When Forster, in the third volume of the ' Life,' became somewhat scared by criticism, and suppressed himself a good deal, there was a serious loss. Again, the having been Forster's friend and protégé, perhaps the only one of the junior writers whom he admitted to his confidence, gives me yet another advantage.

So thus the reader and lover of Dickens may come to the conclusion that there is no one of his sur-

viving friends who, at this moment, could supply so
full and intimate an account of his life and character.
He will have seen how close and familiar were our
relations, and how confidential he was with me;
how much I saw of him, how much I observed
and retained in my memory. Then, too, I was
all but the pupil of this eminent man—I wrote
four or five long novels ·under his supervision,
he suggesting alterations in the plot, devising new
situations, and adding in the proofs innumerable
passages and turns. We used almost weekly to plan
new subjects for new essays. Not long ago, his son
was good enough to state in a little speech that I
was really 'a favourite of his father's.' This close
literary connection gives, therefore, an authority and
an interest to these pages.

I perhaps owe some apology for using the rather
familiar *sobriquet* 'Boz' so often in these pages.
But time was when it was in everybody's mouth, and
was displayed by himself in his title-pages. It then
conveyed a great deal more than it does now. There
is, besides, in it a pleasant tone of affectionate
interest; further, it is short and compendious.

                                PERCY FITZGERALD.

ATHENÆUM CLUB,
        August, 1905.

ERRATA

VOL. I

Page 13, line 5 of footnote, *for* ‘ Randon ’ *read* ‘ Random.’
Page 77, *omit* note.
Page 92, line 17, *omit* ‘ as he had enjoined in his will.’
Page 114, line 16, *after* ‘ years ’ *add* ‘ ago.’
Page 200, line 9, *for* ‘ Land’s ’ *read* ‘ Landor’s.’
Page 206, verse at foot, *for* ‘ tongue ’ *read* ‘ wit.’

VOL. II

Page 20, line 7, *omit* ‘ himself.’
Page 242, line 6, *after* ‘ rollicking ’ *insert* ‘ Pickwick.’
Page 274, *omit* line 13.

CONTENTS OF VOL. I

BOOK FIRST
YOUTH AND MANHOOD IN KENT

CHAPTER I
DICKENS'S LOVE OF ROCHESTER

CHAPTER II

THE BULL INN, AND ITS COMPANY

CHAPTER III

WATTS'S CHARITY—EARLY RELIGIOUS TRAINING

CHAPTER IV

SCHOOLING—DEAN HOLE

CHAPTER V

MANOR FARM—CHRISTMAS WRITINGS—THE MARSHES—COBHAM

CHAPTER VI

BROADSTAIRS—CANTERBURY

CHAPTER VII

DOVER—BOULOGNE—FOLKESTONE

CHAPTER VIII

GADSHILL

CHAPTER IX

JOHN FORSTER

CONTENTS OF VOL. I

BOOK SECOND

PICTURED PLACES IN TOWN AND COUNTRY

CHAPTER X

BOZ AND BATH

BOOK FIRST

YOUTH AND MANHOOD IN KENT

CHARLES DICKENS

CHAPTER I

DICKENS'S LOVE OF ROCHESTER

It is said that since Dickens's death some fifteen
or sixteen biographies of him have appeared. Yet,
perhaps, the best and fullest account, and his real
autobiography, is to be found in his writings. His
childhood and youth was for him, odd to say, the
most fruitful portion of his course ; it was then that
he observed and took stock of life, and garnered
up the knowledge that he later put to such profit.
The scenes and personages about him became his real
microcosm, which he was later to expand and magnify
on a larger canvas. For he later gives us all that
he saw and felt at that early period under innumerable disguises ; and these personal memories
he adapted in the most ingenious, clever fashion to
his stories.

This is no fanciful theory. It can be shown from
even a few chapters in 'Pickwick' how we can restore

the general Rochester life, society, and manners in
the midst of which he had passed his childhood.
He was but ten or twelve years of age when he
quitted the town ; and yet fifteen years later he
could give the most minute and vivid sketches of
the place, showing how the child had been observing
everything that passed before its eyes—seeing and
marking down all its humours, absurdities, and
fashions.   Rochester is one of the most scenic of old
towns.   Its framed houses in the High Street, its
picturesque Guildhall, Market House, and other
buildings, now ' stand where they did'; we almost
expect to see fellows in hoods and jerkins, and bearing
quarter-staves.   As the guide-books put it, ' there is
quite an air of bagwigs and ruffles.'   One cannot be
surprised at Boz's enduring love, or that it was the
first place he wrote about in the opening chapters of
' Pickwick,' and the last that he was writing of when
the pen dropped from his hand.   Even in ' Martin
Chuzzlewit,' when he has got his hero to the United
States, he makes him announce to a native, ' I was
born in Kent.'   As it was with Stevenson, so it
was with Boz.   Both were constantly looking back
to their childhood's days, and drawing from that
source a store of the freshest feelings and impressions.   At that distance of time the retrospect
seemed still inviting and all-important ; the inter-
vening interval was uninteresting compared with

the old childish dramas. They were fairy-tales, full
of pleasing, happy visions.

It is astonishing what a number of persons—
travellers, visitors, and gossips—have found their
way to this good old city, mainly inspired by two
stories, 'Pickwick' and 'Edwin Drood.' I recall
the time when 'Pickwick' was as 'dead as a doornail'
—and that even in Boz's own day. He never spoke
of it himself, nor did he much care to hear it spoken
of. Forster used to say that it was a clever young
fellow's first attempt. Not long since, when opening
the exhibition in London of the Dickens Fellowship, of which I was president, I told the company a little story which has since gone the round
of the press, illustrative of this incuriousness. Once
when I was travelling with Boz, a quiet gentleman,
an amiable enthusiast, gained admission, carrying a
little parcel, which he opened. It was, he assured
Dickens, of enormous value—being, in fact, as he
called it, 'old gold.' 'Yes,' he repeated several
times, 'this is real *old gold*, and I value it as
such, and, depend upon it, it will be valued by-and-
by.' And what was this lump of 'old gold'? A
copy of 'Pickwick,' one of the genuine first issues.
Boz was good-naturedly amused, and encouraged
his devotee, and when the latter had retired, still
repeating that it *was* 'old gold,' he smiled, and
said he was evidently a good, honest fellow, though

he laughed heartily at the 'old gold' notion. The treasure, in fact, was then worth about ten shillings. Well, as I told our Fellowship, this worthy man was infinitely wiser in his generation than either Boz or his friend ; for that copy of ' Pickwick,' supposing it in good and clean condition, and equipped with all the advertisements and addresses, is now worth from fifty to a hundred pounds — a very fair approach to 'old gold.'

Do we not best recognise the tender graces of the garden county of Kent on some soft summer morning when, going down to Dover, holiday-bound, to embark, a Continental journey before us ; the sylvan beauties of the country, the patches of genial red, the thick, rich foliage of the hops, all attracting and giving us a longing for such pastoral charms ? As we draw nearer to Rochester, the grim old Castle on its height, the silvery river winding below, the bridge, even the quaint back view of the houses in the old main street, with the ancient lantern of the Guildhall, come into view. But in a moment all has flashed by. How welcome, too, the first view of Canterbury Towers, cream-coloured, solitary, with something like a village at their feet ! then more hop-fields and poles in their serried and well-foliaged rows. How novel and delightful they look, though seen a hundred times before ! Then, presto ! change to the ports —Dover, Folkestone, and the ever-freshening sea.

Even the Old Kent Road, which starts beyond Westminster Bridge, and toddles on its rickety way for a mile or two, has its associations, with its faded old-fashioned terraces and dismal gardens. Yet is it not the official road to the beautiful garden county?

But those who live in the dreamland of associations, who, as they walk abroad or lie awake, love to entertain themselves with vivid well-coloured pictures and scenes of what is gone by, have quite a different image of this favoured county from the ordinary person. For everywhere they see the figure of Charles Dickens with his magic wand—*i.e.*, pen—in his hand. For myself, I cannot describe how the places I have named—Rochester, Canterbury, Dover—affect me. It recalls the wonderful dream of mail-coaches that ' my uncle ' saw near Edinburgh. Not only Boz himself, and the living persons that he grouped round him, but the figures that he created—the society, the old life that he pictured—people the places. A tender light seems to suffuse it all. To visit Rochester and wander through its cheerful and still old-fashioned streets is almost a distressful thing, like visiting scenes where those that we loved once lived, but who are now no more. At every turn what ghosts confront us! Pickwick and his ' followers ' walking through the streets ; the ballroom at the Bull lit up and crowded with company ; the Dockyard notables ; the military ; the duel

near the fortifications or Lines ; the annual review ;
and the jovial Wardle and his family. Delightful
recreating scenes, pictures, and figures! Then we
turn to 'Edwin Drood,' when quite a new set of
beings present themselves, the old Cathedral as
background, with the tall houses, Minor Canon Row,
the Nuns' House, Durdles, the auctioneer, and the
rest. We wander past the Six Travellers' old
hospice, and call up the delightful Christmas pictures
given in his journal. Then 'Great Expectations,'
with Satis House, where such weird, uncanny doings
went on, and the pompous Pumblechock exhibited
his humours. We take up ' Down at Dulborough,'
and see the boy Dickens at his school. In short,
we cannot call to mind any place so charged with
agreeable and touching memories or so peopled with
figures and images. It sets us looking back as into
our own lives—to some far-off holiday time when
we began to know all these people, and now fondly
think of their doings and what a delightful time we
had of it, that now all are gone, and passed into the
ewigkeit. Such is the potent charm of old Rochester.

One such Rochester vision that comes back on me
of that first visit, forty years ago, is a memory of
'Sir Cloudesley Shovel.' I had gone in on a Sunday
walk from Gadshill and brought back 'Sir Cloudesley
Shovel.' It struck me as having something quaint
in the sound. I suppose someone had told me of

him. But he is, as it were, all over the place. Sir
Cloudesley's portrait hangs in the Guildhall, and
Sir Cloudesley had been more than once Mayor. I
think there is an inscription on one of the buildings,
and I suppose it was thus I picked up the notion.

This constant recurrence to Rochester, from the
first to the last hour (literally) of his life, was, I have
a conviction, based on a peculiar turn of mind and
thought, which is found only in delicate and highly-
strung souls. It was in Rochester, as I have already
shown, that he had learned and studied life, and had
seen the world—a little world, it is true, but for him
full of variety. It seemed to him a very Capital,
the figures of its society great and all-important.
With his quick, vivid observation he had noticed
and studied all. His little mind had worked all into
shape and laid it securely by. It was wonderful in
a lad not yet ten years old ; yet there is no exaggeration, for all his exquisite humours of Rochester—
the rich touches of character—can have been noted
at no other time. Boz, naturally, felt affectionately
towards the *alma mater* which had thus brought
him success. Never, too, had he written with such
ease, fluency, and enjoyment. His boyish days at
Rochester were, besides, happy days for him, and
he recalled with pleasure the balls at the Bull, the
schoolboy parties, and Christmas dances at Cobtree
Hall.

There is a letter of Dickens's, written five years
before his death, and now appropriately placed in
the Eastgate House Museum, which shows what
his feelings were towards the old city.   He writes :
' I beg you to accept my cordial thanks for your
" Curious Visits to Rochester."   As I peeped
about its old corners with interest and wonder
when I was a very little child, few people can
find a greater charm in that ancient city than
I do.—Believe me, yours faithfully, and obliged,
CHARLES DICKENS.'

It is curious to find in him here the note of what
I am contending for—viz., that even in his far-off
childhood he had stored up his knowledge and had
exercised his keenest observation.   He was ' peeping
about with interest and wonder,' studying the place,
in short ; and having done so, he says, he finds in this
the secret of its attraction for him.   This wonderful
boy, as he roved about Rochester with very much
opened eyes, was actually able to take note of a
crying public abuse, and laid by for future use, as it
was to prove, some details which excited his horror
and indignation.   ' I cannot call to mind now,' he
told us in 1858, ' how I came to hear about Yorkshire schools when I was a not very robust child
sitting in by - places near Rochester Castle, with
a head full of Partridge, Strap, Tom Pipes, and
Sancho Panza ; but I know that my first impressions

of them were picked up at that time, and that they were somehow or other connected with a suppurated abscess that some boy had come home with, in consequence of his Yorkshire Guide, Philosopher and Friend having ripped it open with an inky penknife. The impression made upon me, however made, never left me. I was always curious about them, and at last resolved to write about them.' This shows very clearly how much this one of his most powerful delineations owed to childish impressions. He insists on the value of this form of experience in a remarkable passage, where he is so earnest that he really wishes us to believe that he is speaking of himself.

The second chapter of 'Copperfield,' which is entitled 'I Observe,' sets forth in the most minute way his very earliest impressions. But it must refer to the time when he was at Portsea, and not more than two years old.

'Neither, as she approached her old home now, did any of the best influences of the old home descend upon her. The dreams of childhood—its airy fables, its graceful, beautiful, humane, impossible adornments of the world beyond, so good to be believed in once, and good to be remembered when outgrown, for then the least among them rises to the stature of a great charity in the heart, suffering little children to come into the midst of it, and to

keep with their pure hands a garden in the stony
ways wherein it were better for all the children of
Adam that they should often sun themselves.'

When Nicholas took down the dying Smike to the
country, to the place where he had spent his childhood, Dickens indulged in a retrospect of his own
childish days. 'With what longing and enjoyment he would point out some tree that he had
climbed a hundred times to peep at the birds in
their nests, and the branch from which he used to
shout to little Kate, who stood below terrified!
There was the old house with the tiny window
through which the sun used to stream in and wake
him in the summer mornings—*they* were all summer
mornings then—and the very rose-bush, a present
from some little lover, and which she had planted
with her own hands.   There were the hedgerows
where they had so often gathered wild-flowers
together—it all came back upon the mind, as events
of childhood do. Nothing in itself—perhaps a word,
a laugh, a look, but better than the hardest words
or severest sorrows of age.'   He then describes
how they used to go and sit on the graves in the
churchyard, wondering at the silence.   Once the
little girl was lost, and was found here by her
father, fast asleep under a tree, and the father,
taking her up in his arms, said he would like to be
buried where she was.   All this is Dickens's own

self, and his favourite sister's self; it is, in fact, an
epitome of 'the child's dream of a star' in the far-off
Portsmouth days.*

I doubt if ever a great writer was so devoted
to a single place, or made so much of it, as Dickens
did in the case of Rochester; not even the genial,
patriotic Sir Walter cared so much for his native
lakes and fells as did Boz for the obscure Rochester
district.   From the beginning to the end, from the
first to the last, he was perpetually recurring to it :
he wrote of it again and again and again at intervals,
long or short, and lived there continuously 'off and
on.'   He was at Rochester or Chatham—but both are

---

* It is remarkable, when we come to think of it, how many of
our great English stories were cast in this biographical form :
Richardson's three great novels, 'Pamela,' 'Clarissa,' and 'Sir
Charles Grandison'; Fielding's 'Tom Jones' and 'Amelia';
Smollett's 'Humphrey Clinker,' 'Roderick Randon,' and others ;
and 'Robinson Crusoe.'   In the last century Thackeray's 'Vanity
Fair' was the account of the progress of a clever adventuress in
life, 'Pendennis' was that of a young fellow traced from youth
to manhood, while 'The Newcomes' the life and adventures of a
young fellow.

Many of Scott's novels, such as 'Waverley,' 'Quentin Durward,'
'Nigel,' were similarly biographies of young men, but with plots
and subsidiary enlargements superadded.   And who shall say that
the advance of a single character through the various complica-
tions of life is not in itself a sufficient 'plot'? As Horace Walpole
has said, 'If any one ordinary person were without study or
affectation to set down all his experiences, it would be, in whatever hands,' he adds, 'a work of extraordinary interest.'   There
can be found the excitement of a plot in mind as well as in
matter, in thought, feelings, hopes baffled or realized.

one—as a child. He had his schooling there. When
he came to write his first successful book, he chose
Rochester as the subject of the opening chapters;
it was the keynote of the whole. Some of its most
prominent characters, that supply the whole interest
of the book, are found in the neighbourhood of
Rochester. When he came to be married, he chose
a place near Rochester at which to spend the honeymoon. When he resolved to be a country squire, he
selected a house two or three miles from Rochester,
which he had known and admired and coveted as
a lad. Later, to a single building in the town, the
Hospice, he devoted an entire story. In 'Great
Expectations' he returned to it again. In his
weekly journal he wrote papers describing the old
place once again. At last, when the time was
approaching for him to stay his pen and write no
more, he cast about him for a subject, and was
mysteriously drawn to the old subject of his old
town. How strange that his first as well as his
last successful effort was concerned with Rochester!
Finally, he directed in his last will and testament
that he was to be laid in Rochester. As his heart
in life was always with Rochester, so in death he
desired to be placed there.

In the seventies I doubt if any pilgrims had
begun to come to Rochester. I fancy that the
first attempt at Boz topography—now so abundant

—was by an American, Mr. Hassard, who wrote
a little book called 'A Pickwickian Pilgrimage,'
issued more than thirty years ago.   It is very
pleasant reading, and interesting as describing the
places years ago ; since when many changes have
occurred.   Then came one Frost, with his 'Dickens
in Kent,' and later the good, amiable Hughes—an
official of the Birmingham Corporation—who was
almost mad on the subject of Boz.   He came down
with his friend Kitton—no better ally could he have
—and regularly and systematically explored what he
called the 'Dickens Land' of Kent.   A large and
handsome volume was the result.   I myself have
laboured much in the same vineyard, and have
written many a volume on a subject which seems
almost fascinating.   Later came Mr. Hammond Hall
in the pleasant little book 'Mr. Pickwick's Kent';
and there are, no doubt, many more explorers.

No inn in the kingdom enjoys such a curious
literary popularity as the Bull Inn at Rochester.
And what a strange, fantastic idea is that popularity
built upon !   Innkeepers are often proud to enrol the
notable guests who have stayed under their roofs,
and set forth the great and grand patronage they
have enjoyed.   Even the Bull has sheltered Her late
Majesty when Princess Victoria, which, the tradition
runs, was owing to an accident, the old bridge having
broken down, and the royal party being unable to

proceed to London. But I fear that very real and august tarrying did not affect the world so much as the strange, mythical and shadowy group of guests who were described as having put up there, but who never *did*, who, in fact, never existed—that is to say, Mr. Pickwick and his 'followers,' with a number of other characters, all spectral. For years have pilgrims come long distances to see the rooms which these imaginary persons are *said* to have occupied. The rooms are there and the very numbers. Is not this quite a unique thing? Though occurring close on fifty years ago, we believe in it all still, and shall believe it so long as the old house stands.*

I often have read with wonder or surprise the statement in Forster's life how he and Boz and some others made a party and stayed at the Bull. Forster had not the least veneration — it never occurred to him that there were any hallowed associations. To him it seemed some ordinary hotel. The true 'inwardness' of this was that neither Boz nor Forster—'Fuz,' as Carlyle called him—thought

---

* With these feelings I am at this moment looking at a sort of prospectus, issued some time ago when there was an idea of selling the place. Alas that auctioneers and firms should not enter into the romance of the thing ! But though the trade allurements are inviting enough, I was rather saddened to find that they did not consider the Pickwickian associations a commercial asset. There was no allusion to this association, which was perhaps natural enough from their point of view !

much of Pickwick. It seemed to them no more than a comic magazine story. It is curious to think of the author and his friend and the ladies staying in the old hostelry—quite indifferent to the associations—and then contrast this attitude with the wonderful enthusiasm of our time, the visits of pilgrims from far-off countries, etc.

In my own instance the Bull is associated with at least a dozen interesting occasions, scattered through a long life. How grateful one should feel to any object which is thus tenderly associated with some cherished idol! It is a wonderful investment, for it recurs again and again, fills up one's thoughts, and furnishes entertainment for many an hour. It is, in fact, something living. One must pity the poor creatures who have no such things laid up in their mental cabinets.*

---

* I recall one special morn, when I had set off from town, at 5 a.m., on what I called my 'day's tour,' getting down to Rochester before seven, meaning to cover in the twenty-four hours a good deal of ground in France and Belgium. How delightful, and yet novel, was the old city then! The Bull was but half awake, but I turned into the coffee-room, looked out into the street over the blinds, and felt exactly as did Lieutenant Tappleton when he came to rouse up Winkle. I have never experienced anything so real as what I did at that moment. I felt as though Pickwick and Tupman and Winkle were all asleep upstairs, and that look of the street over the blinds, and the coffee-room, I carried about with me the whole day. O magic Bull—rather magic imagination which plays such freaks, and gives us palaces and jewels, and, above all, so many pleasing hours of entertainment!

So ever-welcome is the old inn to Boz's memory
that he seems never to tire of introducing it under
some disguise. Rochester is to be found, under
the name of Winglebury, in the 'Sketches.' Boz
describes it as being exactly forty-two miles and
three-quarters from Hyde Park Corner. 'It has a
long, straggling, quiet High Street, with a great
black and white clock at a small red Town Hall halfway up, a market-place, a cage, an Assembly Room,
a church, a bridge, a chapel, a theatre, a library, an
inn, a pump, and a post-office.' Could anything be
more accurate or more recognisable? He pictures
the inn of the place, the Winglebury Arms. 'It is
in the centre of the High Street, opposite the small
building with the big clock, and the principal inn,
the commercial inn, posting-house, and Excise
office—a "blue" house at every election, and the
Judge's house at every assize.'

There met the whist club of the 'blue' party;
the club of the rival party was held at the other
inn (Wright's, of course), 'a little further down.'
All the travelling jugglers and entertainers gave
their show at the 'elegant and commodious Assembly
Rooms' attached to the inn. The house he goes to
is 'a large one, with a red brick and stone front'—
that is, the porch is stone. 'A pretty spacious hall
terminates in a perspective view of the bar and a
glass case,' etc. 'Opposite doors lead to the coffee

and commercial rooms ; and a great, wide, rambling
staircase—three stairs and a landing, four stairs and
another landing, one step and another landing, half
a dozen stairs and another landing, and so on—con-
ducts to galleries of bedrooms, and labyrinths of
sitting-rooms.' The glamour of the house was
always on Dickens ; his childish dream that it was a
vast palatial edifice clung to him, the fact being that
this staircase is a modest affair enough, and the
' labyrinth' of rooms and passages nothing wonderful
in that way. He describes the London coach coming
in suddenly to the loud notes of a key-bugle. The
coach arrived with a noise, rolling over the uneven
pavement, that ' would have stopped even the large-
faced clock itself.' (How this clock remained always
before his gaze !) ' It is a sedate, odd-faced timepiece
like the dial of an enlarged repeater ! Down got the
outsides, up went the windows, up dashed the ostlers,
and the loungers, and the ragged boys, unstripping,
and un-harnessing, and unbuckling ; dragging willing
horses out, and forcing unwilling horses in.' How
often had he stood watching the scene, always a
bustling one and full of dramatic interest for a child !
It is clear from the fond iteration that the old
Bull was the cynosure, the centre of his admiring
thoughts, the apotheosis of the old town.

'The Bull,' says a sympathetic writer, 'is a pleasant
old house with a great courtyard, an ample and easy

staircase, and an abundance of old-fashioned rooms which promise ease and comfort. At the White Horse at Ipswich they to this day identify the apartment of the lady with the yellow curl-papers, the sanctity of which was disturbed so dreadfully by Mr. Pickwick ; but it is doubtful whether the rooms occupied by the club at Rochester can now be pointed out. But the ballroom in which the club uniform was worn for the first time by Mr. Jingle, while its rightful owner enjoyed his not too sober slumbers, is not at all changed, and much of Dickens's description still applies. It is one of those long assembly-rooms still to be so often seen in old country-town inns, in which agricultural and political dinners and county balls used to take place. The " elevated den " in which the musicians were " securely confined " is still there, with the wall-sconces and old-fashioned chandeliers. It is also the Blue Boar of " Great Expectations," for, although there is an inn of that name in Rochester High Street, the description fits only with the Bull. There was a few years ago a good deal of the Gadshill furniture at the Bull. The great lamp which lights the staircase came thence ; in some of the bedrooms pieces of furniture were ticketed as having belonged to Dickens ; while there was a cosy little sitting-room, almost the entire plenishings of which were said to have been brought from Gadshill at the memorable sale at which its belongings were dispersed.' To the visit of the Princess Victoria and her mother, who stayed there for a night, we owe the change in the name of the old inn, the Victoria and Bull ; but who does not prefer the old name ?

We might speculate, Why did Boz make his Jingle give the hotel and its proprietor so high a testimonial, 'Good house, nice beds'—now to be read on each side of the door in golden letters? Because, it is clear, he knew the people of the house ; he had a warm welcome there; because they let him, as a boy, see the balls and other 'fun' that went on. Even if he could not from experience testify to the 'niceness' of the beds, he may have passed by on one of his reporting journeys. How he would have thrilled had it been whispered to him that over sixty years later the hotel would, in its advertisements say ' *Vide* Pickwick'!

I fancy any Rochester native would be amused if he knew of the romantic interest excited among strangers by this old inn. He would wonder exceedingly. Some time ago an enthusiastic worshipper found his way to Rochester and wrote a very pleasing little work, called ' Mr. Pickwick's Kent.' As though anybody else's Kent was not worth considering! Pickwick, only think of it ! who never existed, to be annexing in this fashion the Kent that *did* exist. Now, this little book of Mr. Hammond Hall's—for such is the name of the

explorer—shows what a living world this Pickwickian one is.   He comes to the Bull—as we all
do—calls up the Pickwickian ghosts around him,
and then, carried away by his honest ardour, proceeds gravely to identify the particular rooms in
which Mr. Pickwick and his friends slept.*

* 'There can be no doubt,' he says, ' that the rooms shown in the
photograph are those in which Dickens put his Pickwickians to
bed ; but, as each room has an outer door, there may be a question as to which is "inside " the other—in other words, which is
Mr. Tupman's and which Mr. Winkle's.   The rooms are numbered
13 and 19, and the reason why the numbers are not consecutive
is that the outer doors belong to separate passages, each with its
own staircase.   No. 13 is on the main or coffee-room staircase,
but the occupant of No. 19, to reach the ballroom, coffee-room,
or bar, must either pass through his neighbour's bedroom or
descend to the commercial-room entrance of the inn and cross
the yard.   The statement that, after dressing in Mr. Tupman's
room, Mr. Tupman and Mr. Jingle "ascended the staircase leading
to the ballroom," suggesting, as it does, that they first descended
to the ground-floor by the staircase of No. 19, favours the belief
that No. 19 was Mr. Tupman's room ; but, on the other hand, we
are told that, after the stormy interview with Dr. Slammer in the
ballroom passage, " the stranger and Mr. Tupman ascended to the
bedroom of the latter," and it is hard to resist the conviction that
they ascended the main staircase to No. 13.

'In putting Mr. Tupman into No. 13 (" the Queen's room ") and
Mr. Winkle into No. 19, I follow what I believe to be the prob-
abilities of the story, as well as the traditions of the inn.   It should
be mentioned, however, that the traditions of the inn are so far
inconsistent that they allot No. 17—a room on the back-staircase
—to Mr. Pickwick.   Mr. Pickwick told the " boots," who knocked
at his chamber door, that Mr. Winkle's was the "next room but
two on the right hand."   Mr. Tupman's room, therefore, was the
next but one, and if Mr. Pickwick's was No. 17 Mr. Tupman's
must have been No. 19.   I prefer to think that Mr. Pickwick and

Ever partial to the Bull, Boz returns to it with fresh praise in 'The Holly Tree Inn.' 'There was an inn in the Cathedral town, where I went to school, which had pleasanter recollections about it than any of these. It was the inn where friends used to put up, and where we used to go and see parents and to have salmon and fowls and be tipped. It had an ecclesiastical sign, the Mitre, and a bar that seemed to be the next best thing to a bishopric,

---

Mr. Tupman, as befitted their age and dignity, occupied rooms 11 and 13 on the principal staircase, and that the young and sportive Winkle slept in No. 19.'

No. 17, if it was not Mr. Pickwick's room, has other points of interest for the pilgrim, for it is known to have been occupied by Dickens on at least one occasion (subsequent to the writing of 'Pickwick'), and it is now filled with furniture from his bedroom at Gadshill. It is believed to be the room referred to in the 'Seven Poor Travellers':

'After the Cathedral bell had struck eight I could smell a delicious savour of turkey and roast beef rising to the window of my adjoining bedroom, which looked down into the inn-yard just where the lights of the kitchen reddened a massive fragment of the Castle wall.'

Again, I say, consider these passages and own to the marvellous persuasion and magic of Pickwick! 'They ascended the main staircase to No. 13.' 'The traditions of the inn' are that Tupman was lodged in No. 13, and Winkle in No. 19.' Or do we 'prefer to think,' with our genial commentator, that they occupied No. 11 and No. 13? 'But if Mr. Pickwick's room was 17, then Tupman's must have been 19,' and so on. I quote all this with the greatest respect and sympathy for the writer; I am always under exactly the same feelings ; it is really a tribute to the magic powers of the story, which really hypnotizes everyone—myself included—that has to do with it.

it seemed so snug.   I loved the landlord's youngest
daughter to distraction, but let that pass.   It was in
this inn that I was cried over by my rosy little sister
because I had acquired a black eye in a fight.'   There
is something pathetic in this, for the parents and the
salmon and the tipping at the inn were not for him,
though he speaks of ' we.'

CHAPTER II

As is now well known, Charles Dickens's father was
a clerk in the Navy Pay-office, one of the public
offices ; on his slender emoluments he had to main-
tain his seven children.   These he had to take with
him from town to town, from port to port, and at
last was sent to Chatham, where he encamped for
three or four years.   In an old ' Court Kalendar '
I lately found a list of employés in the various
Government offices, and turned at once to the roll
of the Chatham Dockyard.   Here we find the name
of the 'Commissioner resident' in 1823, and who is
likely to have been in office in 1827—the pompous
Sir Thomas Clubber of the story.   He is set down
as ' Sir Robert Barlow, Kt.'   In the Navy Pay-
office we find John Dickens as fifth clerk, and it
is curious that in the ' Treasurer's branch ' we should
come upon a fellow-clerk of his bearing the name of
Samuel Tupman.   He was sent to Chatham in the
year 1819.   He was, of course, no more than a

superior clerk, with £250 a year. He first lived
at No. 11 (then No. 2) Ordnance Terrace, on the
border between Chatham and Rochester. He later
removed to a less pretentious tenement, No. 18,
St. Mary's Place, next door to a sort of 'little
Bethel.'

How interesting it is to look on the old, dilapidated
row of houses which stretches off at a right angle
to the road just at the entrance to Chatham, Ordnance
Terrace! Here was one of the houses where the
family resided. We can follow the bright, intelligent
boy as he went about—using even then his keen
powers of observation—taking in the whole Rochester
life, manners, figures, characters — civil, military,
dockyard, and the rest. There was his microcosm,
and here in little he saw a whole world. He knew
his Rochester and Chatham by heart, and, as he
knew, loved both. This is shown by his perpetual
recurrence all through his life to these early scenes.
Everything seemed stamped on his memory, all
to be reproduced later. Were the humours superadded? I fancy all was reminiscence, and that the
child had retained the comic incidents also in his
memory ; though, of course, his mature powers
added point and development. These were certainly happy, buoyant years full of enjoyment, a
contrast to the rueful days and distresses that were
impending. All this little Kent panorama we have

recorded with the utmost minuteness in his 'Pick-wick,' not merely as a story, but as a chronicle also.

Who does not recall the pleasant ball or assembly at the Bull Inn with which 'Pickwick' opens? Boz the child must have been there. He remembered every detail of the scene ; he had friends in the garrison and in the town—was, no doubt, taken in *ex gratia* to look on. He even points out to us the difference between Assembly and Ball, for this was a matter of high etiquette in Rochester life. He recalled the music, and what instruments furnished it. The 'elevated den'—who will ever forget the 'elevated den'?—could not hold more than four musicians, who had fiddles and a harp— say, two fiddles, a bass, and harp. It, however, was enough for the room. From his minute descrip-tion we could easily reconstruct the manners and habits of an English social meeting of the time—the great lady in blue satin, and her daughters also in blue ; the whist-tables ; the snuff-taking with every-body ; the gymnastic dancing ; negus in trays handed about ; waiters in striped jackets, as shown in Phiz's etching.

Boz even tells us something of the furniture with which the inn bedrooms were supplied. For he speaks of a cheval-glass—nothing less!—a token of high civilization ; only 'métropoles' now boast

them. This was Tupman's room, which must surely
have been a lady's.

Among the notabilities of the place was an old
and fat widow—of small stature and wealthy—who
dressed herself out in rich attire and a profusion
of jewels. She was very well off, and followed
assiduously by one, at least, of the officers of the
garrison. Her name was Budger, and such was
the charm of opulence that she would dance in her
absurd fashion without exciting much ridicule,
'bobbing about'; while strangers even got themselves introduced by the M.C. of the ball. Rochester,
like Bath, had its M.C.—no doubt, the local dancing-
master, who took his office quite seriously.* If her
person was fat, so was her face. She took plenty of
negus—and biscuits and other refreshment—and
finally was escorted to her carriage by one of her
admirers ; she must have had a country place or
'box' in the suburbs. She was acquainted with the
Clubbers, Bulders, and other magnates. Of course,
there must have been much amusement—at the
lady's expense—when Jingle's character and profession were in a day or two unveiled ; but, still,

---

* Budger was, perhaps, suggested by Budden, the original of
the Fat Boy. In the first paper that Boz wrote in the *Monthly
Magazine*—the one he dropped with such trepidation into the
letter-box—he was so faithful to his old Rochester love that he
called one of the leading characters by a Rochester name :
Budden.

Tupman belonged to the Pickwick Club, was going
on a visit to a well-known country gentleman's house,
and Winkle was another member ; so the whole
business, altogether, must have been rather flatter-
ing. The doctor's devotion, the danger he had
incurred for her, must have fluttered her ancient
heart, and she could not have long resisted his
advances.

Boz's mother was Miss Elizabeth Barrow, whose
father had been in the navy.* Her sister had
married a Lieutenant Allen, and, being left a widow,
had come to live in Chatham. Here she had
attracted the attention and admiration of an army
surgeon quartered there, whose name was Lammer
—so it sounded—though spelt Lamert. In ' Pickwick' he became Slammer. He was a widower,
and had a son, a great friend and ally of the boy,
who often brought him to the theatre, and helped him
to get up theatricals in the rambling chambers of
the doctor's quarters. Now, anyone speculating
over the ball scene and the attempted duel, might
have guessed that the gallant officer was certain to
win the widow. The fact of his being ready to
expose his life for her would have been so romantic!
And so it proved. Mr. Langton obtained the cer-

* She survived until the year 1863. I possess a copy of 'The
Household Narrative' for 1850 with her name in her own hand-
writing on the title.

tificate of the marriage of Dr. 'Lammer' with Mrs.
Allen :

Matthew Lamert, of this parish, surgeon, widower, and Mary
Allen, of this parish, widow, were married in this church by
license, this 11th December, 1821.

The witnesses were:

ELIZABETH DICKENS.   JOHN BARROW.
JOHN DICKENS.   GEORGE ELLIOTT.

We may be fairly certain that the little Charles—
then nine years old—was looking on at the ceremony
in one of the pews of the old Chatham church.

Thus, in the first chapters of his first famous
work, did our author introduce a little bit of family
history. The army doctor and his new wife were
soon ordered to Ireland, taking with them a servant
named Bonney from the Dickenses' household—a
name Boz used in 'Nickleby'—a regular and affectionate method of his own for registering personal
recollections and feelings, and a very pleasant method
it is.

Sir John Barrow, their relation, was an Arctic
navigator and explorer, and it is hardly fanciful to
connect him with Boz's nautical tastes, and his reading of shipwrecks and hair-breadth 'scapes and adventures at sea. From his weather-beaten, bronzed
aspect, he was often taken for some ancient much-
buffeted sea-captain.

As Barrow reigned at the Admiralty as Second

Secretary for nearly forty years, one might have
hoped that he would have done something important
for John Dickens. But how little could be done in
that sea of embarrassment—Marshalsea, bankruptcy,
etc.! The poor man could not keep even the appointment that he held of £300 a year. ' My wife's
relatives' naturally would grow tired of their impe-
cunious connection. We might be inclined to think
that Mrs. Micawber's references to her influential
relations, and their ignoring of repeated requests,
were suggested by some real experiences of the
kind.

Boz was often severe on inns,* and spoke his mind
about them in a free, almost reckless, way—mentioning their names, even—that must have brought
him threats of actions at law. We know how he
dealt with the Great White Horse, where, it is said,
proceedings were actually threatened. We may
wonder, therefore, why he gives so bad a character
to 'Wright's-next-door' house—'dear, very dear;
half a crown if you look at the waiter.' And then,
if you dined out of the house, they charged for the

* What a strange penchant he had for all inns, old or new !
Here the form and pressure of the outside made itself felt, and
went to his heart. Nothing he enjoyed so much as the cosy and
friendly shelter of the inn. He has put it in the most engaging
attitudes, and makes us long to be with him to share his comfort.
There are over a score of inns described in ' Pickwick ' alone. In
his other stories he has given us pictures of inns of the most
appetizing kind.

dinner all the same. 'Rum fellow, very.' This practice is now common enough. Wright's, which was the Crown, was a more pretentious house with a higher clientele. In an old print there is a view from the other side of the river of the Castle, etc., and the flank of the inn is shown with inscription in large letters—to be seen for a good way off by the traveller crossing the bridge. Boz also humorously declared that the political dinners at the inns were all got up by the inn proprietors to earn the carriage of delicacies from town, fish particularly.

Boz is rather hard on the state of the streets of the four towns—Rochester, Chatham, Strood, and Brompton—though his remarks must have mainly applied to Chatham. Constant smoking, drunken men, and general dirt were the chief characteristics. It is a curious change that there is not much smoking in streets now—certainly not enough to produce the strong flavour complained of by Mr. Pickwick.

The behaviour of the military in the streets of Chatham, as noted by Mr. Pickwick, must have been observed by the young Boz, particularly that of the drunken private who stabbed the barmaid with his bayonet because she refused—'serve' is the technical term—to 'draw him more liquor.' The fellow offered to pass over the matter, and we suspect it was passed over and the matter accommodated, as the publican would naturally be afraid

to lose his military customers.   The drunken soldier,
staggering through the street, was followed by the
jeers and ridicule of the small boys.   Fancy, too, an
officer arrayed in a cloak carrying about with him a
campstool—a cumbrous article as it was in those
days—and sitting down on it magisterially while a
duel was being fought!   No doubt Dr. Payne—
such was the name of the eccentric—was 'a martyr
to gout,' but it was characteristic of Rochester,
surely, that this proceeding was accepted as regular
—no one was astonished.   It is only artists who
nowadays use campstools.   It is likely Boz had
taken stock of this oddity, no doubt as he patrolled
the Chatham streets, carrying this sort of seat.

The review on the Lines made a deep impression on the lad.   He recalled every item—even
to the soldiers wearing white 'ducks,' which they
always donned by regulation after May Day.   No
one has a chance now of seeing these displays, yet
they used to be quite common.   It was the usual
method of celebrating a festival.   The various great
camps, it may be supposed, have drawn the soldiers
away.   Boz certainly overestimates the garrison, for
he says that in the 'sham battle' one side consisted
of six regiments, which implied as many on the
opposing side.   It would have been impossible for
Chatham to find accommodation for so many.
Colonel Bulder, the commander, went through many

antics, 'careering his horse,' shouting and raving in a fashion that would give, say, General Lord Roberts the horrors. Everything now is done in much more gentlemanly fashion.

This power of acute observation in a mere child may be illustrated by another instance. He was describing the trench by the side of Fort Pitt, which seemed to Winkle—who was going to fight a duel— 'like a giant's grave.' Now, everyone that sees the original of the picture will own that nothing could be more appropriate than this similitude, and it is clear that the likeness struck Boz when he was a child, and had remained in his mind ever since.

Few of us, perhaps, could answer the question off-hand, Who was Mrs. Tomlinson,—one of the guests at the ball? She was the Post-mistress of Rochester—an office, it would appear, of importance, and looked up to, for we are assured that she was the leading person of the shopkeepers of the town. The mixture of classes was odd enough, for the trades-folk attended as well as the gentry; but, of course, only the more thriving, as the charge for admission was the very high one of half a guinea. The young Boz, who was certainly present, we may be sure did not pay this high fee; he was, no doubt, brought in by his relation and allowed to look on. We wonder what was the charity for which it was given—the local hospital, perhaps.

Boz's knowledge of Rochester was indeed 'extensive and peculiar.' How well he knew all about the dockyard and military hierarchy! There was the Commissioner of 'the yard'—a really great pundit, Sir Thomas Clubber, a pompous being in a black neckerchief, over which he looked majestically at the crowd—with his stately wife and daughters 'in blue.' 'A great man, remarkably great man.' He and the head of the garrison, Colonel Bulder, were on the most intimate terms, and shared authority, like the two Tycoons of Japan. Poor Mr. Smithie was 'something in the yard,' and was glad to receive a patronizing nod from his superior. The young officer, the Hon. Wilmot Snipe, was of this choice set, and attended on the Misses Clubber —likely enough he was aide-de-camp.

Tupman was so unsophisticated as to ask who was the little boy 'in a fancy dress.' This must have been the Highland garb, which ought to have been familiar enough, as officers then walked the streets in their uniform. It was Slammer's regiment also, and his corpulent person must have looked grotesque enough in such guise.

At this time there were quartered at Chatham a good many regiments of the line. One would have thought that this large force would have been directed by a General, but they were under the command of Colonel Bulder. Among others there

2—2

were the 97th, the 52nd, and the 43rd. The rest
we do not know. Garrison theatricals were got up
by the officers of the 52nd, and were fixed for the
night succeeding the ball—that is, for May 15. It
was, of course, impossible to employ Jingle at the
ball after the exposure, so one of the officers must
have had hastily to get up his part at a day's
notice — or he may have read it. So, with all
these little details, we grow quite acquainted with
the Rochester life.

Lady Clubber looked at Mrs. Smithie through
her glass, while that lady stared at someone else,
'who was not in the Dockyard at all.' So it
descended in the scale. The common officers
had to devote themselves to the families of minor
officials in 'the yard.' The collectors' wives, 'the
wine-merchant's wife'—the young observer marked
that there was only *one* wine-merchant in the place
—headed another grade, who kept to themselves.
There was one exception, the brewer's lady, who
actually was allowed to visit the Clubbers! No
doubt the brewer gave handsome dinner-parties,
and often 'requested the pleasure of Sir Thomas
and Lady Clubber's company.' The rough, brusque
Slammer, being merely a doctor, belonged to the
middle or intermediate class. The army doctor
at that time was held in poor repute, and did
not count as an officer. How wonderfully and

acutely had Boz picked up and recorded all these
things!

It is said that these personal sketches of garrison
life at the time excited much indignation among the
military—and no wonder! for the very numbers of
the regiments were given. An old general officer
has told me that he knew an army doctor who
was quartered there at the time, named Piper, a
peppery personage, who was convinced that the
caricature was intended for him, and was with
difficulty dissuaded from making it a 'personal'
matter.

How wonderful is the touch of Boz! The slightest
thing to which he points his pen becomes magically
glorified. For instance, the white clock is rather
like the enlarged dial of a repeater—not set out
with black and gold and self-assertive, as town
clocks usually are, but a rather insipid, sheepish
thing. So Boz dubbed it 'the moon-faced clock,'
and nothing could be more appropriate.

Strolling along the High Street, as Mr. Pickwick
once did, looking at everything with a pleased
curiosity, we come to the Nuns' House—that is,
Eastgate House, which is enshrined in the fragment,
'Edwin Drood.' It is a remarkable thing that he
should have described almost every stone of the
place, and returned at last to include the few that
had escaped his vivid and romantic touch. There

is even a shadowy image of this Eastgate House in
'Pickwick,' where Mr. Pickwick, hurrying off to
Bury on one of his quixotic expeditions, hides himself in the garden of the young ladies' boarding-
school. He asked what its name was, and was told
Westgate House. 'In the midst of Cloisterham,'
writes Boz, 'stands the Nuns' House, a venerable
brick edifice, whose present appellation is doubtless
derived from the legend of its conventual uses. On
the trim gate enclosing its old courtyard is a resplendent brass flashing forth the legend, "SEMINARY
FOR YOUNG LADIES—MISS TWINKLETON." The
house-front is so old and worn, and the brass
plate is so shining and staring, that the general
result has reminded imaginative strangers of a
battered old beau. Whether the nuns of yore
habitually bent their heads to avoid collision with
the beams on the low ceilings of the many chambers
of the house, whether they sat in its low windows,
telling their beads, whether they were ever walled
up alive in odd angles and jutting gables, is
unknown.' This venerable mansion is an almost
perfect and original specimen of the old English
house—as old, it is said, as the Elizabethan days,
and quite scenic in its disposition of gables, mullioned
windows, and bays. What a character it has, and
what strength and compactness to have stood so
long, in a state of forlorn neglect, regarded, it would

almost seem, with indifference, handed over for any
purpose to anyone that wanted it or would occupy
it ! During the past forty years I have seen it under
all these changes and transmutations, which it seemed
to contemn, defying men—and time—to do their
worst. I first noted it on the memorable day when
Boz himself 'personally conducted' me round the
Rochester 'lions,' good-naturedly acting as show-
man. On many a visit since I have passed it by,
looking at it with interest—at its groined walls and
glistening mullioned panes—the whole lying in a
sort of shadow, seemingly uninhabited. Once when
I went in I found it a workman's club, a sort of
institute or meeting-place; but it always showed
the same ruined and neglected air. One might
have hoped that when it was niched into 'Edwin
Drood,' and called so quaintly 'the Nuns' House,'
a change might have come about in its unhappy
case. But no; it still mouldered on. How it
escaped being regularly pulled down and cleared
away — as being a standing nuisance — seems a
marvel. But it stood and stood, until at last came
the happy day when it occurred to the Rochester
City Fathers that it was a treasure for their town,
and would harmonize well with their ancient Guildhall, and the Corn Exchange, the moon-faced clock,
and Watts's, and the rest. It has now, therefore, been thoroughly and judiciously repaired and

set in order as the Town Museum. One or two
rooms have been set apart and devoted to the
memory of Dickens—as was, indeed, fitting. A
large bust of him in bronzed metal has been set
up on a handsome pedestal—my own work—and
I have also contributed some fifty or so of portraits
and other memorials of the great writer.

It is somewhat significant that as in 'Pickwick'
he made Westgate House a young ladies' boarding-
school, so in 'Edwin Drood' he made Eastgate
House a young ladies' school. Since Dickens's
death—or some time before, I am not certain which
—the house was actually a young ladies' school.

Of all Rochester monuments, there is one
whose disappearance we might most lament, the
ancient and noble bridge which used to cross the
river—a grand and imperishable structure which
might have stood to this hour. Imagine it being
built in the year 1392, in the reign of Richard II.!
I always lament that I did not see it. How fine,
how appropriate, was it as an entry to the old city—
under shadow of its great Castle—with its eleven
arches and gray and solemn aspect! It is extraordinary what a destructive *furia* will at times seize
on men. As 'Alice in Wonderland' has it, the
spirit of uglifying, or of uglification, is as strong as
that of beautifying. In 1850 the Goths and
Vandals of the county had settled to destroy the

old monument. True, it was already destroyed for
pictorial effect by two horrible railway bridges—
each made as ugly as conceivable—and now it was
thought desirable to run a third alongside. One of
Mr. Murray's guide-men tells, in congenial spirit,
the process, and it is amusing to read how fitting
and appropriate it all seems to be to *him*. ' This
bridge,' he says, ' though massive and picturesque,
was too narrow and inconvenient for the wants of
modern traffic, and the foundations of the present
structure were laid by Messrs. Fox and Henderson.'
Then we are told of a ' cluster of iron cylinders sunk
below the bed of the river, as far as the hard chalk.
There is the ' swing-bridge,' an awful gamboge-
coloured thing, crescent-shaped. ' The machinery
here employed should be carefully examined. The
entire weight to be moved is upwards of two hundred
tons, yet it is readily swung by two men at a capstan.'
Alas! what is an old and monumental bridge to this
sort of feat? ' The destruction,' the chronicler goes
on, ' of the massive old bridge was commenced in
1856, under the care of the officers of the Royal
Engineers. . . . Some of the materials have been
used in the Esplanade on the east bank of the
river.'

The view from the bridge that so affected Mr.
Pickwick on his morning stroll always seems to me
the most delightful of pictures. It is an idyllic

scene, and most faithfully expresses even the present 'tone' of the place. 'Bright and pleasant was the sky, balmy the air, and beautiful the appearance of every object around, as Mr. Pickwick leant over the balustrades of Rochester Bridge, contemplating nature and waiting for breakfast. The scene was, indeed, one which might well have charmed a far less reflective mind than that to which it was presented. On the left of the spectator lay the ruined wall, broken in many places, and, in some, overhanging the ruined beach below in rude and heavy masses. Huge knots of sea-weed hung upon the jagged and pointed stones, trembling in every breath of wind; and the green ivy clung mournfully round the dark and ruined battlements. Behind it rose the ancient castle, its towers roofless, and its massive walls crumbling away, but telling us proudly of its old might and strength, as when, seven hundred years ago, it rang with the clash of arms, or resounded with the noise of feasting and revelry.* On either

---

* Longfellow, Dickens, and Forster are associated with Rochester Castle by an odd and awkward incident. Both were about to show their poet friend the old building, when, as Forster says in his best oracular way, 'they were met by one of those prohibitions which are the wonder of visitors and the shame of Englishmen. We overleaped gates and barriers, and, setting at defiance repeated threats of all the terrors of the law coarsely expressed to us by the custodian of the place, explored minutely the Castle ruins.' The only explanation would seem to be that charges for admission were made.

side, the banks of the Medway, covered with cornfields and pastures, with here and there a windmill,
or a distant church, stretched away as far as the eye
could see, presenting a rich and varied landscape,
rendered more beautiful by the changing shadows
which passed swiftly across it, as the thin and half-
formed clouds skimmed away in the light of the
morning sun. The river, reflecting the clear blue
of the sky, glistened and sparkled as it flowed noise-
lessly on ; and the oars of the fishermen dipped into
the water with a clear and liquid sound, as their
heavy but picturesque boats glided slowly down the
stream.'

A charming sketch ! We always think of these
vivid words when looking on the river. There
is a tinge of placid sadness and affection here, and
the genial author, then in the storm and stress of
London life, was, no doubt, recalling the happy old
days spent in the place, when he would wander into
the enclosure and gaze up and down the river. He
may also, like the ' Dismal Jemmy,' have been rue-
fully contemplating his sad prospects—an improvident
father struggling with debt and difficulties, and the
poor chances of anything ever being done to put
him forward in life. Could the brilliant youth have
imagined that years later, when his name was in
every mouth, one of these balusters would have
been presented to him, which he was to fashion into

a sundial and place in his grounds? It was a pretty, suitable tribute.*

But with the old Rochester Bridge he has associated an incident of a more tender sort, in the pilgrimage of the boy Copperfield along the Dover Road. This old Dover Road was full of romance for him. He knew every rood of it, and when entertaining Longfellow held out to him a progress in a chaise along the royal road, the postilions equipped in red jackets. These little touches Boz delighted in. They were his simple pleasures. ' I see myself,' says David, ' as evening closes in, coming over the bridge, at Rochester, footsore and tired. . . . I was afraid of spending the few pence I had, and was even more afraid of the vicious looks of the trampers I had met or overtaken. I sought no shelter, therefore, but the sky, and, toiling into Chatham—which, in that night's aspect, is a mere dream of chalk and draw-bridges, and mastless ships, in a muddy river, roofed like Noah's arks—crept at last upon a sort of grass-grown battery, overhanging a lane, where a sentry was walking to and fro. Here I lay down near a cannon.' We could all of us find our way to this very place. Follows then the bargain with Mr. Dolloby for his ' veskit.' Chatham in those

* The dial is at this moment offered for sale in London, at the price of some £80. As our author says in one of his writings, ' he loved every stone of the place.'

days was a terrible place—as lawless as it was
squalid.

I well recall the old Rochester Theatre, as it
stood—I suppose full forty years ago—when I passed
it one Sunday morning, having walked in from Gadshill, where I was staying. A rusted little bandbox
of a place it seemed, with a portico. At lunch I
made Boz laugh by describing to him the torn and
faded bill pasted on the wall, in which a local actor,
asking for patronage, quoted :

> ' And as the hare, whom hounds and horn pursue,
> Pants to the spot from which at first it flew,
> I still had hopes, my long vexations past,
> Here to return and die at home, at last.'

There was something almost pathetic in this
appeal of the poor player, who must have been
Rochester-born. I was bold enough to suggest to
Boz that it would be a pleasant thing to take the
forlorn little house and give some private theatricals.
What a junketing that would have been, and how
it would be talked of to this hour ! But he did not
care much about it.

I wondered at that moment, did the memories
of the Rochester playhouse of his childhood come
back to him ? In his little paper ' Dulborough '
he revived them all in a delightfully vivid spirit.
How pleasantly he tells of the dealer in wine who
had ' squeezed his trade into the box-office, where

the theatrical money was taken—when it came—in
a kind of metal safe in the passage.' The dealer
must have got under the very stage, too, as he
announced wines in the wood.

Chatham and Rochester must have been lively
enough in those times, for, as we have seen, there
were public balls and 'assemblies'—the former being
of a private character and regulated by patronesses,
vouchers, etc.—a grand review on the Lines, and
garrison theatricals by the officers of the 52nd.
And all this festivity within three days. We have
a pleasant glimpse of the theatrical life of the place,
for was not Mr. Pickwick on the evening after his
arrival hobnobbing with two live actors, Jingle and
'Dismal Jemmy,' *alias* Hutley, and, later *alias*
Trotter? How easily we find out all about them
and the theatre where both were engaged! Jingle,
as we have seen, was to play on the following night
with the officers of the 52nd. His line was, of
course, light, rattling comedy. He no doubt played
'Jeremy Diddler' in 'A Race for a Dinner,' and
played it well. One grows to talk of these Pickwick
scenes and personages as though they were actual
realities. They are blended with the reality.

CHAPTER III

WATTS'S CHARITY—EARLY RELIGIOUS TRAINING

OF all the attractions of this scenic little town, Watts's Charity always seems the most fascinating ; and so, I think, the world has found it. Every traveller finds his way thither. While Boz was living it was like one of the innumerable charities, 'foundations,' and the like, found in every town. But at one Christmas he 'came along,' touched the strings of romance, brought out the associations and fancies, and turned the old mouldering house into a public joy. It is now known all over the English-speaking world ; and a few pages from his magic pen wrought this marvel. Shall I ever forget the day when I first stopped before the door, brought thither by Boz himself ? Then it was really a venerable, crumbling structure, exceedingly interesting to look on ; but in latter days it has been primmed up and refaced with neat new stone. It struck me that the matron was a little cold, certainly not enthusiastic. But then I recalled that she had

47

figured in the 'Seven Poor Travellers,' issued not long before, where she was humorously presented. When we crossed the court to the small row of outhouses allotted to the guests, Boz paused to mark the fact with an amused twinkle in his eye. 'So they are all to sleep out?' he said to her.

The abuses of Watts's Charity, and also of the Free Schools and other charities, had begun to attract attention, and certain reformers to agitate. I remember a clergyman being pointed out to me— a constant frequenter of the Athenæum Club—as the vigorous combatant of the trustees, and final victor. Whiston his name was. He carried on the struggle for a long time in the courts, and finally succeeded in obtaining a new scheme of reform. Dickens in his description gives a scathing account of these abuses : 'Now, the greater part of the property bequeathed by the Worshipful Master Richard Watts for the maintenance of this foundation was, at the period of his death, mere marshland ; but that, in course of time, it had been reclaimed and built upon, and was very considerably increased in value. I found, too, that about a thirtieth part of the annual revenue was now expended on the purposes commemorated in the inscription over the door : the rest being handsomely laid out in Chancery, law expenses, collectorship, receivership, poundage, and other appendages of

management, highly complimentary to the importance of the six poor travellers.'

I well recall the coming out of 'The Seven Poor
Travellers,' and the sensation it caused. It was,
indeed, one of the most delightful of topographical
stories 'written round' a little building in Rochester,
and breathing the whole flavour of Kent, at Christmas
time. No one then had heard much of the old hostel,
or took interest in it, but at once it became famous—
even as a place of pilgrimage. The story suggests
that it must have been written at a 'heat,' so full of
gentle enthusiasm is it, and of pleasant fun and
frolic. The Boots Story which is encrusted in it
is a delightful fancy, and has been often dramatized.
No account gives so elaborate an appreciation of
Rochester and of the author's affection for the place.
We thus have no less than seven or eight of his
writings devoted to the town—'Pickwick,' 'The
Mudfog Papers,' 'Down at Dulborough,' 'The
Chatham Lines,' 'Copperfield,' 'The Seven Poor
Travellers,' and 'Edwin Drood.' A substantial
body of commentaries and fancies. Even the name
'Drood' seems to have been suggested by a local
inhabitant—one Trood, his neighbour and *vis-à-vis*,
the landlord of the Falstaff. How far off now seem
the days when Boz, so full of fancy and spirit, his
imagination at work, touched off those delightful
sketches of his, the Christmas 'Numbers,' as they

were called, into which he really put—hence their value—his whole personality and feelings.

'Strictly speaking,' says he, 'there were only six poor travellers ; but, being a traveller myself, I brought the number up to seven.' This word of explanation is at once due, for what says the inscription over the quaint old door ?

RICHARD WATTS, Esq.,
by his Will, dated 22 Aug. 1579,
founded this Charity
for Six poor Travellers,
who not being ROGUES or PROCTORS,*
May receive gratis for one Night,
Lodging, Entertainment,
and Four-pence each.

' "This," said the matronly presence, ushering me into a low room on the right, "is where the travellers

---

* There has been much jesting as to this coupling of 'rogues with proctors' in the inscription over the door, the superficial assuming it had something to do with legal officials. The meaning of the words is nearly the same, proctor being a deputy or agent. It was lawful for lepers and bedridden folk to appoint someone to go round and beg for them. Naturally, every tramp pretended that he thus represented someone, and so the whole class incurred odium, and were held to be impostors.

The house—a small three-gabled edifice—was rebuilt in 1771, being founded in 1579. When I saw it first, in the fifties, it was in a somewhat ruinous but decidedly picturesque state, mouldering a good deal. When I last saw it it had been newly trimmed and cased with fresh stone, and looked unpleasantly new and spick and span. In the garden we find the common hall, with a range of 'six small neat rooms,' where each man has really good accommodation.

sit by the fire and cook what bits of suppers they buy with their fourpences."

' " Oh! then they have no entertainment ?" said I, for the inscription over the outer door was still running in my head, and I was mentally repeating in a kind of tune, "Lodging, entertainment, and fourpence each."

' " They have a fire provided for 'em," returned the matron, a mighty civil person—not, as I could make out, overpaid—"and these cooking utensils. And this, what's painted on a board, is the rules for their behaviour. They have their fourpences when they get their tickets from the steward over the way—for I don't admit 'em myself; they must get their tickets first—and sometimes one buys a rasher of bacon, and another a herring, and another a pound of potatoes, or what not. Sometimes two or three of 'em will club their fourpences together and make a supper that way. But not much of anything is to be got for fourpence at present, when provisions is so dear."

' " It is very comfortable," said I.

' " Ill-conwenient," observed the matronly presence.

' " Nay, ma'am," said I. "And as to the convenience of the six poor travellers——"

' " I don't mean them," returned the presence. " I speak of its being an ill-conwenience to myself and

4—2

my daughter, having no other room to sit in of
a night."

' " Then, the six poor travellers sleep upstairs ?"

' My new friend shook her head.

' " They sleep," she answered, " in two little outer
galleries at the back, where their beds has always
been ever since the charity was founded.   It being
so very ill-conwenient to me as things is at present,
the gentlemen are going to take off a bit of the
back-yard and make a slip of a room for 'em there
to sit in before they go to bed."

' " And then the six poor travellers," said I, " will
be entirely out of the house ?"

' " Entirely out of the house," assented the presence, comfortably smoothing her hands. " Which is
considered much better for all parties, and much
more conwenient." '

Through whatever portion of Kent we may
wander, we are certain to come on traces of Boz.
At Dartford, for instance, that picturesque and
quaint town on 'the old Dover Road,' they have
a rare, many-galleried old inn, the Bull—another
Bull — with strange little ' hutches ' or cabinets
opening from them.   Here the traditions of Dickens
were long preserved, and it was described how he
used to love to ensconce himself in one of the
' cubicles.'   He loved this old Dover Road, with
the royal red of the postboys.

Dickens, it is pleasant to think, has been never, or 'hardly ever,' mimicked or satirized by the smaller fry. It is, therefore, somewhat astonishing to find Edmund Yates, that most faithful of his henchmen and worshippers, so indiscreet as to write a comic parody of the master's style—and in his lifetime! Boz would, of course, have laughed at this; but he must have thought it was something of a freedom, and scarcely respectful. The imitation appeared in a book called 'Our Miscellany,' and the imitation was supposed to be by Charles Diggins.

I was, however, more astonished lately to find that the genial and amiable Anthony Trollope had introduced a satirical portrait of Boz into his 'Warden' under the title of 'Mr. Popular Sentiment,' which shows hostility. One can hardly realize this nowadays. It seems a serious lack of respect, and almost a profanity.

He particularly ridicules Boz's efforts to reform the Rochester charities. One Hiram, as he describes it, had moneys which he had made as a wool-stapler, to found an almshouse for twelve old men. These used to receive sixpence each, like those of Watts's Charity; but the value of the little estate increased enormously. The Warden of this charity, we may presume, was intended for the reforming Canon of Rochester, who conducted the agitation. He then describes Mr. Popular Sentiment.

'He was very wrong. The artist who paints for the million must use glaring colours, as no one knew better than Mr. Sentiment when he described this almshouse, and the radical reform which has now swept over such establishments has owed more to the twenty numbers of Mr. Sentiment's novel than to all the true complaints which have escaped from the public for the last half-century.'

We rub our eyes as we read this sneering attack.

It is not difficult to discover how Dickens attained such an ingrained dislike of ranting and ranters, which he so denounced in Stiggins and his followers. Next door to his home in St. Mary's Terrace was a sort of little Bethel, while his schoolmaster, Giles, was a minister of the Baptist persuasion. His mother, like Mrs. Weller, may have fallen under the influence of these people, and it is likely that persons, like the Shepherd and Deputy Shepherd, frequented her house. Old Weller ridiculed her doctrine of 'the New Birth.' All the incidents described must have been noticed by the boy at Chatham. Many years later he gave vent to a bitter complaint, bewailing all that he had suffered from these divines, their meetings and services. 'Time was,' he says, 'when I was dragged by the hair of my head, as one may say, to hear too many [preachers]. On summer evenings, when every flower and tree and bird might have better

addressed my young, soft heart, I have been caught
in the palm of a female hand by the crown, have
been violently scrubbed from the neck to the roots
of the hair as a purification for the temple, and
have then been carried off to be steamed like a
potato in the unventilated breath of the Boanerges
boiler and his congregation. I have been hauled
out of the place of meeting at the conclusion and
catechized respecting his fifthly, his sixthly, and his
seventhly. Time was when I was carried off to
platform assemblages, etc. I have sat under
Boanerges when he has specifically addressed himself to us—us, the infants—and I hear his canting
jocularity, and I behold his big, round face, and
I look up the inside of his out-stretched coat-
sleeve, as if it were a telescope, and I hate him
with an unbroken hatred for two hours.' All
which calls up the odious figures of Stiggins and
Chadband, and shows that the family may have been
in these days the prey of such false prophets. In
no way else could he have acquired the knowledge
of their ways. No doubt, too, he may have seen
devout ladies of the place toasting and compounding
hot rum and water for the Shepherd, or collecting
for him when the water was cut off by the impious
rate-collector, 'who he (old Weller) rayther thought
was booked for something uncomfortable.' But to
think of this shrewd little lad observing all this!

When he was writing the story of Little Nell, these memories of the Bethel at Rochester came back upon him, and he revived it again, making it at once serviceable for his plot and a wholesome warning to the fanatical. Kit's mother used to attend one of these places, and was under the influence of its director. It was, he says, 'a particularly little Bethel with a small number of small pews, and a small pulpit in which a small gentleman, by trade a shoemaker, and by calling a divine, was delivering a by no means small sermon.'

The same thing occurred to the baby, whom Kit's mother had brought with her, as occurred to him at Rochester. The preacher got so excited that he seemed to threaten little Jacob, 'by his strained look and attitude'; so it appeared to the child that if he so much as moved a muscle, he, the preacher, would be literally and not figuratively 'down upon him' on the instant. The miserable Jacob sat bold upright, his infant's eyes starting from their sockets. When Kit got his mother away, the preacher called out, 'Stay, Satan!' and said he was carrying off a lamb from the fold. On which Kit answered him, and said the baby was his brother. Then the preacher said, 'He's *my* brother,' etc. In every touch of the picture Boz shows his disgust and thorough dislike of the whole system.

Joe's description in 'Bleak House' of one of these

ranters is still more bitter : ' Mr. Chadbands, he was
a-praying wunst at Mr. Sangsby's, and I heerd him,
but he sounded as if he was a-speaking to hisself
and not to me.   He prayed a lot, but *I* couldn't
make out nothink in it.   Diff'rent times there was
other gen'lmen come down a-praying, but they all
mostly sed as t'other wuns prayed wrong, and all
mostly sounded to be a-talking to theirselves, or
a-passing blame on t'others, and not a-talking
to me.'

This memory of the Chatham church-going never
seemed to leave his mind.   It was *burnt in*, as it
were, and he makes his little Copperfield suffer in
the same way.   ' I remember the tremendous visages
with which we used to go to church, and the changed
air of the place.   Again the dreaded Sunday comes
round, and I file into the old pew first, like a guarded
captive brought to a condemned service.   Again,
Miss Murdstone, in a black velvet gown, that looks
as if it had been made out of a pall, follows close
upon me ; then my mother ; then her husband.
There is no Peggotty now, as in the old time.
Again, I listen to Miss Murdstone mumbling the
responses, and emphasizing all the dread words
with a cruel relish.   Again, I see her dark eyes
roll round the church when she says " miserable
sinners," as if she were calling all the congregation names.   Again, I catch rare glimpses of my

mother, moving her lips timidly between the two,
with one of them muttering at each ear like low
thunder.'

It is not extraordinary that the remembrance of
these religious tortures of his childhood should have
clung to his memory. He never could forget or
forgive those who had worried his younger self.
He was even glad, when starting 'Little Dorrit,' to
give the ranters a fresh buffet, making Clennam
arrive in London on a Sunday evening, which
supplied the cue. 'But its sound (the bells) had
revived a long train of miserable Sundays. "Heaven
forgive me," said he, "and those who trained me.
How I have hated this day!" There was the
dreary Sunday of his childhood, when he sat with
his hands before him, scared out of his senses by a
horrible tract which commenced business with the
poor child by asking him in its title why he was
going to Perdition?—a piece of curiosity that he
really, in a frock and drawers, was not in a condition
to satisfy—and which, for the further attraction of his
infant mind, had a parenthesis in every other line,
with some such hiccupping reference as 2 Ep. Thess.
c. iii. v. 6 & 7. There was the sleepy Sunday of
his boyhood, when, like a military deserter, he was
marched to chapel by a picquet of teachers three
times a day, morally handcuffed to another boy ; and
when he would willingly have bartered two meals of

indigestible sermon for another ounce or two of inferior mutton at his scanty dinner in the flesh. There was the interminable Sunday of his nonage ; . . . There was a legion of Sundays, all days of unserviceable bitterness and mortification, slowly passing before him.'

This early religious tyranny determined in a very marked way his own religion. For it made him, unreasonably, certainly, judge the whole by a corrupt portion, and detest all formal sects—at least, where directed by such individuals. We may assume that the striking profession of religion given in his will gives the true expression of what his feeling was.

There is a very remarkable story of Dickens which has attracted little attention, and which, I fancy, had he worked it out on a larger scale, would have been even more remarkable and enduring. This he wrote for an American firm, and received for it and for another tale an almost ' record price.' It was called ' George Silverman's Explanation,' and it has a particular interest for myself, as he sent me the proof-sheets in advance, with an evident sense of satisfaction in his work. He sent me at the same time 'The Holiday Romance.' How thoughtful and sympathetic was this in so eminent a man, and how amiable his wish to have the approbation of one of his own workmen! What

writer or editor would do such a thing nowadays?
But it is curious to find that there was still before
his mind—and it was only two or three years before
his death—the low 'trading' form of religion which
had been his horror in his childhood. He brings on
a sort of 'Shepherd' and 'Deputy Shepherd'—
Brother Hawkyard and Brother Gimblett—both
good figures. Brother Gimblett's endorsements of
his brother's utterances are very much in the Salva-
tion Army style of our time.

It should be said that Dickens was sometimes
unfortunate in his Biblical allusions—that is, when
dealing with these 'canting' professors. Old Weller's
jesting allusions to 'the New Birth' gave umbrage
to religious persons. Almost the last page he
wrote contained something that brought him protest. A very awkward phrase in 'Little Dorrit'
fortunately escaped notice. He had slipped into
an allusion to 'baptismal water on the brain,' and
forgot to remove it, which he felt was certain to
be mischievously perverted and used against him.
'I wrote it in the text,' he said, 'more as a joke,
which Forster should see in the proof.' Forster did
see it, and hurriedly came to him in infinite alarm.
'The moment I saw it I knew what it was, and
have already taken it out in my mind.' When the
revise was before him 'he most carefully took it
out,' but in fact it somehow remained.

The poor child, besides his peck of family troubles, must have had his nervous temperament, wrought upon by an appalling nurse, who seems to have delighted in agitating him with ghostly and other tales. Long after, in his waking hours, some of these images would come back on him with terrifying effect, particularly 'a figure that I once saw, just after dark, chalked upon a door in a little back lane near a country church—my first church. How young a child I may have been at the time I don't know, but it horrified me so intensely—in connection with the churchyard, I suppose, for it smokes a pipe, and has a big hat with each of its ears sticking out in a horizontal line under the brim, and is not in itself more oppressive than a mouth from ear to ear, a pair of goggle eyes, and hands like two bunches of carrots, five in each, can make it—that it is still vaguely alarming to me to recall (as I have often done before, lying awake) the running home, the looking behind, the horror of its following me; though whether disconnected from the door, or door and all, I can't say, and perhaps never could.'

Hundreds of times, he says, was he compelled to listen to these gruesome things. She had a sort of fiendish enjoyment in his terrors, 'and used to begin, I remember, by clawing the air with both hands, and uttering a long, low, hollow groan.' So

acutely did he suffer that he used to beg to be
let off. This seems to account for the penchant and
curiosity which he always showed for ghostly incidents, and for the skilful, and even masterly, style
in which he treated them. The tale of the phantom
mail coaches is assuredly one of the most dramatic
and creepy tales of the kind ever written; and
'Gabriel Grub' is equally good.

In 'The Holly Tree Inn' he recalls some other
stories related by this terrifying person. 'I found
myself at the knee of a sallow woman with a fishy
eye and aquiline nose and a green gown. She told
of crimes and murders at inns; of the landlord that
made his guests into sausages; the burglar landlord
who always wore a black cap because his ears
had been shaved off in a fight; of the Newfoundland
dog who discovered a murder.'

In 'Copperfield,' still ruminating over the bitter
memories of the past, he says: 'It is a matter of
some surprise to me, even now, that I can so easily
have been thrown away at such an age. A child
of excellent abilities, and *with strong powers of
observation*'—it will be noted how he ever recurs
to this—'quick, eager, delicate, and soon hurt,
bodily or mentally, it seems wonderful to me that
nobody should have made any sign on my behalf.'
But none was made, and he became 'a little labour-
ing hind.'

What a despairing passage is this, and yet, of all that read, few, probably, even dreamed that he was speaking of himself. It was thought to be his own realistic treatment heightening the story of the boy Copperfield. He was telling his tale to himself, and it was not until after his death that the application was known. How tragic! How excellently, too, is here given the leading points of Boz's own character when a man! Nothing could describe it more accurately—'excellent abilities, strong power of observation, quick, eager, delicate, and soon hurt, bodily or mentally.' No words could be better chosen, as his friends will acknowledge, than 'quick, eager, delicate, and soon hurt.' This sensitiveness was a great note of his nature, with the lightning quickness and eagerness always so delightful in him.

But this did not exhaust the wonderful boy's studies and perception. Those who knew Dickens intimately will recall how pleasantly he used to reveal his knowledge of old books, novels, characters and allusions in novels. He was wonderfully fitted in this way ; he left the impression of a well-read man, with a great sympathy in and enjoyment of what he read. Then his own brilliant fancy made him set these incidents in a new and amusing light. This furniture, as we know, all came from the childish days at Rochester. He tells us in

' Copperfield' of the delight he had in the collection
of old novels which he found upstairs in a litter-
room next his own. This was, of course, in
Chatham, when he was about eight or nine years
old. 'From that blessed little room' he took
all the old novels—' Roderick Random,' ' Peregrine
Pickle,' ' Humphrey Clinker,' 'Tom Jones,' 'The
Vicar of Wakefield,' 'Don Quixote,' 'Gil Blas,'
' Robinson Crusoe,' 'The Arabian Nights,' ' Tales
of the Genii,' and others. There were also a few
volumes of ' The Voyages and Travels '—in 'Con-
stable's Miscellany,' most likely, for which he had
always a penchant.

These heroes filled his soul ; for weeks together
they haunted his imagination—he went about acting
the parts in a dream, as it were. He could remember going about the house armed with the
centre bit of a boot-tree, 'copying somebody of the
Royal Navy.'

Then comes his striking and touching passage :
' This was my only and my constant comfort. When
I think of it, the picture always rises in my mind of
a summer evening, the boys at play in the churchyard, and I sitting on my bed, reading as if for life.
Every barn in the neighbourhood, every stone in
the church, and every foot in the churchyard, had
some association of its own in my mind connected
with these books, and some locality made famous in

them.'   Little did he think then the world would
come to associate with his books every stone in
the churches or churchyards.   As we walk through
Chatham we can call up this scene for ourselves—
the church and churchyard perched high, close to
the railway arch.

CHAPTER IV

SCHOOLING—DEAN HOLE

CHARLES DICKENS as a child does not seem to have lacked schools or schooling. He was first sent to a preparatory school, kept by a grim lady, of whom he wrote to his friend Forster in 1846: 'I hope you will like Mrs. Pipchin's establishment. It is from the life, *and I was there*. I don't suppose I was eight years old, but I remember it all.' This reminiscence makes us conjecture that little Paul's grave, old-fashioned ways and 'posers' addressed to this person may have been his own questionings. He was at another school in Rochester, and also at one near London.

Here is a unique and remarkable thing. What writer has given us so many biographies of children? No one understood so well the nature and temperament of the watchful, observing child, whether boy or girl. This faculty would seem to have been the result of sad experience, and in most cases to have been simply the reproducing of his own early recollec-

tions—the life of his own childhood.   He appears
never to exhaust this store.   Oliver Twist, Little
Nell, Little Dombey, Copperfield.   Pip, Little
Dorrit, Tiny Tim, Smike, Lizzie Hexham—how
rich and full are these portraitures!   Into all,
whether boy or girl, he seemed to be infusing his
own early feelings and experiences, which were far
more precious to him than those of his mature life.

At Rochester he was placed under the charge
of a Baptist minister, one Giles.   Mr. R. Langton,
in his pleasant volume, has told us all about these
pleasant school-days.   It was Giles who, long after,
delighted at the rising fame of his pupil, gave him
that grotesque but really appropriate designation,
'the inimitable Boz.'*   No one was so pleased as
Boz, who often thus humorously described himself.
In the playground he had been delivered from the
dangers of Seringapatam, and had been recognised
by his affianced one, Miss Green, 'second house
in the terrace.'   This schoolboy union he has often
dwelt on.   He later transferred its locale to Canterbury, in 'Copperfield.'   There Miss Green appears
again under a fresh name.   Over thirty years later,
grown up and famous, he went down to the old place,
and records his impressions in his touching little
paper, 'Down at Dullborough.'   (Why, by the way,
does he give the old town such odd names?   In

* Moncrieff, the piratical dramatist, also used the term.

another place he calls it 'Mudfog,' in another
'Winglebury.')

When he was here he used to learn from a
companion 'whose father was greatly connected,
being under the Government of a terrible banditti,
known as "the Radicals."' This person under
Government was, of course, 'something in the yard'
—one of the Clubber sort, it might be.

In his visit to 'Dullborough' he tells us rather
pathetically (we think of the passage at every visit
to Rochester): 'We went to look at it only this last
Midsummer, and found that the Railway had cut
it up root and branch. A great trunk-line had
swallowed the playground, sliced away the school-
room, and pared off the corner of the house, which,
thus curtailed of its proportions, presented itself, in
a green stage of stucco, profilewise towards the
road, like a forlorn flat-iron without a handle standing on end.'

I often pass by the site of his London school, to
which he was transferred after the family had left
Rochester, and which was in the Hampstead Road,
at the corner of a side street. It was then among
the fields and trees, but now no part of London has
become so crowded with buildings. It is curious,
too, that we should find here the Sol's Arms, the
only 'public' of the name in London—a name which
figures in 'Bleak House.' It must have been there

in his school-days, and fixed itself in his memory.
'Copperfield' no doubt contains his accurate recollections of the place, and Salem House was drawn
from Jones's Wellington House Academy. Here
Jones is described as an ignorant fellow and a tyrant,
with a huge ruler in his hand, which he used on his
pupils. There was also a rough and gruff serving-
man. Of the white mice that were kept in the desks
Forster has spoken. About the usher Boz is more
distinct, and a capital sketch he gives of him.

There was a vague impression that the head-
master had been in the leather trade, and had
bought the place as a speculation. He seemed to
know nothing but to rule copy-books and to flog.
Boz had some faint memories of the boys. There
was a rich one, who was the favoured boy. So was
Steerforth. How pleasant is his sketch of Dumbledon! 'His special treatment, and our vague association of him with the sea, and with storms, and sharks,
and Coral Reefs, occasioned the wildest legends to be
circulated as his history. A tragedy in blank verse
was written on the subject—if our memory does not
deceive us, by the hand that now chronicles these
recollections—in which his father figured as Pirate,
and was shot for a voluminous catalogue of atroci-
ties : first imparting to his wife the secret of the
cave in which his wealth was stored, and from which
his only son's half-crowns now issued. Dumbledon

(the boy's name) was represented as "yet unborn"
when his brave father met his fate, and the despair
and grief of Mrs. Dumbledon at that calamity was
movingly shadowed forth as having weakened the
parlour-boarder's mind. This production was received with great favour, and was twice performed
with closed doors in the dining-room. But it got
wind, and was seized as libellous, and brought the
unlucky poet into severe affliction. Some two years
afterwards, all of a sudden one day, Dumbledon
vanished. It was whispered that the Chief himself
had taken him down to the Docks and reshipped
him for the Spanish Main.' He also tells of a preparatory day-school, of which he had very shadowy
recollections, kept by a Miss Frost, or some name
like it, with her French pug.

On his late visit to 'Dullborough' he recognised
some familiar faces, and went to call on an old
schoolfellow—now a flourishing doctor, whom he
found married to Lucy Green, his old playmate and
boy-love, and with whom he dined. This lad and he
had read 'Roderick Random' together. It is
astonishing, indeed, in what a number of places he
furnishes little scraps and sketches of his old school-
days—as in 'Copperfield,' where he shifts the scene
to Canterbury and to Mr. Creakle. These are,
of course, much varied and embellished. His official
recollections are given in the humorous paper,

'Our School.' The greengrocer who did not recognise him was to him 'the town, the Cathedral, the bridge, the river, my childhood, and a large slice of my life to me.' How distinct the emphasis here!

Boz talks of Timpson, who used to run the coaches, and who was, no doubt, Simpson. He tells us that he finally left Rochester in the stage-coach, and was forwarded, carriage paid, to Cheapside. He was the sole inside passenger, a boy of eleven or twelve years old. This journey seems to have made an impression on him, for he alludes to it elsewhere in the 'Sketches': 'We have also travelled occasionally with a small boy of pale aspect, with light hair, and no perceptible neck, coming up to town from school, under the protection of the guard, and directed to be left at the Cross-keys till called for.' It is likely that, after his family had removed to town, he had been left at the school to finish his course. A late passage of his story, the departure of the Pickwickians for the Christmas festivities at Dingley Dell, suggests to Boz a reminiscence, which he gives in his own person, an unusual thing with him : 'The salutation between Mr. Weller and his friends (at the public-house) was strictly confined to the freemasonry of the craft, consisting of a jerking round of the right wrist and a tossing of the little finger into the air at the same

time. We once knew two famous coachmen (they
are dead now, poor fellows), who were twins, and
between whom an unaffected and devoted attachment existed. They passed each other on the
Dover Road every day for twenty-four years, never
exchanging any other greeting than this, yet when
one died the other pined away and soon after
followed him.'

There was one schoolfellow of Dickens who was an
exception to the rest, because the connection was continued as he grew up. This was one Thomas Mitton.
They were both law clerks together during Dickens's
struggling days, and when the tide of success came,
Mitton, then a solicitor, was employed by him in
his various difficulties. The solicitor, however, had
but a struggling existence, and was often assisted
by his client. A large number of letters that passed
between them have been preserved. These throw
a good deal of light on the struggles—for there
were such—which attended Boz's first gleams of
prosperity. It is said, however, that Forster had
some quarrel with Mitton, and that this was the
reason of the slight mention of him in his 'Life.'
I well remember, not long after Dickens's death,
a number of his letters to Mitton being exhibited
in the window of a shop in King Street, St. James's,
and my being tempted to read some. They could then
have been secured at very modest prices. The bulk

of these Mitton letters, with a number of others,
making in all near a hundred, came into Mr. Ouvry's
possession. From Ouvry's possession they passed
to a New York publisher. A selection from these
letters was publisbed in the *Times* in October,
1883.

From these papers we learned what the world
little knew, that when Boz had captured a triumphant
popularity, and was presumed to be 'coining money,'
he was still harassed and troubled by pecuniary
difficulties. Some of these seem to have come from
his own family. Fame brought with it additional
cares for him. Attempts were made to make un-
authorized use of his name in connection with pecuniary transactions, which caused him much incon-
venience and annoyance. His executrix* wrote to

* 'CAUTION.

'We, the undersigned, solicitors for Charles Dickens, of No. 1,
Devonshire Terrace, York Gate, Regent's Park, in the county of
Middlesex, do hereby give notice—

'That certain persons having or purporting to have the surname
of our said client have put into circulation, with the view of more
readily obtaining credit thereon, certain acceptances made payable
at his private residence or at the offices of his business agents.

'That no person whatever has any right, title, or authority to
make promissory notes, acceptances, or other pecuniary writings,
payable either at the private residence of the said Charles Dickens,
or at his publishers' or bankers', and that such bills made payable
as aforesaid will not be paid.

'And we do further give notice that from and after the date
hereof the said Charles Dickens will not discharge or liquidate

Mr. Ouvry that, as Mr. Forster had written so freely
of the family money troubles, she did not feel justi-
fied in suppressing the letters and documents refer-
ring to this matter.

Writing about the year 1832 to Mitton, Dickens
tells him that his father has been arrested at the
suit of a wine firm, and begs him to go over
to Cursitor Street to see what can be done.   In
another letter he remarks that he is himself 'desper-
ately hard up, and the smallest contribution will be
thankfully received.'   On one occasion, his father
having disappeared during his difficulties, Dickens
remarked to Mitton : 'I own that at present his
absence does not give me any great uneasiness,
knowing how apt he is to get out of the way when
anything goes wrong.'   In a third letter, which will
show the straits to which Dickens was sometimes
reduced in his early struggles, he asks the loan of
so humble a sum as four shillings for two days.
On another occasion he writes : 'I have an order
in my pocket from my French employer for £5 on
an agent in the City who always pays me.   They

---

any debt or debts save those of his own or his wife's contracting,
and that any application made to him on account of the debts
of any other person whomsoever will be made in vain.

                    'SMITHSON AND MITTON,
                         ' 23, Southampton Buildings,
                                   ' Chancery Lane.
      'Dated this 8th day of March, 1841.'

pay, as the order notifies, "between 2 and 4," and
I did not get it until 5 to-day.   I want to give the
governor some money, and if you will let me have
as much as you can on account of the order, or the
whole, you can have the cheque, or let Hartland
present it—which you please.'   The attitude of
Dickens at this time towards those who caused
him much embarrassment did him great honour.
It seems what is called 'hard lines,' and this noble,
patient being must have all our sympathy.

As we know from Forster, other pressure came
from his publishers, whose accounts of sales brought
him a shock of suspense and astonishment.   He
was in debt to them for a large advance—over
£2,000.   His share of the 'Carol' profits were only
£750 on a sale of 15,000 copies, the price of a
copy being five shillings.   I do not think that
this return was so unreasonable.   Assuming that
the clear profit was half a crown, this would make
some £1,500 or £1,600 to be divided.   When he
changed his publishers, he received about double
from nearly the same amount of copies.

These letters, indeed, which seem to have escaped
Forster, throw an unexpected light on Boz's early
profits from his works.   There was a novel which
he had contracted to write for Macrone, ' Barnaby
Rudge,' or, as it was originally intended to be
called, ' Gabriel Varden, the Locksmith of London.'

Forster was astray when he said that no agreement
to write this work ever existed, for Macrone re-
peatedly advertised it as forthcoming. 'Barnaby
Rudge' did not actually appear until four years
later, when it was published by Chapman and Hall.
Here is the actual agreement on the part of Dickens
to write 'Gabriel Varden':

'*Monday, May* 8, 1836.

'MY DEAR MACRONE,

'I shall have great pleasure in accepting from you the sum
of £200 for the first edition of a work of fiction (in three volumes
of the usual type) to be written by me, and to be entitled "Gabriel
Varden, the Locksmith of London," of which not more than
1,000 copies are to be printed.

'I also agree to your printing an extra number of copies, if it
should appear desirable ; on condition that the profits thereon,
all expenses being first deducted, be divided between us.

'I also understand that the before mentioned £200 are to be
paid by you, on delivery of the entire manuscript—on or before
the 30th day of November next, or as soon afterwards as I can
possibly complete it—by your acceptances, at such dates as may
be agreeable to both of us.

'Very faithfully yours,

'CHARLES DICKENS.

'TO JOHN MACRONE, ESQ.,
'15, FURNIVAL'S INN.'

How sad it is to read that this most successful
writer, when issuing his exuberant 'Nickleby,' was
at one moment so hard pressed that he was, as he
said, thrown upon his beam ends, and hardly knew
where to turn ; while there was a bill of £200 which
he knew not how to meet!

Dickens the father had eight children ; Boz himself ten ; while his father-in-law, George Hogarth,
had fourteen.   Add to these cousins, such as the
Barrows ; brothers-in-law, Austins and Burnetts ;
schoolfellows, like Mitton ; comrades, companions,
such as Kolle, and we have a formidable crowd
encompassing the brilliant young author, with some,
at least, burdening him.   We all know, when there
is one flourishing and successful member of a family,
how the rest look to him for aid in every crisis.   An
amusing story has often been repeated of the redoubtable Forster's correcting his friend, who had
spoken of his ten children.   ' Nine, my dear Dickens
—you have only nine.'   ' Ten ; and I think I ought
to know.'   ' Pardon me, my dear Dickens, only nine.'
The confusion, I fancy, arose from the little girl
Dora, who died when only a year old.   It is hard
to understand what Dickens intended in the selection of names for his male children : Walter Landor,
Francis Jeffrey, Alfred Tennyson, Sydney Smith,
Henry Fielding Edward Bulwer Lytton.*

Not until he came to write ' Edwin Drood ' did
he introduce such Rochester buildings and memorials
as he had omitted to deal with.   Among these were
Minor Canon Row, the Cathedral and its gate-

---

* In the admirable article on Dickens by the late Leslie Stephen
there is a strange mistake.   Enumerating Boz's ten children, he
altogether omits Charles the younger.

houses, and Satis House, a not very interesting
building.   It is, however, made the very core of
'Great   Expectations.'   Our   eyes   are constantly
turned to it.   He explains the origin of the name :

' " Is that the name of this house, miss ?" (the
manor-house).

' " One of its names, boy . . . it's other name was
Satis, which is Greek or Latin or Hebrew, or all
three, or all one to me."

' " Enough House : that is a curious name, miss !'

' " Yes," she replied ; " but it meant more than it
said.   It meant that whoever had this house could
want nothing else."

Rochester Cathedral he did not reckon among his
childish memories ; there is little mention of it in
' Pickwick' save an allusion or two.   But at the
close of his life, from long residence, as it were,
under its shadow, its influence began to affect him.
All romantic associations are, unhappily, chilled by
the gross and heartless 'restorations' carried out
by one Cottingham, a destroyer, who did his worst
with the central tower.   Since Dickens's time, however, there have been praiseworthy and energetic
attempts to abolish Cottingham's 'restorations' and
to destroy what he had set up.   At this moment his
spiky tower is under treatment, and soon will assume
another shape.   ' Edwin Drood' showed Boz's sense
of the poetry of the old building ; he felt much

of what Jingle expressed in his grotesque way :
' Old Cathedral, too—earthy smell—pilgrims' feet
worn away the old steps—little Saxon doors. . . .
Queer customers, these monks—Popes and Lord
Treasurers and all sorts of old fellows with great
red faces and broken noses turning up every day
—buff jerkins, too—sarcophagus—fine place—old
legends, too—strange stories—capital !' As good
an epitome, in a grotesque way, as could be
imagined. Durdles even thirty years later talked
of ' the old uns.' Boz really did for the old
Cathedral what Victor Hugo did for Nôtre Dame.
Jasper is the monk ; Durdles, Quasimodo ; and
Rosa, Esmeralda.

The Rochester of ' Cloisterham ' is altogether a
different thing from the Rochester of ' Pickwick.' It
might, indeed, be hard to recognise it ; it has not
the fresh, brilliant, ' touch-and-go' handling. He
laboriously collects many points of interest, describes
elaborately and minutely ; but still hardly brings the
place before us. Yet he seems to have meant it to
be a complete and exhaustive picture. At any rate,
his first sketch was gay and *riant*, his last gloomy
and heavy. True, Cloisterham was intended to be
embodied altogether in the Cathedral scenes of
' inspissated gloom,' with a murder impending ;
the crypt, Durdles, the ' old uns,' tombstones, gate-
houses, etc., were all foils for Jasper. It is an

interesting subject of speculation why Boz, when he came to deal with Rochester once more—and, alas! for positively the last time — should have chosen to deal with it as an imaginary town in fiction-land, as Cloisterham, a name in which there is something rather artificial.*

He proceeds to describe it as an ancient city and a drowsy city, whose natives seem to fancy that all 'its changes seem to lie behind, and that there are no more to come.' 'The streets of Cloisterham city are little more than one narrow street, by which you get into it and get out of it, the rest being mostly disappointing yards, with pumps in them and no thoroughfare. Exception being made of the Cathedral Close and a paved Quakers' settlement, in colour and general conformation very like a Quakeress' bonnet, up in a shady corner.'

All through the story we come on little sketches or glimpses of Rochester, touched off in a very airy and effective way. He seems to recur to the place, to remind himself of it now and then, and bring it before him. 'In a word,' he goes on, 'a city of another and a bygone time is Cloister-

* Once, when writing a long story for him, the scene of which was laid in a cathedral town, I chose to give it the rather absurd and unnatural name of 'Tweakcuratesnose.' Boz, with an effective stroke of his pen, made it 'Tweakminster'!

ham, with its hoarse cathedral bell, its hoarse rooks,
hovering about the cathedral tower, its hoarser
and less distinct rooks in the stalls far beneath.
Fragments of old wall, saints' chapel, chapter-house,
convent, and monastery, have got incongruously or
obstructively built into many of its houses and
gardens.   The most abundant and the most agreeable evidences of progressing life in Cloisterham are
the evidences of vegetable life in its many gardens.
Even its drooping and despondent little theatre has
its poor strip of garden, receiving the foul fiend when
he ducks from the stage into the infernal regions,
among scarlet beans or oyster shells, according to
the season of the year.'   After a sketch of the
Cathedral precincts, he goes on : 'Among these
secluded nooks there is very little stir or movement
after dark.   There is little enough in the high tide
of the day, but there is next to none at night.
Besides, that cheerfully frequented High Street lies
nearly parallel to the spot (the old cathedral rising
between the two), and is the natural channel along
which the Cloisterham traffic flows ; a certain awful
hush prevails.'

    ' For sufficient reasons,' he goes on to tell us
rather mysteriously, ' which this narrative will itself
unfold as it advances, a fictitious name *must be
bestowed* upon the old cathedral town.'   Now, what
were the 'sufficient reasons'? rather, *what* could

they be? The disguise was so transparent that it might just as well have been called *tout bonnement* Rochester.

These 'sufficient reasons' may have been fears of giving offence, as his Deans, Minor Canons, etc., would have been assuredly taken for portraits of the Rochester dignitaries. Then he adds that 'the narrative itself will unfold these reasons as it advances.' And so it does. Personal application and identification would arise at every moment. The Dean who talked so pleasantly to Tope would have been taken for the existing Dean, and the canons would have been living Canons. But how could the 'reasons' be unfolded with the story? At what stage would he be able to say: 'You can see now why I have concealed my description of Rochester under the guise of Cloisterham; you can see how it never would have done to have talked of Rochester.'

In another passage he talks of 'the hoarse High Street becoming musical' with the cries of farewell. And, again, 'when they'—that is, Rosa and Edwin —'had turned out of the High Street and had got among the quiet walks in the neighbourhood of the cathedral and the river'—an affectionate allusion—'they talked, and as they talked walked on by the river.' The young pair still walked by the river, and did not lean on the old bridge and

look down into water, as Mr. Pickwick had done.
'The sun dropped in the river behind them, and the
whole city lay red before them.   The moving water
cast its seaweed duskily at their feet when they
turned to leave its margin; and the rooks hovered
above them with hoarse cries and darker splashes in
the darkening air.'   Is there not, surely, something
fateful in this gloomy cast of thought which he was
applying to the young pair, but which seemed really
to weigh on his own heart?   Then come more
praises of Rochester in all the seasons.   'It is
so bright and sunny in these summer days that
the cathedral and the monastery ruin show as if
their walls were transparent.'   He expatiates on the
town garden.   The trampers who pass through,
tired and dusty, solace themselves with draughts of
water at the street fountains.   In short, we have
Rochester again and again in its every mood, tense,
and humour.   It is in his 'heart of heart.'

There is a passage in chapter xiv. where he
speaks in his own voice.   It is very significant, as if
he were ruminating on the past.   'Christmas Eve in
Cloisterham.   A few strange faces in the streets; a
few other faces half strange and half familiar; once
the faces of Cloisterham children, now the faces
of men and women who come back from the outer
world at long intervals to find the city wonderfully
shrunken in size.'   How long had this thought been

with him, and how often he would dwell upon it!
His was one of the half-familiar, half-strange, faces
in the street.   I fancy he had walked into the town
on that Christmas Eve before his death.   ' To such
scenes as these,' he goes on with a mysterious sense,
' the striking of the cathedral clock and the cawing
of the rooks from the cathedral tower are like voices
of their nursery time.   To such as these it has
happened in their dying hours afar off, that they
have imagined their chamber floor to be strewn
with the autumnal leaves fallen from the elm-trees
in the Close.   So have the rustling sounds and fresh
scents of their earliest impressions revived when the
circle of their lives was very nearly traced, and
the beginning and the end were drawing close
together.'

This remarkable and forecasting passage shows
clearly how Boz's heart, even to the very end—for
it was written only a few days before his death—was
bound up with his old city of Rochester.

On one of my visits to Gadshill I recall one
of his pleasant speeches or commentaries as we
walked through the High Street.   'I remember,' he
said, ' once thinking this Town Hall one of the
grandest of public monuments, and left the place
with this impression.   I never was so astonished as
when I returned and was struck by its smallness.'
I was amused some years ago at seeing this notion

worked up in his known happy vein : 'I had
entertained the impression that the High Street was
at least as wide as Regent Street. I found it little
better than a lane. There was a public clock in it,
which I had supposed to be the finest clock in
the world, whereas it now turned out to be the most
inexpressive, moon-faced, and as weak a clock as
I ever saw. It belonged to a Town Hall where I
had seen an Indian swallow a sword.' It had
appeared to him then quite ' a glorious structure.'
Now it seemed 'a mean, little brick heap, like
a demented chapel, with a few yawning persons in
leather gaiters lounging at the door and calling
themselves a Corn Exchange.' Oddly enough, however, Boz seems to confuse these two buildings—the
Guildhall and the Corn Exchange—and he certainly
attaches the ' moon-faced clock ' to the former,
whereas it really belongs to the latter. It is
surprising, however, why he should have been so
severe on these buildings, as they are really two
very quaint and original works that would ' hold
their own ' anywhere. The whole High Street is,
indeed, one of the best things we have in England.

In whatever direction we turn, we find this contact
of Dickens with the outer world displayed in the
most striking way. At the risk of being thought self-
sufficient, I merely mention a trifling matter where,
I fancy, I was a little concerned. In his last and

fatally interrupted story it will be remembered how,
after the murder of Edwin Drood, a watch and pin
were recovered from the weir. This watch was
much insisted upon, with the date of its last winding,
etc., no doubt with a view to the chain of incidents
that were to be linked together later. Dickens deals
with the incident in quite legal style, and it is
evident that much was to turn on it. Crisparkle
found the watch at the weir, and it was identified by
the jeweller as one that he had wound and set for
Edwin Drood at twenty minutes past two on that
same afternoon. It had run down before being
cast into the water, and it was the jeweller's positive
opinion that it had never been rewound. This would
justify the hypothesis that the watch was taken from
Edwin Drood not long after he left Jasper's house
at midnight, and that it had been thrown away
after being retained some hours. Why thrown
away? If he had been murdered and artfully disfigured, the murderer hoped that identification would
be impossible except by something that he wore; and
assuredly the murderer would seek to remove from
him the most easily recognisable things.

All this had a rather familiar air to me, and there
came back to my memory a case of murder in which
I had been concerned professionally some three or
four years before. It had been first tried without
issue ; on the second trial the man was convicted and

hanged. The chief evidence was the silent one of a watch found in the river Laggan, near Belfast, and which was an inducement to the crime. This dramatic case made a deep impression on me, and I wrote a highly coloured account for Dickens's journal, where it appeared under the title of 'The Fatal Watch.' Dickens was much struck with it. When he came to deal with the murder in his story, this element of the watch may have suggested itself as a new and telling incident.

The links or strands that join the people of to-day with Boz and Thackeray are being sharply severed; one by one their old intimates—all more or less remarkable—are falling away. While a fair number of survivors remain, we are still in touch with the two great writers. But by-and-by, when all are gone, what a great gulf will be between! The cheerful, interesting Dean Hole who has lately departed is a loss in this way. He was the Dean of Boz's own diocese, Dean of the 'Kinfredral,' of Watts's Charity, of Minor Canon Row, of the Nuns' and Satis Houses, and of Gadshill itself! He knew Boz well, as he tells us in his 'Memories,' though he did not come to the Deanery till after Dickens's death. It was appropriate, however, that one of Dickens's friends should have held the post. I remember the coming out of the 'Little Tour in Ireland,' with Leech's (his co-traveller) brilliant woodcuts, some, I think, coloured—a lost fashion now. How bright and gay it was, and how full of fun and joviality! Once he asked me to come down and lecture on 'Boz' in the Town Hall, when he would take the chair. I see (and admire, too) his imposing, stately, truly remarkable figure—what is called a fine presence—as he promenaded it about his beautiful Deanery garden, so embowered in trees and luxuriant foliage, beyond the Cathedral. Here would he show us his roses, walking on himself a little in front, making stately strides, and pointing with his stick.

Next I see him in the High Street of his own city, a fine imposing personage, highly impressive, 'a man to stop and look after,' as Carlyle might put it, six feet and more of height, long-legged, with really a fine, well-cut, monumental face. His walk was in keeping. It was a summer's day when we were to keep a little festival of the Boz Club with Dickens's admirers, who had come down to Rochester specially. He had promised to join us about one o'clock in the old Town Hall which Boz thought so poorly of. Dine he could not. I met him in the High Street as he was striding up to the place for the tryst. He was in great good-humour.

Presently gathered the London visitors just arrived : Henry Dickens (Boz's son), Fildes, R.A.,

Sir F. Burnand, Parkinson, and many more, all members of the Boz Club. The genial Dean met us, greeting us with an antique ceremonial, and took his place on the black oak rostrum, the old portraits, Sir Cloudesley Shovel and the rest, looking grimly down in a shadowy way on the party who had come to disturb them. Then our Dean began, as if about to preach from the pulpit ; but what a lay sermon it was!—warm, refined, witty, touching ; his heart seemed to be in it, for the memories of the one great event he had known so well were coming back to him. He kindled up, told us many things, and made some admirable critical remarks on the influence of the great Charles. It was a curious ceremonial, not without a certain *devotional* air. Here was the old darkened hall ; the ancient town that Boz so loved, where he had lived, and where he had died, and where he desired to be buried ; and this excellent Dean panegyrizing him to a congregation composed of Boz's own friends and relatives. To this happy discourse Boz's son replied in some feeling, well-delivered words.

When he brought us to the Cathedral, and was expatiating on the Edwin Drood localities, Fildes the R.A., ventured some casual speech differing from the diaconal view, and was, as I thought, a little curtly answered, on which I whispered to him that here was the actual illustrator in the flesh of Edwin Drood, who knew a good deal about these matters, and the story itself.

How many things he told us, and in how pleasant a style! Then we set forward to Gadshill, where a member of the club, Mr. Latham, now the occupant, welcomed us. Finally, after an enchanting day that stirred all sorts of images for those who had lived there, we returned to the town, to the good Bull, where the banquet was set forth in the Pickwickian ballroom, with a Pickwickian bill of fare, a pleasant night after a pleasant day. But I must say we missed our agreeable, handsome Dean. We should have been glad to have him with us. On that festive occasion we little dreamed that he was to be so soon called away to his rest beneath, as it is likely, the red roses that he knew so well.

Seated in his Fechter châlet—that white elephant of a present—on the last afternoon of his life, the amiable and genial Boz penned what were to be his last sentences. These had a sort of significance; for they referred to the chalk score by which one of his odd characters had a way of marking his meals; only on this occasion we are told he 'takes his bit of chalk from its shelf, adds one thick line to the score, extending from the top of the cupboard door to the bottom, and then falls to with an appetite.' There was a sort of finality in this, for previously he had

made only short strokes.   Then came the significant
saying : ' The score debited with what is against
him ; the scorer not committed '—an odd, strange
fancy.

Then he came to this : ' A brilliant morning
shines on the old city. Its antiquities and ruins
are surpassingly beautiful, with the lusty ivy gleaming in the sun and the rich trees waving in the
balmy air.   Changes of glorious light from moving
boughs, songs of birds, scents from gardens, woods,
and fields—or rather from the one great garden of
the whole cultivated island in its yielding time—
penetrate into the Cathedral, subdue its earthy odour,
and preach the Resurrection and the Life.   The
cold stone tombs of centuries ago grow warm, and
flecks of brightness dart into the sternest marble
corners of the building, fluttering there like wings.'
It was truly remarkable that this glowing passage
was written not two hours before his death, so that
almost his last studied picture was that of the
Cathedral interior and the old city he had so loved
all through his life.

When Dickens died he was but fifty-eight years
old, a young man comparatively, as we reckon nowadays—certainly for a writer.   I well remember the
general shock and horror of that fateful morning when
we opened the *Times* and read the news.   We had
been so long accustomed to our great writer, he was

such a part of life, and of London life, that no one really dreamed of such a separation. He might have gone on for years more. He was always there, we knew, behind the curtain, ready to come out and recreate all. The style was then a little worn and used, and very familiar ; by-and-by it would have been 'good old Dickens,' with a joke. Had he lived to this year he would have been ninety-one !

The incidents connected with Dickens's interment are not generally known, while Forster, not unnaturally, has despatched the matter as briefly as possible. Mr. R. Prothero, the author of the ' Life of Dean Stanley,' has thrown more light on the matter, and shown how Dickens came to be laid in the Abbey, and not in Rochester Cathedral, as he had enjoined in his will. Mr. Prothero says that the plan had to be abandoned, as it was found that an Order of the Privy Council had closed the graveyard. Yet it would seem that this prohibition was unknown to the Rochester authorities, for a grave had been dug in the churchyard.

I possess what is, I think, the most striking and dramatic of known Dickens curios. The last letter written to Charles Kent, now in the British Museum, has a sad kind of interest; but the relic I speak of is really tragic. It is the agitated telegram for medical aid, sent off from Gadshill just after the

seizure.   It was sent to the household of the
faithful Holsworth, a worthy fellow, and, for as
many years as I can remember, office clerk under
father and son.   I knew him well, and saw him about
once a week when I came on business.   It runs :

'Charles Dickens, junior.   Received at Higham.   G. Holsworth,
    All the Year Round Office, 26, Wellington Street, Strand,
    London.   Dated Somerset House, W.C., June 9, 1870.

   ' *Go without losing a moment to Russell Reynolds, thirty-eight
Grosvenor Street, Grosvenor Square.   Get him to come by next
train to Higham or Rochester and meet Cara (?) Beard at Gadshill.   If Reynolds not to be found go to Radcliffe, twenty-five
Cavendish Square.   Mr. Dickens very ill.   Most urgent.*'

Dickens died on Friday, June 9.   Saturday,
Sunday and Monday passed without anything being
settled.   Westminster Abbey had been mentioned
or suggested, and there was certainly a feeling that
it was the proper place for so great a man.   The Dean
had made a rule never to offer the Abbey to relatives,
always waiting to be approached by them.   It was a
strange thing that only a few weeks before Dickens
had gone to dine with him at the Deanery, and was
now, alas! again to be received by the same host.
Stanley, departing from his rule, had sent an intima-
tion through a friend to the family that if they asked
him he would consider the matter.   This was on the
day of Dickens's death, but, by a strange chance, it
seems the communication had gone astray and never

reached the family. But on the Monday an elaborate
article appeared in the *Times* strongly urging Westminster Abbey as the fitting place. The effect
was overpowering. Even Forster, who as executor
would have held sternly by the terms of the will,
felt that they were called on to apply.

'At eleven o'clock on Monday morning,' writes
Dean Stanley, 'arrived Mr. Forster, accompanied
by the son (Charles Dickens the younger). Mr.
Forster said' (we can hear his emphatic, porten-
tous tones): '"I imagine that an article in the
Times must have been written with your con-
currence." I replied, "No ; I had no concern
with it."

'"After this strong expression in the *Times*, of
course, all further solicitation is unnecessary, and I
at once consent." He seemed thus to convey that
they had to thank the great journal for the conces-
sion. Forster replied, "Do not consent till you
hear what are the conditions upon which alone I
can allow it." I answered, "Let me hear them."
Mr. Forster said, "The first condition is that there
shall be only two mourning-coaches, with mourners
sufficient to fill them." "That," I said, "is entirely
an affair of the family. Do as you like." "The
second condition is that there shall be no plumes,
trappings, or funereal pomp of any kind." "That,"
I replied, "is a matter between you and the under-

taker, and is no concern of mine." " The third condition is that the place and time of the interment shall be unknown—beforehand." '

There was really no reason why Dickens should not have been followed to his grave by the most dignified attendance, or that the approaches to the Abbey should not have been filled by overpowering and tumultuous crowds eager to see the last of one who had been so long their friend and entertainer. But 'the place and time shall be unknown beforehand.' As the Dean said reasonably, what with the *Times* article, the public knowledge, the removal from Rochester—how was the secret to be kept? But it was kept. The body was brought to London in the night. As soon as the Abbey was closed the grave-diggers set to work. 'At nine on Tuesday,' says Mr. Prothero, 'a solitary hearse, with two mourning-coaches, drove into Dean's Yard without attracting any attention whatever. There were about ten or twelve people—mourners—present. Still, no doubt Dickens himself wished for privacy.

As the small procession quitted the Abbey, Dean Stanley suggested to Forster that it might be well to give the public a chance of showing its feeling and affection, and allow the grave to remain open for the day. Forster agreed, saying: 'Yes; now my work is over, and you may do what you like.'

At eleven, goes on the Dean all the newspaper
reporters began to arrive 'to know when the
funeral was to take place.' Meantime the rumour
had spread, and thousands came to see the grave.
I was one of them, and well recall looking down into
the deep grave. Every class was there, and the
Dean describes the enormous amount of flowers
dropped down into the grave; but this is a mistake,
for I recall reading the name 'Charles Dickens' on
the coffin.

His directions as to his funeral show in a quaint
but perfectly genuine fashion his old disgust at the
undertaker's ritual. He directed that not more than
three mourning coaches should be employed, 'and
that those who attend my funeral *wear no scarf,
cloak, black bow, long hat-band, or other such
revolting absurdity.*' One cannot restrain a smile
at this vehement and characteristic reprobation,
strong as it were in death. All through his writings
he had made the undertaker and his antics the
topic of his ridicule, as in the case of Sowerberry,
Joram, and others, and very amusing characters
they are.

There is a tablet, however, set up in the
Cathedral, with an inscription, no doubt, written
by Forster :

CHARLES DICKENS,

BORN AT PORTSMOUTH, 7TH FEBRUARY, 1812; DIED AT
GADSHILL PLACE, NEAR ROCHESTER, 9TH JUNE,
1870; BURIED IN WESTMINSTER ABBEY.

TO CONNECT HIS MEMORY WITH THE SCENES IN WHICH
HIS EARLIEST AND HIS LATEST YEARS WERE PASSED,
AND WITH THE ASSOCIATIONS OF ROCHESTER
CATHEDRAL AND ITS NEIGHBOURHOOD,
WHICH EXTENDED OVER ALL
HIS LIFE,

THIS TABLET,

WITH THE SANCTION OF THE DEAN AND CHAPTER,
IS PLACED BY HIS EXECUTORS.

The question of the prohibitory clause in the will is one rather of sentiment than of logic. It is now quite an antique matter, and after over thirty years since his death, the question assumes a different aspect. During the years succeeding his death it would have been indelicate and unfeeling to touch the subject; but now, after new generations have grown up, it is different. Then he was appealing to his large group of personal friends and admirers, who would rush in a tumult, make passionate speeches and call for subscriptions—a thing he detested. It was to these friends that he appealed, but they are now nearly all gone. It should be noted that he did not make the same request to the greater public. He merely said that he relied on his *books* to be the best memorial of him. And there is the unanswerable argument : if it were right to set aside his wish as to his burial-place, why may not this wish also be disregarded ?*

Dickens has, indeed, done as much for Kent as Scott has for Scotland. He has made the picturesque even more picturesque, and has filled it with the most delightful living associations. The county is, therefore, under the deepest obligations to him for thus devoting his talent to it and serving it with all his affection.

* 'We understand,' says a Rochester paper, 'that on Saturday application was made to the Home Secretary to bury deceased under the castle wall in the St. Nicholas Burial-ground. Answer was given that no new vault could be made, but the remains might be placed in one already erected ; and on Sunday James Edwards, Esq., placed his vault at the disposal of the Dickens family. On Saturday Archdeacon Grant offered Rochester Cathedral, and was visited by Mr. C. Dickens junior at Aylesford to talk the matter over ; and on the following day (late in the evening) the family decided to bury the deceased at Shorne, as they feared he could not be buried privately at Rochester Cathedral. But on the Archdeacon writing to assure them that everything should be strictly private, the family on Monday, through Mr. Homan, consented to the burial taking place in the cathedral at noon on Tuesday. Mr. Foord, having communicated with Mr. Homan on Monday morning, and finding the offer had been accepted, commenced work immediately after morning service, Mr. Homan proceeding to London to obtain the consent of the Secretary of State. This could not be obtained, and the family, having been pressed to allow the remains of Mr. Dickens to be taken to Westminster Abbey, gave their consent on Monday afternoon.'

CHAPTER V

MANOR FARM—CHRISTMAS WRITINGS—THE MARSHES—COBHAM

Boz's experiences of tramps, so amusingly recounted in the 'Uncommercials,' were all gathered in the Kentish roads and lanes. And what types they were! His walks were often dramatic, and on the principle of the child's tale of 'Eyes and no Eyes.' His quick eye, ever roving, saw a hundred things which would have escaped common folk. Once given a hint, he could garnish and supply, with unerring truth and certainty, a vast number of things which were behind and must have existed, though unseen or unknown. Many know the little patch of green which is found between the Falstaff Inn and Gadshill Place. This spot was very dear to Boz, for it was virtually a piece of his own territory. He has described it, too, after his loving way, in this chapter on 'Tramps,' which so clearly shows that he knew his Kent by heart. He does not say that the spot is on Gadshill or near his house, but every Rochester citizen will recognise the touches.

'I have my eye upon a piece of Kentish ground,
bordered on either side by a wood, and having on
one hand, between the road-dust and the trees, a
skirting patch of grass.   Wild-flowers grow in
abundance on this spot, and it lies high and airy,
with the distant river stealing steadily away to the
ocean, like a man's life.   To gain the milestone
here—which the moss, primroses, violets, bluebells,
and wild-roses would soon render illegible but for
peering travellers pushing them aside with their
sticks—you must come up a steep hill, come which
way you may.   So all the tramps with carts or
caravans—the gipsy tramp, the show tramp, the
"Cheap Jack"—find it impossible to resist the
temptations of the place, and all turn the horse
loose when they come to it, and boil the pot.   Bless
the place, I love the ashes of the vagabond fires
that have scorched the grass!   What tramp children
do I see here, attired in a handful of rags . . .
making a toy of the hobbled old horse who is not
more like a horse than any cheap toy would be,' etc.
This favoured spot, upon which Boz 'had his eye,'
was lately seriously threatened by an invasion of
the tramway.

Boz was recalling another of his 'Seven League
Boots' walks when he described how he met a
particular kind of tramp, on what he (the latter)
described as 'the public I-way.'   He encountered

him, he says, 'this bright summer day, say, on a
road with the sea-breeze making the dust lively,
and sails of the ships in the blue distance beyond
the slope of the downs. As you walk enjoyingly
on, you descry in the perspective at the bottom of
a steep hill up which your way lies a figure that
appears to be sitting airily on a gate. This is a
well-spoken young man, who asks his way to Dover
and the distance.' Marching intrepidly on and
knowing his man well, Boz informs him that his
way to Dover is straight on, and the distance some
eighteen miles. These many pictures of Kent and
Kent life, touched off so airily, show how well he
knew every foot of the ground. It brings the Kent
country vividly before us. Anyhow, he loved the
sunshiny days, the long, straight roads, and the
hills ; how well he knew the distances, and how
he treasured it all in his memory as pictures !

I wonder, has the landlord of the Falstaff ever
thought of Boz's engaging description of his rural
hostelry ; or does he know that such was written
by his sympathetic neighbour ? If not, I would be
inclined to suggest to him that he should have it
printed in large, handsome characters, framed, and
hung up that all might read. For it is a delightful
sketch, done with ardour and enthusiasm and much
power of language.

'Within appropriate distance of this magic ground,

though not so near it as that the song, trolled from
tap or bench at door, can invade its woodland
silence, is a little hostelry which no man possessed
of a penny was ever known to pass in warm
weather. Before its entrance are certain pleasant
trimmed limes, likewise a cool well, with so musical
a bucket-handle that its fall upon the bucket-rim
will make a horse prick up his ears and neigh upon
the droughty road half a mile off. This is a house
of great resort for hay-making tramps and harvest
tramps, inasmuch as they sit within drinking their
mugs of beer, their relinquished scythes and reaping-
hooks glaring out of the open windows, as if the
whole establishment were a family war-coach of the
Ancient Britons. Later in the season the whole
country-side, for miles and miles, still swarm with
hopping tramps.'

There are many other incidental tokens of this
affection for Kent. Boz even delighted in adopting
names that he found in places in the county, such
as Upchurch for the chemist in the Bardell trial,
Upchurch being not very far from Rochester. And
in a paper in his *Household Words* he gives
to some personage the name of Briggs—a name
familiar enough in Rochester. Flintwich, Magnus,
and Weller, are also Rochester names.

Some of Boz's most delightful Kentish pictures
were drawn from the life at Manor Farm, near

Maidstone, where he had been a guest in his boyish
days. Of this we have a positive certainty, based
on the vividness of his recollections. Here he
found all that charm of Christmas enjoyment which
clung to him through life, and with which he
succeeded in inspiring the community at large.
Everything about Manor Farm was present to him
nigh twenty years later—the dancing, the blind-
man's buff, the kissing under the mistletoe, and
all the jocund sports described with such joyous
animation. When he was famous, and halfway
through his 'Pickwick'—that is, in 1837—his eyes
turned back to these old Kentish days, and, dropping
his narrative for a moment, he gives us this touching
retrospect: ' We write these words now, many miles
distant from the spot at which, year after year, we
met on that day, a merry and joyous circle. Many
hearts that throbbed so gaily then have ceased to
beat; many of the lights that shone so brightly then
have ceased to glow; the hands we grasped have
grown cold; the eyes we sought have hid their
lustre in the grave; and yet the old house, the
room, the merry voices and smiling faces, the jest,
the laugh, the most minute and trivial circumstances
connected with those happy meetings, crowd upon
our mind at each recurrence of the season, as if the
last assemblage had been but yesterday! Happy,
happy Christmas, that can win us back to the

delusions of our childish days; that can recall to the old man the pleasures of his youth; that can transport the sailor and the traveller, thousands of miles away, back to his own fireside and his quiet home!' He was writing in London, 'many miles distant' from the scene, which, therefore, must have been in the country. Where else could he have spent those delightful festivals? It must have been long ago, also, or so many would not have passed away; and it was an 'old house.' We have the most minute pictures of the place—no doubt described by him to 'Phiz'—and his own sketch of the interior. 'The best sitting-room at Manor Farm was a good, long, dark-panelled room with a high chimney-piece, and a capacious chimney, up which you could have driven one of the new patent cabs, wheels and all. At the upper end of the room, seated in a shady bower of holly and evergreens, were the two best fiddlers, and the only harp, in all Muggleton. In all sorts of recesses, and on all kinds of brackets, stood massive old silver candlesticks, with four branches each. The carpet was up, the candles burnt bright, the fire blazed and crackled on the hearth; and merry voices and light-hearted laughter rang through the room. If any of the old English yeomen had turned into fairies when they died, it was just the place in which they would have held their revels.'

Rook-shooting he must have seen at Wardle's—
that is, at Cob Tree—where there is, or was lately,
a rookery as well as a pond. I have always the
fancy that the lad was asked hither for the Christmas
festivals, and that with these good and hearty people
he picked up all this knowledge of the country.   At
the same hospitable house he had seen the Muggleton—*i.e.*, the Maidstone—cricket.   The truth was
he was as precocious at ten years old, and just as
old and observing as one of fifteen or sixteen.

Dickens was an extraordinary walker, and
thought little of twenty miles.   Rochester to Maidstone was a distance of about seven miles, and this
he would have trudged to see a cricket match or go
on a visit to friends.   Muggleton was certainly
intended for Maidstone, as I have been assured by
one of Boz's family, and there the famous match
came off.   The name Muggleton, I am certain, was
suggested by the Stigginses and other ranters whom
he loathed, and whose doctrines were 'Muggle-
tonian.' Who that has read and enjoyed the Manor
Farm Christmas scenes can doubt that they were
reminiscences, and that the young fellow was fondly
recording what he had himself so enjoyed?   The
Wardles have been tracked to earth there by the
Pickwickian antiquaries.   The late Mr. Hughes,
treasurer of Birmingham, and my old friend, really
discovered Manor Farm in the shape of Cob Tree,

Sandling, not very far from Maidstone. The evidence for its identity is striking enough. If we compare it with the two sketches in 'Pickwick' ('Mr. Pickwick Slides' and 'The Arbour,' which furnish both back and front views), we shall recognise the likeness. Both houses are two stories high, have wings and gabled roofs. But what settles the point is that there is a pond exactly in front of Cob Tree, and also a rookery. In Dickens's time it would seem that the owners were a family of Spongs, and a modern commentator has contended that they were the originals of the hospitable Wardles. This may be so, and logically follows from the identification of Cob Tree with Dingley Dell. However, this may be assumed as a certainty, from the reality of Boz's description, that he himself was a guest at the Manor Farm Christmas festivities. The Spongs had also some connection with the Bull.

Boz's knowledge of Kent in these days was certainly extraordinary. Even his most casual allusion is always correct, and he is constantly introducing something local, as a person in real life might do. Thus, the clergyman at Dingley Dell, when giving 'The Madman's Story' to Mr. Pickwick, spoke of 'our county lunatic asylum'; and, as Mr. Hammond Hall points out, the asylum is only a few miles from Cob Tree—a further point in the identity.

Two of the best ghost stories that we have are to

be found in 'Pickwick'—that of Gabriel Grub, and
of the spectral mail-coaches at the close of the book.
An abbey, introduced into the picture at the front,
has caused some difficulty and confusion, as it
clearly represents that of St. Albans in Hertfordshire.   Now, old Wardle speaks of an old abbey
church 'down here'—that is, in Kent.   There was
at the time," as Mr. Hammond Hall notes, some
abbey near Maidstone, but this was an abbey 'in
being.'   One might suggest the abbey church of
Minster, though that is a good way off.   There is
also Mayfield.

There is an extraordinary charm and power in
Dickens's dealings with this topic of Christmas.   It
is difficult to read any of these old sketches without
kindling and glowing, and feeling a longing sympathy for what he describes.   Boz's heart was in
every sentence of what he wrote.   There was a
tender affection, a longing to diffuse comfort and
happiness, and, as I said, a thorough belief in the
unique character of the season.   I defy anyone to
read over his many Christmas pieces without being
to some extent filled with the feeling.   It is impossible to resist.   Who would not wish to have
been at Dingley Dell?   For myself, I can only say
that for twenty happy years, as each recurring
Christmas arrived, it became—all owing to him—a
delightful festival.

Many must have smiled at Boz's simple belief
that the mere advent and pressure of the season
compelled family reconciliations, caused angry
brethren to 'make it up,' and diffused an amiable
and benevolent good-nature over all the parishes of
the land. He amiably enforced all these themes
with such conviction, and in so picturesque a way,
that he persuaded all. And it must be said that his
account of the hard Scrooge being softened gained
the whole kingdom, and was one of the most per-
suasive agents of such proselytism that ever appeared. For years it was fervently believed that
the sight of abundant holly and ivy, contrasted with
snow upon the ground, with the 'waits' and the
bells and the modern imitation of wassail, exercised
a sort of holy and softening influence on the sternest
souls.

There were all manner of touching stories based
on these seasonable reconciliations of the wild
brother who had run away and 'gone to the bad,'
and who, by a strange chance, returned *exactly* on
Christmas Eve ; the snow thick on the ground, the
family banqueting inside the Grange ; he, the outcast, looking in through the mullioned panes ! Some
sound betrayed him ; he was brought in, fell into
his brother's arms, was placed at the fire, filled with
good things, and all was forgiven ! How often have
I seen this favourite topic treated most artistically

in the pictures—the old Grange, the lights within, the dark figure peering in!

There is a curious passage which a sort of mysterious reference underlies, and which would escape the notice of those not in his secret. 'How many families whose members have been dispersed and scattered far and wide are then re-united, and meet once again in that happy state of companionship and goodwill which is a source of such pure and unalloyed delight, and one so incompatible with the cares and sorrows of the world that the religious belief of the most civilized nations, and the rude traditions of the roughest savages alike, number it among the first joys of a future condition of existence provided for the blest and happy.' This passionate reference to the hope of meeting again and being reunited refers clearly to the one great loss of his life.

About seven years after 'Pickwick' appeared, he was to give even more formal expression to his Christmas thoughts by the issue of the first of his little books written specially to glorify the season, the famous 'Christmas Carol,' that one entire and perfect chrysolite. Here his feelings as to the holy season seem almost tumultuous. The idea was truly original, and carried out in the most artistic and suitable fashion. The dainty little volume was all but perfect in its writing, dramatic arrangement,

printing, paper, illustrations, and even binding.   So
good and choice is the material used that even
now, after sixty years, a copy still looks fresh, fair,
unfaded, and attractive.   The print and paper are
delicate ; the plates by Leech, when coloured, are
brilliant and spirited to a degree ; even the title-
page is inviting.*   The life, spirit, and enthusiasm
which the author infused into his work was extraordinary ; the contrasts between the humorous and
pathetic portions are alternated like changes of scene,
while the Christmas flavour is almost obstreperous.

There was a regular series of these graceful little
books.   ‘A Christmas Carol,’ ‘The Cricket on
the Hearth,’ ‘The Chimes,’ ‘The Haunted Man,’
and ‘The Battle of Life.’   The four last were
decorated with exquisitely fanciful illustrations by
Doyle, Maclise, and others, some delicately inter-
mingled with the text.   But it was noted that the
Christmas flavour gradually evaporated, the last two
stories rather flagged, and lacked inspiration.   Still,
allowing for this exhaustion, they are tender, elegant
trifles—unique in their way—and which we would
not part with.   All were dramatized.   One regards
these little Christmas volumes with a wonderfully
tender affection.   The very look of them in their

* Book-collectors are curious as to the variations of the title.
One edition has ‘Stave One,’ another ‘Stave I.,’ and the lines of
the title are printed in some copies in different colours.   There
are, moreover, the ‘green end papers.’

genial, glowing crimson binding—elegant-looking
little things—sets all the Christmas fires aglow.
Boz put his whole self, his faith, his enthusiasm,
into each.

In these Christmas stories—gems of feeling and
true romance—written with all his glowing fervour
and sympathy for the poor, how charmingly and
poetically is the association of animal life with
human feelings glorified! In 'The Cricket on the
Hearth,' how the chirping of the little insect is
bound up with the fates and fortunes of the carrier
and his wife! So with 'The Chimes,' when the bells
of the city take their part in the little drama; so
with 'The Haunted Man,' when a painted window
and motto in one of the old Inns of Court supply
the text. This uniting of non-sentient things with
grace and poetry and life, so that we turn back and
think of them again, is surely a marvellous gift.

Dickens himself, after his fifth Christmas book,
recognised the truth that the novelty had worn
away. As he was later to complain, in the case
of the Christmas number, there were too many
imitations, and the waste of exertion for so small
a result was costly and excessive. A good deal
of the labour necessary for engendering a book was
expended on mere ephemeral production. He was
always thus sagacious in recognising signs of failing
attraction.

The art displayed in the 'machinery' and treatment of these little volumes was as original as it was effective. It was shown in the humanizing, as it were, the making probable, and even natural, the supernatural element. These were either actual ghosts, or the embodied sound of bells, or the apparition of sprites rushing with the chimes from old steeples. But they were left misty and indistinct; they might be of such stuff as dreams are. Something of the same kind was attempted by La Motte Fouqué, but these were professedly ghostly visitants, and treated as such.

Dickens, as I said, for many years continued—fitfully, perhaps—to touch the same note, until he had exhausted the subject and found no more to say. Still, he tried to believe in it to the last, and in his Christmas utterances there was always the note of these tender feelings, though he may have felt that they had grown cold and dead. The same view had already dawned on my old friend Edmund Yates, who in one of his 'Loungers at the Club' made a rather sour protest against the exaggeration of the festival. He was very droll on the artificial fashion in which the sentiment was pumped up, though the well often 'sucked dry.'

It would take us long to give all the tempting, picturesque glimpses of Kent Boz has furnished us with. As when he says: 'There are some small out-

of-the-way landing-places on the Thames and Medway where I do much of my summer idling.   I like
to watch the great ships standing out to sea or coming
home richly laden.   These, with the creaking little
jetty on which I sit, and the broken bank and broken
stakes and piles leaning forward, will melt into any
train of fancy.   One of these landing-places is near
an old Fort.   I can see the Nore light from it with
my pocket-glass.'   What painting is here, and in
so few strokes!   In his *Household Words* he describes the hop-fields in very vivid fashion.   He has
also limned the Chatham Dockyards in his own
lively and yet practical way.   ' My good opinion
of the yard's retiring character was not dashed by
nearer inspection.'   He describes the great sheds,
the clattering and hammering of iron, etc.   ' For all
that, the yard made no display, but kept itself snug
under hillsides of cornfields, hop-gardens, and
orchards ; its great chimneys smoking with a quiet,
almost lazy air, and the great shears moored off
it.'   He has also an account of the Dartford
paper-mills.

Nothing could be more thorough or more complete
than Dickens's survey, as it might be called, of his
favourite county.   He saw it in every aspect.   Wood,
city, churches, road, copse, coast, watering-place,
inns—we have it all.   More particularly he took
note of the sad, low-lying stretches of land and water

that spread away under the side of his Gadshill,
and known as the 'meshes' or marshes. On this
he actually wrought his story of 'Great Expectations,' to which it furnished the keynote. When
we think of the story, the first impressive scene on
the 'meshes' ever rises before us. It was only a
poetical and romantic pen that could invest the
topic with a dramatic interest, and it was thus that
Boz 'read off' his Kent and interpreted it to his
public.

Chalk is two miles from Cobham and five from
Rochester. The porch of the church at Chalk is
truly remarkable from its grotesque ornaments—two
figures, one of which holds a jug, while both grin at
each other. I recall as well as though it were
yesterday, though it is now nigh forty-five years,
the brilliant Boz, his face glowing with the walk,
standing with me before it and laughing responsively
as he pointed out these oddities. Chalk had also its
romantic associations for him, for thither he had
gone for his honeymoon and to wait the news of
the 'Pickwick' successes. The house still stands,
though not known to many. We must have passed
it on that walk, but he made no reference to it.

Beyond Gravesend the whole shore was a series
of these marshes—Gravesend Marsh, Cliffe Marsh,
Cooling Marsh, and Higham Marsh. The river
here begins to widen out; the sea-air is stormy and

makes its way in.   Boz had not, therefore, far to go
from Gadshill for inspiration.

The weird and solemn fascination of 'the marshes'
—which he was ever contemplating—was sufficient
to inspire and engender a story.   Thus, as I have
before said, place and story will act and react, even
in the instance of smaller writers, on each other.
The place will raise up thoughts, speculations,
characters, incidents, which can be appropriate to
such a place only ; while the story will, in its turn,
lend a new charm and poetry to the place.   'The
old Battery,' he says in ' Great Expectations,' ' out
on the marshes, was our place of study.   It was
pleasant and quiet out there, with the sails on the
river passing beyond the outwork.   I watched the
vessels standing out to sea with their white sails.'
One of the characters then ' struck across the marsh
in the direction of the Nore.'

He speaks of the churchyard by the marshes,
where were 'five little stone lozenges arranged
in a neat row, sacred to the memory of five little
brothers of mine.'   'Ours was the marsh country
down by the river, within, as the river wound,
twenty miles of the sea.   The flat, dark wilderness
beyond the churchyard, intersected with dykes and
mounds and gates, with scattered cattle feeding on
it, was the marshes ; and this, the low leaden line
beyond, was the river ; and that, the distant

8—2

savage lair from which the wind was rushing, was the sea.'

Again he recurs to the same striking picture : 'The marshes were just a long, black, horizontal line then, as I stopped to look after him ; the river was just another horizontal line, not nearly so broad nor yet so black, and the sky was just a row of long awry red lines and dense black lines intermixed. On the edge of the river I could faintly make out the only two black things on all the prospect that seemed to be standing upright : one of these was the beacon by which the sailors steered—like an unhooped cask upon a pole—an ugly thing when you were near it ; the other a gibbet, with some chains hanging to it, which had once held a pirate.'

Kent must certainly, and beyond question, be considered Dickens's own county, though he was not born there. This matter of birth has for all time little to do with the connection of a distinguished man with a particular place. No one, for instance, ever notes the slightest relation between Lamport, where Boz 'first saw the light,' and the writer. It is not known generally that Kent has the credit of vividly engendering and developing another brilliant writer—the ever-delightful and inimitable Jane — Jane Austen, whose family was thoroughly Kentish, having been settled at Godmersham and Godne- stone. And it is a quaint notion that among Jane's

progenitors should have been a Weller. When Jane
and her family had to go and settle at Steventon
in Hampshire, she looked back wistfully to Kent,
declaring humorously that 'people get so horribly
poor and economical in this part of the world that I
have no patience with them. Kent is the only place
for happiness ; everybody is rich there.' Here, then,
are two brilliant writers on which the fair county
may well plume itself. Nothing in England could
match so gifted a pair. Boz and Jane against the
world ! We should have a portrait of the latter in
our Rochester Walhalla !

'I have discovered,' wrote Boz once to Forster,
'that the seven miles between Maidstone and
Rochester is one of the most beautiful walks in
England.' How often do I lament that I did not
make use of my opportunities to learn from him
interesting particulars as to the localities of his
stories ! It would have been so easy to do so. I
could have suggested this very walk, and then asked
him about Muggleton and Dingley Dell and a dozen
such matters. But at that time no one much cared.
The thing was assumed to be concluded. It was
enough to read your ' Pickwick ' then without
troubling about details—a sensible course enough,
after all. And there was Dickens always ready to
write new ' Pickwicks.' The new school of explorers
had not yet arisen, and, above all, the author was

alive. Boz had long since dismissed Muggleton
from his thoughts.

But it was along this charming road that the Pickwickians, after their disaster with horse and chaise,
had to trudge, leading the dreadful quadruped.
They passed by Horsted, Binband Wood, Bridge-
wood Gate, Upper Bell, and Blue Bell. Passing
Kit's Coty House, we come to cross-roads and the
Lower Bell Inn, which is just four miles from
Rochester. Here it certainly was that the Pickwickians tried to put up their led horse. They then
walked past Warren Cottage and Lyland. A mile
and a half further on, when half a mile to their right,
they would see Cob Tree House. The Lower Bell
Inn, where they were suspected of having stolen the
horse, is minutely described, with its signpost in
front, one or two ' *deformed haystacks* behind, a
kitchen-garden at the side, and rotten sheds and
mouldering outhouses, jumbled in strange confusion,
all about it.' What a picture! Here they were told
that it was ' better er seven miles ' to Dingley Dell.
Boz, it will be seen, had retained his recollection of
the Kentish dialect, of which this is a specimen. In
other counties they might have said ' better *nor*
seven miles.' They trudged the seven miles, leading the horse, and this brought them to Dingley
Dell, which they reached late in the afternoon, say
at five o'clock. Thus, they had walked about thirteen

miles in six hours. This does not exactly fit with the waiter's computation, but ''twill serve'; for in the country there are 'long miles' and 'better er' miles, and such lax estimation of distance.

Sandling was Dingley Dell, and in his weird story of 'The Convict's Return' he gives an inviting sketch of its old-world charm. 'His nearest way lay through the churchyard. The man's heart swelled as he crossed the stile. The tall old elms, through whose branches the declining sun cast here and there a rich ray of light upon the shady path, awakened the associations of his earliest days.' He then entered the church. 'Nothing was changed. The place seemed smaller than it used to be' (again Boz's favourite fancy), 'but there were the old monuments, the little pulpit with its favourite cushion. . . . He walked down the hill.'

The present Maidstone is described as consisting of four main streets, with several smaller ones, which meet at the Market Cross. The High Street, a broad and handsome thoroughfare, ascends the hill from the bridge, and opens upon the breezy country towards Milton. What a cosy, friendly, natural scene that is, the reception of the Pickwickian travellers on their arrival at Manor Farm, with the glimpse it furnishes of some Kent folk! We have, indeed, the whole household set before us—master, his mother and daughters and sister, guests, servants, etc.   We like the two Kentish men—the fat one and the hard-headed, pippin-faced, intrusive Miller—both perfect characters.   Miller, the pippin-cheeked one, was an enthusiast in agriculture, and knew nothing better than Kent.   He told Mr. Pickwick that it was the finest bit of land 'in the whole country'—half as wanting something to say, half to please the host, who thought it a self-evident proposition.

Of horses, dogs and birds Boz was an admirer and a skilled acute observer.   Of horses he had practical knowledge, and was fond of a ride, such as he often took with his friend Forster up to Jack Straw's Castle.   I have often wondered, by the way, why it was that The Spaniards of Hampstead was introduced into 'Pickwick,' and not the Jack Straw's Castle, which he knew so well.   The omission was the more remarkable as the passage was written just about the time he was taking these rides with Forster.   Boz, too, had but little scruple as to naming his inns.   I fancy the reason was that The Spaniard was better adapted scenically to Mrs. Bardell's arrest than the Jack Straw's Castle, for there was the garden, arbours, alcoves, etc. ; and, further, The Spaniard—how and when has it become plural nowadays : Spaniards ?—was a lower class than the other, and more suited to Mrs. Bardell.   Boz, I fancy, was the first novelist to treat a horse humorously or as a humorous character. I think there is no more genuinely diverting sketch than that of Winkle's embarrassment with the tall quadruped; it is of high comedy. This, of course, does not imply knowledge, but observation, though what old Weller said might seem to be true in Boz's case, that 'a man who is an ackerate judge of a animal is a ackerate judge of anything'; and the man who drew Whisker in 'The Old Curiosity Shop' could have drawn anything.

But of all these interesting localities, the eye rests with the most particular interest on the delightful route to Cobham, and on that little hamlet itself. It is easy to see what a charm it had for Boz himself, and what an impression it had left on his childish imagination. He knew every foot of the way, the woods, the pleasance, the demesne. Some fifteen years after he had left the district, its tranquil and romantic fascination was still at work. As in the case of the old bridge and the winding river at it's foot, he wrote with an amazing power of description because his heart was in the work. Who will forget the passage which so faithfully reflects the whole tone of the pretty scene ? The three friends had set forward again in the afternoon to walk to Cobham. 'A delightful walk it was; for it was a pleasant afternoon in June, and their way lay through a deep and shady wood, cooled by the light

wind which gently rustled the thick foliage, and
enlivened by the songs of the birds perched upon the
boughs. The ivy and the moss crept in thick
clusters over the old trees, and the soft green turf
overspread the ground like a silken mat. They
emerged upon an open park, with an ancient hall
displaying the quaint and picturesque architecture of
Elizabeth's time. Long vistas of stately oaks and
elm-trees appeared on every side ; large herds of
deer were cropping the fresh grass ; and occasionally
a startled hare scoured along the ground with the
speed of the shadows thrown by the light clouds
which swept across a sunny landscape like a passing
breath of summer.'

There is yet another description of the woods,
written over thirty years later, showing that it still
had its attraction for him : 'As for me, I was
going to walk by Cobham woods, as far on my way
to London as I fancied. . . . And now the mists
began to rise in the most beautiful manner, and the
sun to shine, and as I went on through the evening
air I felt as if all Nature shared in the joy of the
great Birthday. . . . By Cobham Hall I came to
the village and the churchyard, where our dead had
been quietly buried.'

' " If this," said Mr. Pickwick, looking about him,
" if this were the place to which who are
troubled with our friend's complaint came, I fancy

their old attachment to this world would very soon
return." "And really," added Mr. Pickwick, after
half an hour's walking had brought them to the
village, "really, for a misanthrope's choice, this is
one of the prettiest and most desirable places of
residence I have ever met with."'

'One of the prettiest and most desirable places of
residence I ever met with.' And this was clearly Boz's
own opinion. The Leather Bottle has been often
described, and will ever be associated with Pickwick.
At the recent Dickens Exhibition an ancient leather
bottle was exhibited, stated to be the original 'sign'
that hung over the door. This little inn is a great
place of resort for the tourists, and is actually described in Murray's and other guide-books as the
house 'to which Mr. Tupman retired when giving
up the world.' Mr. Tupman retired! As usual, he
becomes as real as the inn itself. The little party
spent the night there, and our author, with his
poetic instinct, contrives to leave quite a romantic
impression—such as one would experience when staying at some such old-world place in a tranquil village
under the shadow of an old church with its bells.
To give a further effect, he makes his hero pass
a rather restless night, reading a very startling and
exciting story. 'Having been directed to the
Leather Bottle, a clean and commodious village
alehouse, the three travellers entered a long, low-

roofed room, furnished with a number of high-
backed, leather-cushioned chairs, of fantastic shapes,
and embellished with a great variety of old portraits
and roughly-coloured prints of some antiquity. The
evening was devoted to festivity and conversation.
It was past eleven o'clock—a late hour for the little
village of Cobham—when Mr. Pickwick retired to
the bedroom which had been prepared for his reception. He threw open the lattice-window, and,
settling his light upon the table, fell into a train of
meditation on the hurried events of the two pre-
ceding days. The hour and the place were both
favourable to contemplation ; Mr. Pickwick was
roused by the church clock striking twelve. The
first stroke of the hour sounded solemnly in his ear,
but when the bell ceased the stillness seemed in-
supportable ; he almost felt as if he had lost a
companion. He was nervous and excited ; and
hastily undressing himself, and placing his light in
the chimney, got into bed.

' Everyone has experienced that disagreeable
state of mind in which a sensation of bodily weari-
ness in vain contends against an inability to sleep.
After half-an-hour's tumbling about, he came to the
unsatisfactory conclusion that it was of no use trying
to sleep ; so he got up and partially dressed himself.
Anything, he thought, was better than lying there
fancying all kinds of horrors. He looked out of

the window—it was very dark. He walked about
the room—it was very lonely.

'Mr. Pickwick's candle was just expiring in the
socket, as he concluded the perusal of the old
clergyman's manuscript; and when the light went
suddenly out, without any previous flicker by way
of warning, he communicated a very considerable
start to his excited frame. Hastily throwing off
such articles of clothing as he had put on when he
rose from his uneasy bed, and casting a fearful
glance around, he once more scrambled hastily
between the sheets, and soon fell fast asleep.

'The sun was shining brilliantly into his chamber
when he awoke, and the morning was far advanced.
The gloom which had oppressed him on the previous
night had disappeared with the dark shadows which
shrouded the landscape, and his thoughts and
feelings were as light and gay as the morning itself.
After a hearty breakfast, the four gentlemen sallied
forth to walk to Gravesend, followed by a man
bearing the stone in its dead box. They reached
the town about one o'clock (their luggage they had
directed to be forwarded to the city from Rochester),
and, being fortunate enough to secure places on the
outside of a coach, arrived in London in sound
health and spirits on that same afternoon.'

The description of Lord Darnley's demesne is
really charming, and as truthful and exact as it is

charming. It is only two or three lines, but it
brings the scene perfectly before us. The eye
gazes on it as on some real landscape. It is something to think of, and look back to, that I was taken by
Boz himself on this very walk, and was really affected
by it much as he describes. Alas! that is long, long
ago, and there are many milestones between.

Years afterwards Boz turned fondly back to the
old hall, and he figured himself coming by as
a sort of clock-mending tramp—a pleasant fancy
suggested by the delightful Kent roads and hamlets
where he had so often wandered. 'Likewise,' he
says, 'we foresee great interest in going round by
the park plantations, under the overhanging boughs
(hares, rabbits, partridges, and pheasants scudding
like mad across and across the chequered ground
before us)'—the very images he had used in
'Pickwick' nigh thirty years before—'and so over
the park ladder, and through the wood, until we
came to the keeper's lodge. Then the keeper
would mention that there was something wrong
with the bell of the turret stable clock up at the
hall, and that if we thought good of going up he
would take us. Then, should we go, among the
branching oaks and the deep fern, and by silent
ways of mystery known to the keeper, seeing the
herd glancing here and there as we went along,
until we came to the old hall, solemn and grand.

Under the terrace flower-garden and round by the
stables would the keeper take us in, and, as we
passed by, we should view spacious and stately
stables ; and how solitary all, the family being in
London ! Then the housekeeper, sitting in state at
needlework in a bay-window, looking out upon a
mighty grim red-brick quadrangle guarded by
lions disrespectfully throwing somersaults over the
escutcheons of the family. Then at liberty to go
and be told to keep round over yonder by the
blasted ash, and so straight through the woods till
we should see the town's lights right afore us.
The job done, our fanciful clock-mender would go
his way, and be told by a pointing helper to " keep
round over yinder by the blasted ash, and so straight
through the woods." We keep on until suddenly
the stable bell would strike ten in that doleful way.
Then should we make a burst to get clear of the
trees, and should soon find ourselves in the open,
with the town lights bright ahead of us. So should
we lie that night at the sign of the Crispin and
Crispianus—*i.e.*, The Old Leather Bottle.'

There is a tone of affectionate reminiscence in
all this, and most accurate is the description, but
coloured romantically. The house of Darnley is
likely ever to be associated with Boz, though
mistily. How fondly touching it all is, and how
it corresponds with the old Pickwickian scene !

In the delightful paper 'A Christmas Tree' he
has another allusion to Lord Darnley's mansion :
' There was the daughter of the first occupier of
the picturesque Elizabethan house, so famous in our
neighbourhood.   You have heard about her ?   No !
Why, she went out one summer evening at twilight,
when she was a beautiful girl, just seventeen years
of age, to gather flowers in the garden; and
presently came running, terrified, into the hall to
her father, saying, "Oh, dear father, I have met
myself!"   He took her in his arms, and told her it
was fancy, but she said, "Oh, no! I met myself in
the broad walk, and I was pale and gathering
withered flowers, and I turned my head and held
them up!"   And that night she died; and a picture
of her story was begun, though never finished, and
they say it is somewhere in the house to this day,
with its face to the wall.'

Yet another sketch of his walk along the 'low-
lying, misty grounds, through fens and fogs, up long
hills, winding dark as caverns between thick plantations, almost shutting out the sparkling stars; so, out
on broad heights, until we stop at last, with sudden
silence, at an avenue.   The gate-bell has a deep,
half-awful sound in the frosty air; the gate swings
open on its hinges; and, as we drive up to a great
house, the glancing lights grow larger in the
windows, and the opposing rows of trees seem to

fall solemnly back on either side, to give us place. At intervals, all day, a frightened hare has shot across this whitened turf; or the distant clatter of a herd of deer trampling the hard frost has, for the minute, crushed the silence too. Their watchful eyes beneath the fern may be shining now, if we could see them, like the icy dewdrops on the leaves; but they are still, and all is still. And so, the lights growing larger, and the trees falling back before us, and closing up again behind us, as if to forbid retreat, we come to the house.'

Strange it was that his last walk was on the evening of June 7, when he drove to Cobham Woods, and, sending away the carriage, walked round the park and back. On the following day he was seized with his fatal illness.*

* The Lord Darnley of that day was a great friend of his, and was ever eager to show his appreciation of his distinguished and interesting neighbour; and Dickens on his side, as I noted, relaxed the sort of indifference he felt for what are called 'nobs'—'swells' and persons of title. There was no radical feeling in the matter, but he always disdained being patronized or 'encouraged.' Lord Darnley was ever kindly to him. He and his family used often to dine at Cobham. As is well known, Fechter's châlet, which used to stand on Boz's little property across the road, was given by the family to the Darnleys, and it now is set up in their grounds.

CHAPTER VI

BROADSTAIRS—CANTERBURY

Of all Kentish spots, perhaps Boz fancied most the little quaint and original port of Broadstairs. He found an attraction in its calm and repose, and perhaps a solitude that he did not obtain elsewhere. Ramsgate and Margate he did not care for much. They were, no doubt, too public and too noisy. But Broadstairs had for him a recurring charm which did not wear off until many a year had passed. A great many of his books were inspired and written here. And this would seem to show that the breezes and the view of the open sea were favourable to his work. A portion of 'Pickwick' the immortal was written at Broadstairs in September, 1837—to wit, No. 18, with other 'parts.' He was once very ill there. He stayed at the well-known Albion, which still flourishes, and where he discovered that the landlord 'had the most delicious Hollands.' He wrote that he had walked to Ramsgate at low-water by the sands, and enjoyed the place exceedingly.

' I have found out that our next-door neighbour has a wife and somebody else under the roof—the wife deaf and blind, the somebody else given to drinking.' This strange story he has told somewhere.

The closing chapters of ' Nickleby' were written at this favoured little place about September, 1839. This time he had taken a house two doors from the Albion, 'where we [he and Forster] had that merry night two years ago.' He was hard at it winding all up, but these windings-up went on slowly. The publishers came, bringing down sketches with them, and dined. ' It has been blowing great guns for the last three days, and last night there was such a sea. I staggered down to the pier, and, creeping under the lee of a large boat, which was high and dry, watched it breaking for an hour. Of course I came back wet through.' This is what is always so interesting in Boz—his enjoyment and magnifying of cheap, ordinary pleasures, such as are to be had at any moment. And with what a few sharp strokes he could touch off such a scene !

About August in 1841 he found his way again to Broadstairs. He had to tell his friend of some important items of news, but the charm of the place led his pen astray. It was something that would surprise him who was pent up in dark and dismal Lincoln's Inn Fields. We wait to learn—but no ! he goes on : ' It is the brightest day you ever saw.

The sun is sparkling on the water so that I can hardly bear to look at it. The tide is in, and the fishing-boats are dancing like mad. Upon the green-topped cliffs the corn is cut and piled in stacks, and thousands of butterflies are flitting about.'

He stayed at his favourite Fort House by the sea until October. This prominent beetling building, so observed of all visitors from its conspicuous, eerie position, used to be invariably, and foolishly, known as Bleak House. It had been asserted again and again that it was the model of that house, though most people knew well that a house in quite another part of the country had been the subject of the story. It was later transformed and rebuilt, and now has been levelled to the ground.

' It is more delightful here '—this was written in June—' than I can express. Corn growing, larks singing, garden full of flowers, fresh air on the sea. Oh, it is wonderful!' A perfect picture, if ever there was one, of Broadstairs and its speciality. That note particularly must have struck many—corn growing and looking golden yellow, and just touching the rich cobalt of the sea.

At Broadstairs in 1842 he wrote a good portion of his American notes. The sea and the sunshine, however, had their drawbacks, for the open windows and the shimmering sun and the blue sea were a perpetual invitation, and we constantly find him throwing down his pen and dashing out to have a bathe.

He was here once more in 1843, and again for three weeks in 1845. 'Everything here is the same as of old,' he wrote to his friend. 'I have walked twenty miles a day since I came, and I went to a circus at Ramsgate where " Mazeppa " was played in three long acts, without an *h* in it.' In 1847 he began to complain bitterly of the vagrants, 'so impossible to be escaped from that I fear Broadstairs and I must part company in time to come. Unless it pours with rain, I cannot write for half an hour without the most excruciating organs, fiddles, bells, or glee-singers.' He went over to Margate for the play, and saw a son of the old Dowton, 'but the theatre was a dusthole.'

At Broadstairs in 1847 'Dombey' was being written, and also 'The Haunted Man,' but these two contending interests distracted him. 'I'm *blowed* if I know what to do !' In July, 1849, he was again at his favourite resort, walking fourteen miles a day. He was now at work on 'Copperfield.' He remained until he had finished No. 7. It brought him his sleep, which he had lost. 'As for news, you might as well ask me for dolphins ; nobody in Broadstairs to speak of—certainly nobody in Ballard's.' Ballard's was the house within two of the Albion, and where he had been three years

before. In 1850 he returned once more, but this
was to be one of his last visits.

As Forster said, he had always a kindly word
for Broadstairs. 'It is more delightful here,' he
wrote on June 1, 1851, 'than I can express.
Oh, it is wonderful! Fancy the preventive men
finding a lot of barrels on the rocks here, the
day before yesterday. Nobody knows anything
about the barrels, of course. They were intended
to have been landed with the next tide, to have been
just covered at low-water. But the water being
unusually low, the tops of the barrels became revealed to Preventive Telescopes, and a descent
was made upon the brandy. They are always at
it hereabouts, I have no doubt, and of course B.
would not have had any of it. O dear no, certainly
not!'

These sprightly pictures and comments show us
how constantly he was observing. The amount
of stories that he wrote here, encouraged by the
influence of a pretty place, lays us all under
obligation.

I often wonder that he did not lay some scenes of
a story here. As at Dover, he delighted when the
storms and tempests came on, on which he could
look out from his bow-windows, two doors from the
Albion. No wonder, then, that we find him here
again and again, and for months at a time. Here,

too, his greater stories were written and inspired.
Steerforth's drowning, as we know, he placed at
Yarmouth, a place of which he knew little ; but
his experiences of storms and shipwrecks were
drawn from Dover and Broadstairs. I believe a
careful study of his stories—page by page—with
Forster's Life and the Letters, and the various
light papers beside one, would furnish the most
abundant details of his personal feelings and actua
experiences. For there can be no question that he
transferred most of these into his writings. And he
found, as was only natural, that under such conditions he wrote with most effect and animation.
But it would have to be a very searching and
elaborate investigation.

Another passage in 'Our English Watering-
Place' seems to refer to the portion of the place
in which he was residing—'in this sunny window,
on the edge of a chalk cliff;' the backs of the houses
in the High Street seeming to be thus perched.
The sojourner will recognise every touch, while
those who have never seen it have it brought
before their eyes. In these sketches Boz was at
his best, for he gave free play to his fancy, and let
his pen gallop away with him. There was none of
the effort and constructed wit he was obliged to use in
his official work. Happily, at this moment Broadstairs stands exactly where it did as regards its sea,

though inland it has been built out of all recognition.
It has more character and originality than any of
our watering-places.

I have mentioned that in 1837, when he was
busy with the last portion of the ever-glorious
' Pickwick,' he was staying at No. 12 in the High
Street. ' Pickwick ' was, indeed, written at many
places. Begun at Furnival's Inn, it was continued
on his honeymoon at Chalk, then at Broadstairs
in 1837, and finally at 48, Doughty Street. Furnival's
Inn has been levelled to the ground, but the other
homes, I believe, are standing. I have entered the
Doughty Street house—a modest, compact dwelling,
now a lodging-house—with feelings of veneration,
and stood in the little room where he wrote, which
must have been the front-parlour.*

In one of his letters he describes Broadstairs :
' A good sea, fresh breezes, fine sands, and pleasant
walks, with all manner of fishing. Boats, light-
houses, piers, bathing-machines, are its only attractions, but it is one of the freshest little places in the
world.' A storm, too, is described : ' A great to-do
here—a steamer lost on the Goodwins, and our men
bringing in no end of dead cattle and sheep. I
stood supper for them last night, to the unbounded
gratification of Broadstairs. A lean-faced boatman

---

* Few persons, perhaps, recall that Tony Weller is mentioned
in Thackeray's first public success, ' Vanity Fair.'

looking at the carcases, murmured : " Couldn't sassages be made on it ?" '

'This is a little fishing-place,' he wrote to Felton, ' intensely quiet, built on a cliff whereon, in the centre of a tiny semicircular bar, our house stands, the sea rolling and dashing under the windows. Seven miles out are the Goodwin Sands (you've heard of the Goodwin Sands ?), whose floating lights perfectly wink after dark, as if they were carrying on intrigues with the servants. Also there is a lighthouse, called the North Foreland, on a hill behind the village, a severe sort of light which stares gravely out into the sea. Under the cliff are rare good sands.' Again I must repeat that of all the traditions that have grown up out of Boz's stories, none is so baseless as that Fort House was the original of Bleak House. There is no likeness. It was a mere seaside villa. Bleak House was a sort of manor-house down near St. Albans in Hertfordshire, with possibly an estate attached.

He was eager to secure this Fort House, which stood at the top of a breezy hill on the road to Kingsgate, with a cornfield between it and the sea ; but he had to be content with Lawn House, a small villa between the hill and the cornfield. The closing scenes of ' Nickleby ' were written also at Broadstairs. The story of ' Copperfield ' was completed at Broadstairs, and the plan of his periodical

worked out there in 1849. 'Such a night and day of
rain I should think the oldest inhabitant never saw.
And yet in the old, familiar Broadstairs I somehow
don't mind it much. The change has done Mamey
a world of good, and I have begun to sleep again.'
How simple was this enjoyment! How easily was
he satisfied! and how much he 'got' out of a homely
lodging at the seaside! 'We are in the part, which
is the house next door to the hotel itself, that we
once had for three years running, and just as quiet
and snug now as it was then.' Next year he was
there again, but at his favourite Fort House.

This account of Broadstairs is 'word-painted'
with such feeling and partiality as to become recognisable by anyone who has seen the place :

'Half awake and half asleep, this idle morning in
our sunny window on the edge of a chalk-cliff in the
old-fashioned watering-place to which we are a
faithful resorter, we feel a lazy inclination to sketch
its picture. The place seems to respond. Sky,
sea, beach, and village lie as still before us as if they
were sitting for the picture. It is dead low-water.
A ripple plays among the ripening corn upon the
cliff, as if it were faintly trying from recollection to
imitate the sea ; and the world of butterflies hovering over the crop of radish seed are as restless in
their little way as the gulls are in their larger
manner when the wind blows. But the ocean lies

winking in the sunlight like a drowsy lion—its glassy
waters scarcely curve upon the shore—the fishing-
boats in the tiny harbour are all stranded in the mud
—our two colliers (our watering-place has a maritime
trade employing that amount of shipping) have not
an inch of water within a quarter of a mile of them,
and turn, exhausted, on their sides, like faint fish of
an antediluvian species.   Rusty cables and chains,
ropes and rings, undermost parts of posts and piles,
and confused timber-defences against the waves, lie
strewn about in a brown litter of tangled seaweed
and fallen cliff, which looks as if a family of giants
had been making tea here for ages, and had observed
an untidy custom of throwing their tea-leaves on
the shore.

'In truth, our watering-place itself has been left
somewhat high and dry by the tide of years.   Concerned as we are for its honour, we must reluctantly
admit that the time when this pretty little semicircular sweep of houses, tapering off at the end of
the wooden pier into a point in the sea, was a gay
place, and when the lighthouse overlooking it shone
at daybreak on company dispersing from public
balls, is but dimly traditional now.   There is a bleak
chamber in our watering-place which is yet called
the Assembly "Rooms," and understood to be
available on hire for balls or concerts. . . . As to
subscription balls in the Assembly Rooms of our

watering-place now, red-hot cannon-balls are less improbable. Sometimes a misguided wanderer of a Ventriloquist, or an Infant Phenomenon, or a Juggler, or somebody with an Orrery that is several stars behind the time, takes the place for a night, and issues bills with the name of his last town lined out, and the name of ours ignominiously written in, but you may be sure this never happens twice to the same unfortunate person. . . .

'We have a pier—a queer old wooden pier—fortunately without the slightest pretensions to architecture, and very picturesque in consequence. Boats are hauled up upon it, ropes are coiled all over it ; lobster-pots, nets, masts, oars, spars, sails, ballast, and rickety capstans, make a perfect labyrinth of it. For ever hovering about this pier, with their hands in their pockets, or leaning over the rough bulwark it opposes to the sea, gazing through telescopes which they carry about in the same profound receptacles, are the Boatmen of our watering-place. Looking at them you would say that surely these must be the laziest boatmen in the world. They lounge about, in obstinate and inflexible pantaloons that are apparently made of wood, the whole season through. Whether talking together about the shipping in the Channel, or gruffly unbending over mugs of beer at the public-house, you would consider them the slowest of men. The chances are a thousand to

one that you might stay here for ten seasons, and
never see a boatman in a hurry.'

Mr. Howard Paul, the American, has an agreeable
picture of Dickens, whom he met at Broadstairs.
He had, in fact, two walks with the novelist—one
from Stratford-on-Avon to Warwick, and the second,
which he describes more particularly, from Broadstairs to Margate and back by way of the coast.
Walking was at one time among Dickens's chief
pleasures, and toward the end of his life his chief
hope of vanquishing insomnia. 'My last notable feat,'
he told Mr. Paul, ' was turning out of the streets at
2 a.m., after a day of labour, and walking twenty
miles into the country to breakfast.' His biographer,
Forster, was quite undecided whether he owed his
death ' to too much walking, too much rail-roading,
or too much going to the United States.' Arrived
at Broadstairs, Dickens and Mr. Paul had what the
latter describes as a ' simple, homely dinner.' There
were oysters from Whitstable, a sole browned to a
turn, a roast leg of mutton snatched from the fire at
the auspicious moment, the bone of which had been
removed, and the space supplied with oysters and
veal stuffing.

And then Dickens asked his guest if he had ever
tasted gin punch—*his* gin punch. ' Well, you shall,'
he replied to Mr. Paul's negative, and proceeded to
brew it.

' The brass kettle was placed over a spirit lamp,
a lemon was cut and peeled, a jug was produced
and carefully rubbed with a napkin, glasses ditto, a
bottle of old gin was in evidence, and the delicate
task proceeded.   The boiling water was poured in,
the lumps of sugar counted and added, the spirit
measured in a wineglass then followed, the chips of
lemon being added ; the mouth of the jug was closed
by stuffing in the napkin, rolled up to do duty as
a cork, and then the illustrious brewer, watch in
hand, timed the commingling of the work of his
hand.   In about six minutes the precious brew
was ready to be reverently quaffed, and as he
handed me, with a smile, a full tumbler, he kept
his eye on my face, as if to watch my first impression.'

There is a most curious, minute description of
Boz as he was in his villegiatura, during those days
at Broadstairs, which appeared many years ago, and
attracted but little notice.   It was the recollection
of a lady who was on intimate terms with the family,
in all the gay relaxation which attends families who
are away together on their holiday; and, though not
without lapses in the matter of taste, really furnishes
a delightful picture of the buoyant Boz, now at his
best and in the highest spirits.   I have asked members
of the family about this fair reporter, and found that
I had brought to their memories the image of one

who had long since faded out. The name, however, need not be given.

'I vividly recall the flutter of delight that I felt when told I was to meet Boz, and dine at the same table with the great author and his wife. My introduction to Mrs. Charles Dickens took place in the bedroom before dinner, while "fixing" our respective toilettes. She was a pretty little woman, plump and fresh-coloured, with the large, heavy-lidded, blue eyes so much admired by men. The nose was slightly retroussé, the forehead good, mouth small, round and red-lipped, with a genial smiling expression of countenance, notwithstanding the sleepy look of the slow-moving eyes. Her manner to me was friendly and informal, but could not quite allay my nervousness as I went down to be introduced to her husband.

'The first thing that riveted me was the marvellous power of his eyes. Nondescript in colour, though inclining to warm gray in repose; but lighting up suddenly into a luminous depth of hue, they instantly arrested me, and I could see nothing else for the moment. Then I became aware of a rare harmony of features, a combination of strength and delicacy of preception, a breadth and grandeur united to spiritualized refinement, which compelled a prolonged study of the whole countenance. . . . The collar and lapels of his surtout were very wide, and thrown

back so as to give full effect to a vast expanse of
white waistcoat.   He wore drab-coloured trousers,
ditto boots, with patent-leather toes, all most inconsistent with the poetic head and its flowing locks,
and the genius that glowed in his fine, well-opened
eyes.

' He talked but little during the evening, seeming
rather to allow the lead to be taken by Mr. Forster,
who was also one of the guests, and whose greater
fluency seemed to interest and impress him.   His
own speech had a certain thickness—it was a family
characteristic—as if the tongue was too large for the
mouth, and his tones were low and hurried, as though
his ideas and words were racing against each other.
His humorous remarks were generally delivered in
an exaggerated, stilted style, and sometimes with a
complete perversion of facts, quite astounding to
matter-of-fact minds, and were accompanied by a
twinkle in the eyes and a comic lifting of one eye-
brow.   I was surprised to find that, instead of the
piercing satirical expression one expected, he usually
wore a rapt, preoccupied, far-off look which was
exceedingly misleading.   When I came to know
him better, I found this was nothing but a trap for
the unwary.   During these outward semblances of
reverie nothing escaped him ; he was quietly and
unsuspectingly " taking in " every incident going on
around, and making notes thereon. . . .

'Soon after I became acquainted with him and his family, they went, as they usually did every autumn, to Broadstairs, and they induced my friends, Mr. and Mrs. Smithson, to follow them, after finding a suitable house for their occupation. . . .

'We were daily together, and on the most friendly footing. At this time, too, his mother and sister, Mrs. Burnett, with her husband, came to stay with him, and these two latter added greatly to the general enjoyment, as both sang extremely well. They were students at the Royal Academy of Music, where they first met. She was very sweet and amiable, in delicate health, and she died quite young. Old Mrs. Dickens was very agreeable, and entered into youthful amusements with much enjoyment; she had a worn, deeply-lined face, evidently roughly ploughed by "carking care." Dickens's sister Letitia (Mrs. Austin) came also for a short time. She struck me as not being so full of fun as the rest of the family. She was like Frederick Dickens, but rather tall. . . .

'Her husband appeared younger than she did, and was a plump, good-looking man, rather an "old buck" in dress, but with no resemblance to Micawber that I could detect; no salient characteristics that could be twisted into anything so grotesque, except that he indulged occasionally in *fine* sentiments and long-worded sentences, and seemed to take an airy, sunny-sided view of things in general. He avowed himself an optimist, and said he was like a cork—if he was pushed under water in one place, he always bobbed "up to time" cheerfully in another, and felt none the worse for the dip.

'It was wonderful how the whole family had emancipated themselves from their antecedents, and contrived to fit easily into their improved position. They appeared to be less at ease with Charles than with anyone else, and seemed in fear of offending him. There was a subdued manner, a kind of restraint in his presence, not merely the result of admiration of his genius, or respect for his opinion, but because his moods were very variable. Sometimes so genial and gay that one became excited and exhilarated (as if champagne had been flowing freely) merely from his contagious spirits ; at other times abstracted, and even morose—we wondered how we could possibly ever have been so friendly with him. He pretended to be engaged in a sentimental flirtation with my friend Millie (who was of a certain age) as well as with me, calling us rhapsodically in turns, " My charmer," " Beloved of my soul," " Fair enslaver," " Queen of my heart," to the infinite amusement of Mrs. Charles Dickens, and he would solicit a dance in the old English style.

' " Wilt tread a measure with me, sweet ladye ?

Fain would I thread the mazes of this saraband with thee."

" 'Ay, fair sir, that will I right gladly ; in good sooth I'll never say thee nay."

' Needless to say, the measure we trod was probably as unlike a saraband as anything imaginable ; but Charles edified the spectators by his Turveydrop deportment and Malvolio airs of smirking conceit.

' Once we proceeded to tread this measure in an imposingly majestic style, when suddenly Dickens burst into an unearthly howl expressive of mortal agony. We all stopped, appalled. He subsided into groans and moans, accompanied by contortions that outdid the writhings of the Laocoön. After a few seconds of grotesque facial and muscular performance, he turned to Mr. Smithson with an injured and upbraiding air, and faltered out: "When next you *tread a measure* in my vicinity, be humane enough to *measure your tread*, and don't stamp down with your fourteen-stone-avoirdupois-weight on that unlucky cornfield, my poor foot. I might be tempted to wreak a dire revenge, and repay you the same *measure for measure.*" . . .

' About this period his brother Frederick, whom I now saw for the first time, arrived by steamer, and we all went to meet him. He had the same *wearied* expression as Mrs. Burnett, the raised eyebrows, small nose, and large full-lipped mouth,

10—2

and spoke with the thick utterance of his father and
brother. I thought him, on the whole, more comic
in society than Dickens.   He had a positive genius
for representing commonplace matters in an absurd
light, and with exaggerated facial expression, so
that he contrived to convert the most meagre
material into ludicrous combinations. They both
occasionally indulged in puns, which, if not always
very clever, produced shouts of laughter from their
hearers, owing to the absurd way in which they
were uttered. . . .

' I have never met with anyone who entered into
games with as much spirit and boisterous glee ; the
simplest of them he contrived to make amusing, and
often instructive.   His fun was most infectious, and
he had three able partisans in his brothers and
Mr. Mitton, and under the incentive of his prompt-
ing they became irresistibly comic.   Under their
manipulation " Vingt-et-un," " Loo," etc., became
so totally altered as to be scarcely recognisable, and
generally ended in unblushing cheating and conse-
quent uproar.   The stakes were usually thrown into
a heap, and distributed honestly at the end of the
evening. . . .

'We used to play a game named "Animal,
Mineral or Vegetable," and we succeeded in puzzling
Dickens the first time he joined in it, though he
easily routed us afterwards. After exhausting all

his questions and displaying a good deal of classic and mythologic lore, he could get no further, and admitted himself beaten. He had got so far, that the object was Vegetable, mentioned in mythological history, belonging to a queen, and that the final destiny was pathetic. Great was his pretended anger and disgust when he was triumphantly informed that all this puzzling, all this parade of learning and research, had been expended on THE TARTS made by the Queen of Hearts, and stolen by the knave, who " took them quite away."

'We promised not to offend again by introducing such trivial subjects, but he pulled my hair viciously, later on, because I gave him " *the wax* that Ulysses stuffed into the ears of his crew, lest they should yield to the songs of the Syrens." How proud and elated we all felt if any clever answer gained a word of approval from the *maestro !* We were on one occasion playing, " How, when, and where do you like it ?" Fred was the questioner, and the word was *scull.* In answer to how I liked it, I answered, " With the accompaniment of a fine organ."

' " When ?"

' " When youth is at the helm, and pleasure at the prow."

' " Where ?"

' " Where wanders the hoary Thames along his silver winding way."

' "Why, of course, you little goose !" exclaimed
Dickens, crossing to where I sat. "Your answers
betrayed the word to the most simple compre-
hension ; but they were good answers and apt
quotations, nevertheless, and I think it would add
considerably to the interest of the game if we all
sharpened our wits by trying to give a poetical tone
to it with good quotations."

' He did so after this, introducing so much clever-
ness and quoting so aptly that we were literally
driven to our wits' ends trying to keep up with him.

' We went one evening in " the whole strength of
the company " to spend a few hours at the Tivoli
Gardens, a place purporting to be Vauxhall on a small
scale. Some respectable people were dancing in a part
set aside for that purpose, and we young ones were
seized with the desire to get up a quadrille among ourselves.   As no one knew us, we decided on enjoying
ourselves, with the exception of Dickens, who feared
to be recognised in these "halls of dazzling light,"
and therefore walked about outside. . . .

' We were strolling along the sands next day, our
party increased by the addition of Mr. Fletcher,
who had just arrived on a visit to Dickens. He
was a very eccentric man, impulsive and erratic—
indeed, most "unexpected" in his behaviour. He
suddenly ran some yards in front of us, careering
along with a frolicsome air, and indulging in sundry

odd and unaccountable antics, thereby attracting the
attention of several passing strangers.   They stood
still and stared after him,   " Ah !" sighed one with
profound commiseration, wagging his head mournfully.   "How sad!   You see it's quite true.   Poor
Boz ! what a pity to see such a wreck !"

'Dickens glared at him, and called to his friend.
" Halloa, Fletcher, I wish you'd moderate your
insane gambollings!   There are fools among the
British public who might mistake you for me." . . .

' To watch the sea was his greatest delight ; for
hours he would remain as if in a trance, with a face
of rapt, immovable calm, and the far-off gaze of his
marvellous eyes turned seaward, totally oblivious of
everything around him.   At first I did not understand his change of moods—in the evening full of
friendly converse and fun ; in the morning he would
pass us by with gruding recognition, as if it annoyed
him to be obliged to mutter, " How d'ye do ?" '

As we recall the absorbing story of Copperfield,
the eye always settles, somehow, upon Canterbury,
Dover, and the district between, where so much that
was dramatic and exciting took place.   We seem to
see Canterbury as we see Rochester.   Nothing can
be more accurately described than these places—the
downs, the old streets, the dwelling-houses—and the
whole tone is quite distinct from the high-comedy
spirit of Rochester.   He seems to have felt the

influence of the Cathedral and its precincts, the tranquil, slumbering, tender air of the place. The corresponding influence at Dover was that of the port and the great sea outside—so responsive his delicate nature. As I have said, when we think of Copperfield, we think mostly of these Canterbury and Dover scenes, and these are still the impressions of a lad of some twelve years old. The two towns were not more than a few miles or so away—an hour or two's journey—and he was likely enough to have often repaired thither.

The County Inn, Canterbury, where Mr. Dick put up every alternate Wednesday, was, no doubt, as Mr. Hughes suggests, the old Fountain Inn; while Micawber's inn, we may assume on the same authority, was the old Sun Inn in Sun Street, overhanging the street in picturesque fashion. It quite corresponds with Boz's description: ' I looked in the old house from the corner of the street.' It stands at a corner : 'the evening sun, we are told, was striking on its gables and lattice-windows.'

There have been several houses in Canterbury suggested as Wickfield's. There is one nearly opposite the Catholic Church, which has always been used, so runs the tradition, as a lawyer's office. It is a two-storied house of brick and timber and lime-washed front. The door is low and arched, and opens on a sort of hall, or square, with panelled walls.   On your left is the clerk's office, which might be Uriah's room, except that there is no turret.   On the right is a panelled waiting-room, and beyond the office of the aged clerk.   Looking out on the garden at the back is a large room, which appears to fit in exactly with the dining-room in which Uriah was ultimately denounced by Micawber.   The stairs also deserve a word.   Broad, with shallow oak steps and a hand-rail almost wide enough to walk upon, they seem to correspond exactly with the description in the novel.   · The main objection is the absence of gables and carved woodwork in the front, and the fact that there is no turret-room. . . .   An enterprising clerk, some years ago, carved " U. Heep" on his desk in one of the downstairs rooms, and the name is shown to this day to American and other tourists, some of whom believe it to be genuine.'

It was to Canterbury that David came to propose for Agnes, when he tells us that 'the well-remembered ground was soon traversed, and I came into the quiet streets, where every stone was a boy's book to me.   I went on foot to the old house.'   He looked through a low window of the turret-room, then stood in a window and looked across the ancient street at the opposite houses, recalling how he had watched them on wet afternoons.   He had watched the tramps, too, as they limped past, which

shows that it must have been the main street.
After being articled to the Proctor he visited
Canterbury; in fact, through the book he is constantly going back to the place, and every time it
is mentioned with affectionate reminiscence. Often,
too, he repeats the same description, as though
never tired of the topic. 'Coming into Canterbury I loitered through the old streets with a sober
pleasure that calmed my spirits and eased my heart.
There were the old signs, the old names. It
appeared so long since I had been a school-boy
there that I wondered the place was so little
changed; strange to say, the great influence which
was inseparable in my mind from Agnes seemed
to pervade even the city where she dwelt, the
venerable Cathedral towers, and the old jackdaws
and rooks.' His praise of Canterbury for its
appreciation of his readings should make the place
rejoice: 'The most delicate audience I have seen in
any provincial place is Canterbury—an intelligent
and delightful response in them.'

He has a little sketch of the approach to Canterbury at Christmas time: 'How I recollect that
wintry ride! the loud clatter of the horses' hoofs
beating in time upon the ground; the stiff tilled
soil; the snowdrift slightly eddying in the chalk-
pit. The smoking team, with the waggon of old
hay, stopping to breathe on the hill-top, and shaking

their bells musically ; the whitened slopes and sweeps
of down-land, lying in darkened relief, as if they
were drawn on a huge slate.'   Who knew his Kent
so well as he ? He had it by heart, every town of it.

Of Deal he gives this pretty and truthful sketch :
'At last we came into the narrow streets of Deal,
and very gloomy they were upon a raw, misty
morning.   The long, flat beach, with its little
irregular houses, wooden and brick, and its litter
of capstans, and great boats and sheds, and bare
upright poles with tackle and blocks, and loose,
gravelly waste places, overgrown with grass and
weeds, were as dull in appearance as ever I saw.
The sea was heaving under thick white fog, and
nothing else was moving but a few early rope-
makers, who, with yarn twisted rounded their bodies,
looked as if they were spinning themselves into
cordage.'

A vivid and truthful and poetical description of
the little place which all frequenters will recognise.
Then there was the old hotel in the main street,
where are rooms like a ship's cabins, and the more
modern and pretentious ' Queen's.'

He describes the fog rising like a curtain, ' when
numbers of ships we had had no idea were near
appeared.   I don't know how many,' said he, ' the
waiter told us were then lying in the Downs.'   All
of which brings Deal vividly before us

CHAPTER VII

DOVER—BOULOGNE—FOLKESTONE

THERE was a curious charm, quite unequalled, in Boz's touch which marvellously conveyed the *tone* of a place. Every town and bit of country—however like to another—with him is distinct, and has a fashion and garb which only those with the true instinct can appreciate. Thus, the little Copperfield's walk to Dover, how thoroughly Kentish it is! On the downs we breathe the full Kentish sea-breezes ; we seem to be drawing nearer and yet nearer to the town. He once wrote of the place :

' I particularly detest Dover for the self-complacency with which it goes to bed. It always goes to bed when I am going to Calais with a more brilliant display of lamps and candles than any other town. Mr. and Mrs. Birmingham, host and hostess of the Lord Warden Hotel, are my much-esteemed friends, but they are too conceited about the comforts of the establishment when a night-mail is starting. I know it is a good house to stay at, but I don't want the fact insisted upon in all its warm, bright windows at such an hour. I know the Warden is a stationary edifice that never rolls or pitches; I object to its big outline seeming to insist upon this circumstance, and, as it were, to come over me with it when I am reeling on the deck of the boat. Beshrew the Warden, likewise, for obstructing that corner, and making the wind so angry as it rushes round.'

'As I wait here, on board the night packet, for the South-Eastern train to come down with the mail, Dover appears to me to be illuminated for some intensely aggravating festivity; in my personal distresses all its noises smack of taunting.'

How many of us, who in our chequered course have come down by night to go abroad, will not recognise the faithfulness of his description of that waiting on a fine but menacing night while the preparations go on—the town lights ranged as in an amphitheatre, with quite a festive character —the train gliding down so smoothly! Boz felt and appreciated the dramatic varieties of the situation. What life, too, he gives to the tall Lord Warden Hotel, thrusting its big shoulder forward to meet the wind, looking out to the sea, by day and by night, and encountering all the storms!

It was in 1852 that he came to Dover, and stayed there three months—a long time for him. Nine

years later, when on a reading tour, he was turning away 'half Dover' from the doors : 'the audience
wouldn't go, but sat applauding like mad.'

Some of us have, no doubt, been detained at such
a place—weather-bound, it may be—and found what
a weary restlessness came on us, and how impossible
it was to do anything. The feeling is a peculiar one,
and Boz, in his own analytical way, has interpreted
it for us. He could, indeed, write upon anything, and,
like Swift, upon a broomstick, even. But we must go
back to the old Dover of fifty years ago—the Dover
of the ' old Ship '—of the small inner harbour before
the Admiralty Pier was, and of the rude, imperfect
transfer from the station. As at Calais, the boats
came in quite close to the town, just under the old
Ship Inn. And there was the pier clock, which
drew his attention as he looked out from his window.

'It became a positive duty to look at the packet
preparing to go across, aboard of which the people
newly come down were hurrying in a great fluster.
The crew had got their tarry overalls on, and one
knew what *that* meant, not to mention the white
basins ranged in neat little piles of a dozen each
behind the door of the after-cabin. The mail-bags
—O that I had the sea-legs of a mail-bag !—were
bundled aboard, the packet left off roaring, warped
out, and made at the white cone upon the bar. One
dip, one roll, one break of the sea over her bows,

and Moore's Almanac could not have told me more
of the state of things aboard, that I know.'

Reading ' Out of the Season,' as his paper was
called, we seem to be spending the monotonous
hours there with Boz—no bad company, however.
How accurately he analyzes the curious feeling!—
everything ' shut up,' etc.   On this visit there was
a tremendous gale, which he described in his own
picturesque way, and which he did not scruple to
' throw away ' on a letter : ' The storm was most
magnificent. All the great side of the Lord Warden
next the sea had to be emptied, and the break of
the waves was so prodigious and the noise so utterly
confounding.   The sea came in like a great sky of
immense clouds, for ever breaking suddenly with
furious rain ; all kinds of wreck were washed in :
among other things a very pretty brass-bound chest
being thrown about like a feather.   The unhappy
Ostend packet, unable to get on or go back, beat
about the Channel all Tuesday night, and until noon
yesterday, when I saw her come in with five men at
the wheel, a picture of misery inconceivable.'

Exceptional touches like this last always impressed
him, and he was fond of repeating them as dramatic
incidents.

My friend Mr. Ashby Sterry, who has made so
many ingenious investigations into the localities of
Dickens's stories, once turned his attention to the

discovery of Miss Trotwood's house at Dover, and in one of his most pleasant 'Cucumber Papers' seems to have arrived at a satisfactory conclusion.

It will be remembered that the outcast David Copperfield, when he found himself in Dover inquiring hopelessly for his aunt's house, was standing at a street close by the Market Place, and was directed by a good-natured flyman, 'who pointed towards the Heights. "If you go up there and keep right on till you come to some houses facing the sea, I think you'll hear of her."' Our explorer followed this direction implicitly, and 'went up there and kept right on,' but found no house that would 'do.' He then took a turn round by a disused road, and going to the right, facing the sea, found a short turn to the left, down a narrow street that recalled the rows of old Yarmouth, and finally noted a general shop that corresponded with the one where David met Janet. 'I pass the shop, turn down a narrow passage on my right, and I come upon a road leading up to the Downs upon my left.' This looks like the right track. He goes on :

'In the distance I see what I fancy must be her house. It is perhaps not quite so neat as it was in Miss Trotwood's time, but there is no doubt that it is the house ; here are the bow-windows, there is the room above. The window must have been in the next room where Miss Trotwood sat. There is the garden. It still stands high, meeting the fresh breezes from the sea and the Downs. It has still a view of the sea, though much built about.'

Boz's sketch of 'Our French Watering-Place,' an account of his residence at Boulogne, is one of his most charming efforts. He has given a captivating account of that ever-brilliant little port, its gay colouring and cheerful natives. He was there in the years 1853 and 1856. The old 'High Town' had for him an extraordinary attraction—as, indeed, it must have for anyone with a feeling for the old world. As he truly said, if it had been some thousand miles off it would have drawn innumerable pilgrims and sightseers, but being only a couple of hours' journey from England no one thinks of it. The solitude of the venerable ramparts, where so many forlorn exiles make their daily promenade, the small streets slumbering below, where the poet Campbell and the greater Le Sage ended their days, have a strange charm. And so Dickens was attracted to it. For he pitched his camp, not by the bustling port, but high up on the very crest of the hill, on the downs, well beyond the Old Town, and in one of those pleasant French country-houses so complimentarily styled 'châteaux.' It was a steep and toilsome walk from below. He has described it in his brightest and most enthusiastic style.

Last year, being in Boulogne, I set forth on a sort

of voyage of discovery, or pious pilgrimage, to see
if I could find this pleasant retreat of a celebrated
man ; but no one knew of it, or even that Dickens
had been in any way associated with the place.
This is not surprising, as it was nigh half a century
ago. I had even heard that it had been partially
levelled or rebuilt. But a friendly English bookseller, living high up, in the Grande Rue, knew all
about the matter, and put me on the right track.
I took my way, accordingly, to the left of the Old
Town, struck out of the Boulevard Mariette, past
the coquettish little dancing-garden known as the
Tintilleries, went on higher and yet higher, until
I reached the Rue Beaurepaire, where I was told
I would assuredly find the château. This road, or
lane, scarcely deserves the name of street, for there
were but a few houses here and there ; but in Boz's
day it was a charming country road, always rising,
and that pretty steeply. How fresh was the air at
that elevation ! How rich all the greenery, with a
pleasant wilderness and uncultivation ! Before me
was a rude stone wall, built of cobbles, and within
the stone wall was 'the property' of M. Beaucourt,
Boz's landlord, and whom he has described so
humorously. But the château itself, where was it !
There were two châteaux, both occupied by Dickens
at different visits, and bearing different names. The
first was gone—levelled, I presumed. Instead, here

was a huge monastic building, with an imposing
church or chapel in front, of a Gothic kind, whose
windows were filled with stained glass—a most important place indeed.   Now it seemed all silent,
dusty, and deserted—' shut up,' in fact ; and so it
was, as a little mean advertisement affixed to the
wall told us—' Maison à Vendre ou à Louer.'   The
late Law of Suppression had been at work here,
and the good nuns and their protégés had been
ejected.   The building seemed of recent erection,
and must have cost much.   But, again, where was
the château ?   The convent ' stood in its own
grounds,' as auctioneers have it, and attractive
grounds, too.   There was a large growth of trees
rich in foliage at the back, on the rising hill, planted
over fifty years ago, before Boz's tenancy.   But at
the corner, nestling among them, I noted a modest,
unpretending building — large villa rather than
château—yellow all over, with a triangular pedi-
ment, its windows, three in a row, garnished with
green ' jalousies.'   All the ground about it, a large
field of a couple of acres, sloping to the road, formed
' the property ' or estate of which the admirable
Beaucourt (' M. Loyal ' in the sketch) was so proud.
A steep road, with another cobbled wall, ran up the
hill beside it, and led on still higher.   Boz no doubt
tramped it often enough, while on the spacious field
his children gambolled.   It was here that the English

servant kept guard with a gun, bent on taking the life of the wild-cat, to the terror of the tradesmen. ' Ne tirez pas, monsieur !   C'est moi—boulanger !'

In his account of the humours of the place Boz was at his best, because his heart was engaged. He loved his worthy host, and studied him *con amore.* He could see from the windows the cherished Old Town below.   The place was then altogether in the country, but during the fifty odd years houses and streets have grown, and the view was intercepted.

What will become of this château and of the monumental structure beside it ? It is clear the château was used by the Sisters as a house for visitors.   It will by-and-by come down, while its great neighbour will be turned into some sort of institution.   It was with rather sad and mixed emotions that one turned away from the old house so fast decaying.   The genial, buoyant Dickens at rest ; his amiable host gone ; the excellent nuns gone also ! What merry parties in that château ! For the hospitable Boz would invite over all his friends —the doughty Forster, the sparkling Jerrold, and many more.   All gone !

Beaucourt-Mutuel had another property to the extreme south of Boulogne, and many miles from the first.   But it is said in the district that Dickens actually came over here to Hardelot, and was so delighted with the place that he put up with his host.　The Mayor of Condette, M. E. Huret-Legache, told Sir F. Burnand, who was the first to call attention to this interesting episode, that he well recollected meeting Dickens at Hardelot, who, he said, gave away many a little souvenir to the natives. They still religiously preserve them, and are glad to show them.　But I fear some of this Hardelot legend, however interesting, is somewhat shadowy; for the good Mayor fixes the date of the visit as being in 1864, when Boz was not at Boulogne. Boz, he said, remained eight days.　As Sir F. Burnand suggests, Boz most probably would have preferred to take one of his rousing walks over to Hardelot, returning on the same day to the 'property.'

After his last visit to Boulogne, Boz does not appear ever to have returned to the good landlord's enticing 'property,' so Beaucourt-Mutuel fades out, and we see no more of him, as we would have liked to have done.　Boz parted from him in 1856, and died, as we know, in 1870; but his host survived him eleven years, and was buried at Condette, a pleasant village south of Boulogne, and many miles away from his 'property,' at the north of the town.　He lies beside the church, which boasts a modest Gothic steeple.　His tomb is a stone with a huge plain stone cross reared upon it, and with this inscription : ' Ici repose le corps de Monsieur Ferdinand Beaucourt, époux de Françoise Mutuel, né à Bethune, décédé à Condette, le 8 mai, 1881, à l'âge de 75 ans et 8 mois.'

From this little record might one 'speculate out' some scraps of his life. It is likely, from his using the name 'Mutuel,' that his wife had brought him the 'property.' Further, that she heartily bewailed his loss, from the pretentious character of the monument as well as from the affectionate calculation as to the months even of his age.

On the other side of the stone is a most touching tribute paid to Dickens, and one, too, that would have gladdened his heart. The widow, in her natural pride at the celebrity which the grand *romancier* had given her husband, had caused to be 'cut' on the stone a passage from 'Our French Watering-Place': 'The Landlord of whom Charles Dickens wrote, "I never did see such a gentle, kind heart."'

All which makes a truly pleasing pastoral, equally delightful to read of or to think over.

Thus has Dickens done something for the bright and interesting little port, linking it, as he could do so well, to a sort of romance. We would all have liked to have seen, to have known, 'le brav' Beaucourt.' I think Mr. Merridew, the well-known bookseller at Boulogne and tourist's friend-in-need, might usefully reprint, with notes, Dickens's account

of the gay town—the charming little sketch 'Our
English Watering-Place'—and put it at the end of
his familiar guide.

And how vivid is his account of Calais, which
everyone who has been there by night or day will
recognise !—'The passengers were landing on the
pier, a low-lying place and a low-spirited place, with
the tide ebbing out towards low-water mark, the
meagre lighthouse all the while haunting the sea-
board, the long rows of gaunt black piles, slimy and
wet and weather-worn.   Every wave-dashed, storm-
beaten object was so low and so little that the
wonder was that there was any Calais left, and that
its low gates and low wall, and low roofs and low
ditches, and low sand-hills and low ramparts, and flat
streets, had not yielded long ago to the under-
mining and besieging sea.'

This was the old Calais of fifty years ago, which
many of us will recall, when the packet came up to
the town, and not, as now, to the far end of the pier.
Then the railway-station was close by.

Boz, who took care to see everything stirring
that was going on, found himself about 1840 at
the Thanet Races, held on the road from Margate
to Acol, and of which he wrote : ' I saw—oh, who
shall say what an amount of character in the way of
inconceivable villainy and blackguardism ! I even
got new wrinkles, in the way of showmen, con-

jurors, pea-and-thimble men, and trampers generally.'
This is interesting and worth noting, for at the time
he was staying there, in the June and September
of 1840, he was busy with the fortunes of his
Little Nell, and may have there found the characters
of Codlin and Short and their fellows, while the
Thanet Races might have furnished him with details
of the race during which Nell and her father made
their escape.

In these almost confidential *communiqués*—his
' Uncommercials' and other light papers—we see
the simple, engaging nature of Boz at its best. We
think of his high position—one of the greatest
men in the kingdom, every eye turned to him—
and yet we find him living in the most simple,
unaffected fashion, by himself and attending on
himself, without a valet, having the keenest enjoyment in staying a few days at some familiar English
port out of the season, and entertaining himself by
looking on at the humours of the place! Though
no one loved home and fellowship more, and he
might have said with the elder Dumas, ' Sans moi
j'en serai bien *embêté*,' there is nothing more
pleasing or interesting than this unfeigned sim-
plicity. It is a great and even precious gift, this
finding pleasure in observing what is round about us.

Returning again to Dover I've often found him
dwelling on ' praises of the land, and dispraises of the

gloomy sea.   The drums upon the heights have gone
to bed, or I know they would rattle taunts against
me for having my unsteady footing on this slippery
deck.   The many gas eyes of the Marine Parade
twinkle in an offensive manner as if with derision.
The distant Dogs of Dover bark at me in my mis-
shapen wrappers as if I were Richard the Third.
A screech-owl and a bell and two red eyes come
gliding down the Admiralty Pier with a smoothness
of motion rendered more smooth by the heaving of
the boat.   The sea makes noises against the pier, as
if several hippopotami were lapping at it, and were
prevented by circumstances over which they had no
control from drinking peaceably.   We—the boat—
become violently agitated—rumble, hum, scream,
roar, and establish an immense family washing-day
at each paddle-box.   Bright patches break out in
the train as the doors of the Post Office open,' etc.

David Copperfield's distressful walk to Dover is
one of the most dramatic passages in Boz's writings ;
he knew the road so well.   I always think of his
approach to Dover as the train draws near the
town, when the first fresh breezes of the sea give
note of the approaching coast, with the undulating,
swelling downs and patches of white chalk.   He
makes David romantically associate the memory
of his mother's girlhood with various stages of
the journey, more particularly with her love of

Canterbury. 'I have associated it ever since with the sunny streets of Canterbury dozing, as it were, in the hot light; and with the sight of its old houses and gateways, and the stately gray Cathedral, with the rooks sailing round the towers.'

The first scene, too, of 'A Tale of Two Cities' was laid on 'the Dover Road,' which lay before the Dover mail as it lumbered up Shooter's Hill. When it got down to Dover the coach stopped at the George. This inn was probably the old Ship, long since in ruins. According to the old system, the rooms at the George had odd names—'Show Concord!' 'Gentleman's valise and hot water to Concord,' etc. When Mr. Lorry had finished his breakfast, he went out for a stroll on the beach. The little, narrow, crooked street of Dover hid itself away from the beach, and ran itself into the chalk cliffs like a marine ostrich. The beach was a desert of heaps of sea and stones tumbling wildly about, and the sea did what it liked, and what it liked was destruction. It thundered at the town and thundered at the cliffs, and brought the coast down madly. A little fishing was done in the port, and a quantity of strolling about by night and looking seaward. Small tradesmen who did no business whatever sometimes unaccountably realized large fortunes, and it was remarkable that nobody in the neighbourhood could endure a lamplighter.'

Close by was another port to which he was
affectionately devoted. In those days it was not
at all developed. Boz is united to Folkestone, not
merely by his own personal liking and feelings, but
by his writings. His knowledge of its 'ways' and
doings is shown in his letters to friends, full of
genial sketches and touches, and, finally, in the
truly lively and graphic picture of the place written
for his own magazine, and in which all its charm
is set forth with a pleasant engaging humour and
truthful accuracy. Folkestone is not likely to be
ever again celebrated by so accomplished a master.

Almost fifty years have elapsed since Boz was
staying there, at No. 3, Albion Villas, whither he
had retired to write the opening chapters of a new
novel. His sketches of the place are lively and
graphic. In a letter written for the benefit of his
friend Wilkie Collins, he says : 'We have a very
pleasant little house overlooking the sea. It rained
in honour of our arrival with the greatest vigour.
I went out after dinner, and I stopped in the rain
about halfway down a steep crooked street, like
a crippled ladder, to look at a little coachmaker's,
where there had just been a sale, speculating on the
coachmaker's business, and what kind of coaches he
could possibly have expected to get orders for in
Folkestone. I thought, "What would bring together
people now, in this little street, at this little rainy

minute ?"   On the instant a brewer's van, with two
mad horses in it, and the harness dangling about
them, dashed by me, and in that instant such a
crowd as would have accumulated in Fleet Street
sprang up magically.   Men fell out of windows,
dived out of doors, plunged down courts, precipitated themselves down steps, came down water-
spouts instead of rain, I think ; and I never saw so
wonderful an instance of the gregarious effects of
an excitement.   A man, a woman, and a child had
been thrown out on the horses taking fright and the
reins breaking.   The child is dead, the woman very
ill but will probably recover, and the man has a head
broken and other mischief done to him.'

This shows Dickens's admirable power of observation : to anyone else it would have seemed but
a common street accident.   And how lifelike it is,
and with what pains and many touchings is the
scene painted !   It might be a sketch in one of his
stories.   We recognise the tone and colouring of
the old Folkestone of fifty years ago, the ' crooked
street like a crippled ladder ' (a good stroke).   I
suppose it is there now.   I fancy, however, that the
present Folkestone coachmaker gets more orders
than Boz ' wotted of ' at the time.

He gives the drollest account of the launching of a
Folkestone fishing-boat, but everything this pleasant
man touched he made humorous : ' All the fisher-

men in the place, all the nondescripts, and all the
boys pulled at it with ropes from six a.m. to four p.m.
Every now and again the ropes broke, and they all
fell down in the shingle.   The obstinate way in which
the beastly thing *wouldn't* move was so exasperating
that I wondered they didn't shoot it or burn it.
Finally, when it was quite given over, someone
tumbled against it accidentally (as it appeared to
me, looking out at my window), and it instantly
shot about a mile into the sea, and they all stood
looking at it helplessly.'

Folkestone is particularly dignified by being what
Elia calls 'the kindly engendure' of ' Little Dorrit.'
The place seems to have inspired Boz : for he held
to his work, ' sticking at it day after day.'   He
seems to have no idea of holding a pen for any
other purpose but that book.   ' How I work, how
I walk, how I shut myself up, how I roll down hills
and climb up cliffs ; how the new story is everywhere, heaving in the sea, flying with the clouds,
blowing in the wind ; how I settle to nothing and
wonder (in the old way) at my own incomprehen-
sibility.'   He had fashioned here three numbers, in
the last of which he had relieved his 'indignant soul
with a scarifier'—that is, he blew off a little of
indignant steam 'which would otherwise blow me
up, and with Gods' leave I shall walk in the same
all the days of my life.'   At Folkestone, also, he read

the 'Carol' in what he described as 'a long car-
penter's shop, which looks far more alarming as a
place to hear in than the Town Hall at Birmingham.'

The old Folkestone of some fifty years ago was,
as may be gathered from the foregoing, a very
different place from the new and almost resplendent
watering-place of to-day. It had then an old-
fashioned, sleepy air and a somewhat shabby aspect.
Boz, who at the time he wrote his sketch 'Out of
Town' lived close to the South-Eastern line—his
station was at Higham: how familiar in those days
was the heading on his blue note-paper, 'Gadshill Place, Higham, by Rochester, Kent'!—was
frequently tempted to run down to the Pavilion,
or pass through it, making a little flight to Paris.
He believed heartily in the romance of travelling—
in the flitting by night through the darkness, the
lights, the shadowy figures; above all, in the entering a foreign country at midnight, with the unfamiliar
gendarmes and douaniers waiting, and the clock of
the old Town Hall or the Market Place chiming
forth the hour. No one of real sentiment can help
being thus affected on landing at the old familiar
ports. It is a show that never palls on one, and
though we cross to the Continent a dozen times in
the year, we never can get over the sense of surprise
on finding ourselves of a sudden in a new land and
among new people dresses and decorations. How

odd the feeling as we pass the quaint and curious
rows of houses along the port at Boulogne—with
the clattering progress through narrow streets—the
cracking whip, which denotes that the inn is at
hand! Then how delightful some old Louis XV.
bedroom, with the crimson velvet sofas, the mirrors,
the clocks, and the stately rococo doors! Familiar
as is all this, and seen over and over again, the
feeling never grows stale. You ever wonder how
it is that you are there.

The Pavilion Hotel being on the line to Paris,
and hospitably at hand after stormy passages,
Boz naturally had a tender interest in the place
which had received him so kindly and bound up
his wounds. It was one of the incidents of his
high position and reputation, that at every hostelry
he was made much of, with extra attention, accommodation, cookery, etc.—though I imagine that
these attentions often found their way into the
bills. But apart from this, he was deeply interested
in the establishment—chiefly, as I have said, because
it was associated with so much that was agreeable.
No one was more modest or unassuming, or put on
less 'side'; but I always noted that he liked little
deferential attentions from railway-guards and such
persons, and also to feel that he was well known
and looked up to in his own district. This he
felt was a homage to his craft. On his own line,

the South - Eastern, he was known and saluted by all.

The Pavilion, as it appeared in those old days of the fifties and sixties, would seem to us now a very modest affair—a rambling brick building, lying low under the cliff. But everyone all over the kingdom knew the Pavilion, mainly because most travellers passed by it, and with every boat a stream of guests found their way to its hospitable halls.

In his essay Dickens's special partiality for the Pavilion is displayed. He shows an almost affectionate sympathy for the place ; it is full of loving touches, and is done with wonderful spirit and vivacity. In another, 'The Flight,' a vivid description of a journey to Paris, he still returns to his favoury hostelry, though giving it another name. It is astonishing with what delightful and accurate vividness he has touched the incidents and curious 'feeling' of the journey. So with the approaching end of the journey, the sense of the sea being at hand, the glimpses of the great chalk cliffs —who does not know well these symptoms, and how curious and indescrible the sense, though ever so familiar ?

Altogether—if hotels are subject to feelings of vanity, or to what is known as 'swelled head'—the Pavilion, and the town where it is situated, may be very well pardoned for having thus gained the affections of this distinguished and engaging man.

His picture of the hotel and the seaport which enshrines it is a very enticing one. 'Sitting, on a bright September morning, among my books and papers at my open window on the cliff overhanging the sea-beach, I have the sky and ocean framed before me like a beautiful picture. A beautiful picture, but with such movement in it, such changes of light upon the sails of ships and the wake of steam-boats, such dazzling gleams of silver far out at sea, such fresh touches on the crisp wave-tops as they break and roll towards me—a picture with such music in the billowy rush upon the shingle, the blowing of morning wind through the corn-sheaves where the farmer's wagons are busy, the singing of the larks, and the distant voices of children at play —such charms of sight and sound as all the Galleries on earth can but poorly suggest. . . .

'The South-Eastern Company have brought Pavilionstone into such vogue, with their tidal trains and splendid steam-packets, that a new Pavilion-stone is rising up. I am myself of New Pavilion-stone. We are a little mortary and limey at present, but we are getting on capitally. Indeed, we were getting on so fast at one time that we overdid it, and built a street of shops, the business of which may be expected to arrive in about ten years. We

are sensibly laid out in general, and with a little
care and pains (by no means wanting, so far) shall
become a very pretty place. We ought to be, for
our situation is delightful, our air is delicious, and
our breezy hills and downs, carpeted with wild-
thyme, and decorated with millions of wild-flowers,
are, on the faith of a pedestrian, perfect. In New
Pavilionstone we are a little too much addicted to
small windows with more bricks in them than glass,
and we are not over-fanciful in the way of decorative
architecture, and we get unexpected sea - views
through cracks in the street doors; on the whole,
however, we are very snug and comfortable, and
well accommodated. But the Home Secretary (if
there be such an officer) cannot too soon shut up
the burial-ground of the old parish church. It is in
the midst of us, and Pavilionstone will get no good
of it, if it be too long left alone.

'The lion of Pavilionstone is its Great Hotel. A
dozen years ago, going over to Paris by South-
Eastern Tidal Steamer, you used to be dropped
upon the platform of the main line Pavilionstone
Station (not a junction then) at eleven o'clock on a
dark winter's night, in a roaring wind; and in the
howling wilderness outside the station was a short
omnibus, which brought you up by the forehead
the instant you got in at the door; and nobody
cared about you, and you were alone in the world.

You bumped over infinite chalk, until you were turned out at a strange building which had just left off being a barn without having quite begun to be a house, where nobody expected your coming, or knew what to do with you when you were come, and where you were usually blown about, until you happened to be blown against the cold beef, and finally into bed.   At five in the morning you were blown out of bed, and after a dreary breakfast, with crumpled company, in the midst of confusion, were hustled on board a steamboat, and lay wretched on deck until you saw France lunging and surging at you with great vehemence over the bowsprit.

' Now, you come down to Pavilionstone in a free and easy manner, an irresponsible agent, made over in trust to the South-Eastern Company, until you get out of the railway carriage at high-water mark. If you are crossing by the boat at once, you have nothing to do but walk on board and be happy there if you can—I can't.   If you are going to our Great Pavilionstone Hotel, the sprightliest porters under the sun, whose cheerful looks are a pleasant welcome, shoulder your luggage, drive it off in vans, bowl it away in trucks, and enjoy themselves in playing athletic games with it.   If you are for public life at our Great Pavilionstone Hotel, you walk into that establishment as if it were your club, and find ready for you your news-room, dining - room, smoking-room, billiard-room, music-room, public breakfast, public dinner twice a day (one plain, one gorgeous), hot baths and cold baths. If you want to be bored, there are plenty of bores always ready for you, and from Saturday to Monday in particular you can be bored (if you like it) through and through. Should you want to be private at our Great Pavilionstone Hotel, say but the word, look at the list of charges, choose your floor, name your figure—there you are, established in your castle, by the day, week, month, or year, innocent of all comers or goers, unless you have my fancy for walking early in the morning down the groves of boots and shoes, which so regularly flourish at all the chamber-doors before breakfast, that it seems to me as if nobody ever got up or took them in. Are you going across the Alps, and would you like to air your Italian at our Great Pavilionstone Hotel? Talk to the Manager— always conversational, accomplished, and polite. Do you want to be aided, abetted, comforted, or advised at our Great Pavilionstone Hotel? Send for the good Landlord, and he is your friend. Should you, or anyone belonging to you, ever be taken ill at our Great Pavilionstone Hotel, you will not soon forget him or his kind wife. And when you pay your bill at our Great Pavilionstone Hotel, you will not be put out of humour by anything you find in it.

'A thoroughly good inn, in the days of coaching and posting, was a noble place. But no such inn would have been equal to the reception of four or five hundred people, all of them wet through, and half of them dead sick every day in the year. This is where we shine in our Pavilionstone Hotel. Again, who—coming and going, pitching and tossing, boating and training, hurrying in and flying out— could ever have calculated the fees to be paid at an old-fashioned house? In our Pavilionstone Hotel vocabulary there is no such word as "fee." Everything is done for you; every service is provided at a fixed and reasonable charge; all the prices are hung up in all the rooms, and you can make up your own bill beforehand, as well as the bookkeeper. . . .

'We are a tidal harbour at Pavilionstone, as, indeed, I have already implied in my mention of tidal trains. At low water we are a heap of mud with an empty channel in it, where a couple of men in big boots always shovel and scoop, with what exact object I am unable to say. At that time all the stranded fishing-boats turn on their sides, as if they were dead marine monsters; the colliers and other shipping stick disconsolate in the mud; the steamers look as if their white chimneys would never smoke more, and their red paddles never turn again; the green sea-slime and weed upon the rough stones at the entrance seem records of obsolete high tides never more to flow; the flagstaff-halyards droop; the very little wooden lighthouse shrinks in the idle glare of the sun.   And here I may observe of the very little wooden lighthouse, that when it is lighted at night—red and green—it looks so like a medical man's, that several distracted husbands have at various times been found, on occasions of premature domestic anxiety, going round it trying to find the Night-bell.

'But the moment the tide begins to make the Pavilionstone Harbour begins to revive.   It feels the breeze of the rising water before the water comes, and begins to flutter and stir.   When the little shallow waves creep in, barely overlapping one another, the vanes at the mastheads wake and become agitated. As the tide rises the fishing-boats get into good spirits and dance, the flagstaff hoists a bright red flag, the steamboat smokes, cranes creak, horses and carriages dangle in the air, stray passengers and luggage appear.   Now, the shipping is afloat, and comes up buoyantly to look at the wharf.   Now, the carts that have come down for coals load away as hard as they can load.   Now, the steamer smokes immensely, and occasionally blows at the paddle-boxes like a vaporous whale, greatly disturbing nervous loungers.   Now, both the tide and the breeze have risen, and you are holding your hat on (if you want to see how the ladies hold *their* hats on with a stay, passing over the broad brim and down the nose, come to Pavilionstone). Now, every-thing in the harbour splashes, dashes, and bobs. Now, the Down Tidal Train is telegraphed, and you know (without knowing how you know) that two hundred and eighty-seven people are coming. Now, the fishing-boats that have been out sail in at the top of the tide. Now, the bell goes, and the loco-motive hisses and shrieks, and the train comes gliding in, and the two hundred and eighty-seven come scuffling out. Now, there is not only a tide of water, but a tide of people, and a tide of luggage—all tumbling and flowing and bouncing about together. Now, after infinite bustle, the steamer steams out, and we (on the Pier) are all delighted when she rolls as if she would roll her funnel out, and are all disappointed when she don't. Now, the other steamer is coming in, and the Custom House prepares, and the wharf-labourers assemble, and the hawsers are made ready, and the Hotel Porters come rattling down with van and truck, eager to begin more Olympic games with more luggage. And this is the way in which we go on, down at Pavilionstone, every tide. And, if you want to live a life of luggage, or to see it lived, or to breathe sweet air which will send you to sleep at a moment's notice at any period of the day or night, or to disport yourself upon or in the sea, or to scamper about Kent, or to come out of town for the enjoyment of all or any of these pleasures, come to Pavilionstone.'

This old snug and interesting Pavilion, for which Boz was so enthusiastic, was some years ago altogether rebuilt in glorified fashion, after the pattern of our modern 'Métropoles.' It might have been a shock to Boz to have seen this destruction. How many a time and oft had he found welcome shelter within its walls!

What an illustration of Dickens's enthusiastic nature is all this praise of an ordinary hotel! But he loved it, and he liked its people, who made him happy there. So he could not resist giving them this very unusual tribute.*

* The proprietors have, at my suggestion, reprinted Dickens's paper of praise in a tempting little volume, which they entrusted to my editorship, and which every guest of theirs can read and carry away.

CHAPTER VIII

GADSHILL

Boz looked back fondly to his first aquaintance with Gadshill, when he was a 'very small boy.' The image of the place, magnified to palatial size, was before his eyes for over thirty years. Once, going abroad in state with courier and well-laden carriage, he took the old Dover Road, and, when beyond Gravesend, his child's dream came back on him, and he dressed it up in this pleasing and fanciful way : 'The widening river,' as he noticed, 'was bearing the ships, white-sailed or smoke-blacked, out to sea,' when he met, in this dreamy retrospect, a very queer small boy. '"Halloo," I said, "where do you live?" "At Chatham," says he. "What do you do there?" says I. "I go to school," says he. I took him up in a moment, and we went on. Presently the very queer small boy says : "This is Gadshill we are coming to, where Falstaff went out to rob those travellers and ran away." "You know something about Falstaff, eh?" said I. "All about

him," said the very queer small boy ; "*I am old
(I am nine*), and I *read all sorts of books.* But do
let us stop at the top of the Hill and look at the
house there, if you please." "You admire that
house ?" said I. "Bless you, sir ! when I was not
more than half as old as nine, it used to be a treat
for me to be brought to look at it. And now I am
nine I come by myself to look at it. And ever since
I can recollect, my father, seeing me so fond of it,
has often said to me : 'If you were to be very
persevering and were to work hard, you might
come one day to live in it '—*though that's impossible,*"
said the very queer small boy, drawing a low breath,
and now staring at the house out of the window with
all his might. I was rather amazed to be told this
by the very queer small boy, for that house happens
to be *my* house, and I have reason to believe that
what he said is true.' A little bit of his biography,
and charmingly told. The passage illustrates the
graceful tenderness of Boz's nature. He cherished
this thought. The only portion that is fiction is the
'half as old as nine.'

For this was about the year 1821, when he was
nine years old. Thirty-five years passed away, during
twenty of which Boz had been in the full enjoyment
of his fame. Yet the image of the old house was
still with him. Now and then we find him somewhere on the Kent Road, or perhaps at Gravesend.

It came to the February of 1855—he was setting out on a trip to Paris, and he put his friend Wills off, who had settled to meet him on business, with this excuse: 'When I was at Gravesend t'other day I saw at Gadshill, just opposite to the Hermitage where Miss Lynn used to live, a little freehold to be sold. The spot and the very house are literally a dream of my childhood, and I should like to look at it before I go to Paris. I want you, strongly booted, to go with me.' They went down, accordingly, but it is likely that Boz made some mistake as to its being offered for sale, or found on inquiry that it could not be obtained, for nothing then came of the matter. This is shown clearly by his letter to his friend Cerjat, written nearly a couple of years later, where he mentions and describes this very expedition. The board announcing the sale probably was erected on the ground of another property—the Hermitage, perhaps, belonging to Miss Lynn.

'Down at Gadshill, near Rochester in Kent, Shakespeare's Gadshill, where Falstaff engaged in the robbery,' he wrote to Cerjat, 'is a quaint little Country House of the time of Queen Anne. I happened to be walking past a year and a half or so ago, with my sub-editor of *Household Words*, when I said to him, "You see that House? It has always a curious interest for me, because when

I was a small boy in these parts I thought it the most beautiful house" (I suppose because of its famous old cedar-trees) "ever seen. And my poor father used to bring me to look at it, and used to say that, if I ever grew up to be a clever man, perhaps I might own that house, or such another house. In remembrance of which I have always, in passing, looked to see if it was to be sold or let, and it has never been to me like any other house, and it has never changed at all." We came back to town, and my friend went out to dinner. Next morning he came to me in great excitement, and said: "It is written that you were to have that house at Gadshill. The lady I had allotted to me to take down to dinner yesterday began to speak of that neighbourhood. 'You know it?' I said. 'I have been there to-day.' 'Oh yes,' she said, 'I know it very well. I was a child there in the house they call Gadshill Place. My father was the Rector, and lived there many years. He has just died, left it to me, and I want to sell it.' So," says the sub-editor, "you must buy it, now or never!" I did. I hope to pass next summer there, though I may perhaps afterwards let it furnished from time to time.'*

* In 1804 Mr. Lynn, the father of Mrs. Lynn Linton, became Perpetual Curate of Strood, and some time between that year and 1814 bought Gadshill House, which he retained to his death in 1855, when he was seventy-eight. In that year she, being the

I always think that in the ever-attractive 'Christmas Carol' he intended to make yet one more allusion to Rochester and to this house. He describes Scrooge as having been a boy at a market town which they saw as they 'walked along the road, in the distance, with its bridge, its church and winding river. They soon approached, leaving the highroad—by a well-remembered lane—*a mansion of dull red brick, with a little weather-cock-surmounted cupola on the roof, and a bell hanging within it*'—an exact suggestion of Gadshill.

Gadshill! At this moment the name works with the potency of a charm. It has become a shrine, known all over England and America. Yet I recall the time when it was hardly at all familiar; and I also remember well the mystic enchantment of my first visit, which afforded me one of the prettiest, most entrancing pictures of a literary man's domestic life—golden and glittering and almost fascinating.*

---

sole executrix, disposed of it to Boz, a chance he had long been waiting for. 'I used,' she said, 'to go to his parties with all the rest of the world, but I never saw Gadshill again when it was his. He would say that I must go down, but never fixed a time.' Her biographer mentions what he calls 'an amusing fact' in this connection : that Charles Dickens, disputing the value she had placed on the timber—viz., £40—an arbitrator was named, who fixed it at £70.

* I have in my possession some interesting letters on the subject of the purchase of Gadshill. They are from Mr. Frederic

Gadshill is a *riant* (as the French have it), cheerful house. Its effect is almost dramatic. The windows and their disposition have a character ; so has the roof, with its piquant cupola. No one could pass it without being attracted by it. The back, also, has character of its own. How well I recall one bright morning, when I had risen betimes and strolled out

---

Ouvry, Boz's man of business—an interesting, genial man—whom I had met, and whose contact with Dickens lent a particular and affectionate interest in his affairs. The first is addressed to Mr. Wills, and runs :

'66, LINCOLN INN FIELDS,
'*17th March*, 1856.

'MY DEAR SIR,
'Gad's Place. I have settled this purchase, paying as under :

	£	s.	d.
Purchase money	1,750	0	0
Timber	45	2	6
Half-year's rent to Lady Day ...	51	6	8
	£1,846	9	2
Cash received of Mr. Dickens ...	1,790	0	0
Balance due to me	£56	9	2

'It appears the rev. tenant pays £110 per annum, which includes the house and leaseholds. He will therefore have to pay back to Mr. Dickens the £51 6s. 8d.
'Mr. Soaden (of Waden) will pay the school rent to Lady Day, but there will be a trifling difference, as the old rent of the leasehold was £28, and is now raised to £32.
'Where does Mr. Dickens wish his title-deeds to be deposited ?
'Yours very truly,
'FREDERIC OUVRY.'

It will be noted that the little property is here entitled 'Gad's Place,' which must have been the current name, as his solicitor

down the steps into the garden, wandering about! Presently I heard a light step. It was the daughter of the house, coming out to look after her flowers. Later came the cheery breakfast, Boz going over to the side-table and recommending certain savoury dishes —say kidneys, dressed in very appetising way. Yet he was nothing of a gourmand, but the rather delicate appetite had to be roused by something piquant and tasty.

There was something almost romantic in this idea of his now at last living in the house on which his mind had been fixed so long ago, when he was a lad. I have often thought how fitting it was that Sir Walter Scott should have shown the same *territorial*

---

was not likely to mistake. Dickens would naturally wish to re-vive the familiar Falstaff name, the inn so named being *vis-à-vis*. The price was really about £1,800, not £1,750, as he put it. This would be equivalent to a rental of about £70 a year. But the property must have gradually swallowed up thousands. A completely appointed mansion would have been cheaper in the end. But, then, there was his special fancy for romantic associations.

With his usual promptitude, Boz settled the account on the next day, for we found Ouvry writing :

'18*th March*.

' MY DEAR SIR,
      ' Thanks for the cheque. I cannot send the title-deeds, as the conveyance is not yet stamped. I wish also, before they are deposited, to make a schedule of them. When these things are accomplished, I will send them to Coutts's to be deposited.'

Thus prudently did he arrange his business. Instead of leaving his deeds with his solicitor, as is commonly done, he consigned them to his bankers' safe.

longings, as we might call them.   His eyes had been long fixed on Abbotsford.   It is pleasant to follow Boz's ardour when he was set up as a country squire. For years he had been going from house to house in London—Doughty Street, Tavistock House, Devonshire Terrace.   One can quite understand his feelings, and there is nothing more interesting in his life than this passage of it—the turning back of his eyes to Rochester after so many years' absence. It was over thirty years since he had left it, and here was he now eagerly seizing the opportunity to establish himself in the county he so loved.

And at this moment has not the name Gadshill become a wondrously suggestive thing for all the world, like Stratford-on-Avon or Abbotsford?   It means the brilliant, ever-living Personality, which we wish to call up before us by a visit, or by even thinking of the place.   The pilgrims arrive and drive out there, and gaze reverently.   But what must be the feelings of those who, like myself, have been there, have lived under its sheltering roof, have heard the genial, cheery voice, have taken the generous open hand, have walked under his guidance —here, there, and everywhere—over his fair Kent and its green lanes!   It is a curious, strange thing that this should be so; for how few are there that can say it!   But Boz seems about as far off now as the Laird of Abbotsford himself.   Nothing was more wonderful than this presence of his; it was so filling, so ennobling. I was at the house recently, and it seemed to me much smaller and unpretentious than I had imagined. It was his animation and protean shapes that furnished the idea of spaciousness and of palatial dimensions.

Boz was delighted with his purchase and his new position as a squire. But, outside sentimental associations, it was hardly a suitable residence for him. It was a long way from the station, and also a good walk from Rochester, and even the neighbours were some way off. This at once entailed carriages and horses and servants. Then, like all old houses, it proved to be dreadfully out of repair, and £1,000 had at once to be laid out. Above all, there was no water. 'The house,' he wrote to a friend, 'is so old-fashioned, cheerful, and comfortable that it is really pleasant to look at.' So it was, and so it is. 'The good old rector has lived in it twenty-six years, and so I have not the heart to turn him out'—*i.e.*, at once. Boz was always thus, amiable and indulgent. It is, as all know, highly 'cheerful' in aspect, from its mellow rubicund tint and quaint outlines. How good and satisfactory is the deep porch, within which Boz so often stood, framed, as it were, and looked out across the flowers! Within it was delightfully old-fashioned, with its 'well' staircase, which rose upwards, every landing seem-

ing the same.   The latest occupant before his owner-
ship began was Mr. Hindle, the Vicar, with whom
Forster had a talk when writing the biography.
I remember him myself coming to the house at
Christmas time.

I heard my old friend Marcus Stone, at a meeting of
the Boz Club, make the statement that in all matters
relating to household arrangements—dining and
cookery—Dickens was far in advance of his day.
Nothing could be more true.   Long before dinners
à la Russe were thought of, he had introduced them.

It always seemed to me a pleasant-looking, picturesque house, with a comfortable, glowing, even
rubicund air.   In winter, at Christmas time, it was
at its best—the snow covering the spreading fields,
and the lights glowing in the scattered houses—a
warm background for Christmas, while the genial
owner furnished interior heartiness and good spirits.

Three years later, in July, 1858, he wrote to
Cerjat : ' At this present I am on my little Kentish
freehold, looking out on as pretty a view out of my
study window as you will find in a long day's English
ride.   My little place is a grave red-brick house
(time of George I., I suppose), which I have added
to and stuck brick bits upon in all manner of ways,
so that it is pleasantly irregular and as violently
opposed to all architectural ideas as the most hopeful
man could possibly devise.   The robbery was com-

mitted before the door on the man with the treasure, and Falstaff ran away from the identical spot of ground now covered by the room in which I write. A little rustic alehouse is over the way—has been over the way ever since—in honour of the event. Cobham woods and park are behind the house.' Again, on October 25, 1864 : 'I have altered this place very much since you were here, and have made a pretty (I think an unusually pretty) drawing-room. My being on the Dover line, and my being very fond of France, occasions me to cross the Channel perpetually. Whenever I feel that I have worked too much, or am on the eve of overdoing it and want a change, away I go, and turn up in Paris, or anywhere else that suits my humour, next morning. So I come back as fresh as a daisy, and preserve as ruddy a face as though I never leant over a sheet of paper.'

It will have been seen that Boz puts the date of the house as Queen Anne's or early Georgian. But, according to Forster, it was built so lately as 1775 by an illiterate functionary who wrote his name and his office as 'Mare of Rochester.' I think most visitors, judging from the little lantern and the general style, would consider it much older. The bricks, too, seem to have the tilelike tone and texture of Queen Anne's day.

Nothing was more delightful in Boz than his

unfailing *gaieté de cœur*, shown by gay remarks
and trifling jests.   There was no pretence in these
little quips.   A most delightful being, surely!   He
could be often what is called 'waggish.'   A most
pleasing feature in him was his welcome of any
natural little story, or supposed good thing, and he
seemed to be almost grateful and under an obligation
at it being told him.   A trifling instance of this kind
comes back on the moment, but it is no bad illustration of his way.   At Gadshill, a visit to which
was ever a delightful sort of holiday, I was telling
him of an English opera I had been to see or hear ;
and I described to him the absurd introduction of a
game of cricket played *secundum artem* on the stage,
with wickets pitched, bowling, etc.   But this was
not all the absurdity, for all was set to music, and
there was a grand chorus of rustic spectators, fielders,
and others.   The words were something of this
kind :

    ' Here we play the game of Crick-et !
    The glo-ri-ous game of Crick-et !'

This tickled Boz immensely, and often when I met
him he would allude to it—'just like your friends
with their "glo-ri-ous game of Crick-et !" Un-
commonly droll that !'   This is what made him so
engaging to his friends.   How good-naturedly, too,
used he to welcome anything in the shape of a jest
—feeble though it might be, he making the best of

it! I remember when he took me out to see the new châlet, and described how quickly it had been put up, I said in a rather feeble way, 'Nothing shilly-shally, I see.' This amused him, and he repeated it at dinner. I suppose there never was a man of his high position so modest and unobtrusive, or that gave so cordial a welcome to what others would say. And I cannot help comparing him with Scott in this. Sir Walter was, no doubt, an engaging man also in his own household, but it is easy to see that he took the lead, as it were, and furnished the entertainment. He was not quite so receptive as Boz. Scott was a business man, so was Boz; but Scott, genial as he was, could be despotic, and at times hard, in business.

There are not many now alive who can have played billiards with Boz in his own house. I see him now, stooping over the table,* his coat off, his large double glasses on—which gave him rather an antique, 'old-mannish' look. And yet how comparatively young at this time—only fifty-eight! Since his day middle-aged folk have become younger and yet younger, and a man anywhere in the fifties is now comparatively a juvenile. But what a neighbour to have! Only fancy it, Charles Dickens! Boz *lui-même*, and not one of your

---

* This billiard-table was sold for the 'song' of £3. It is to be lamented that all these relics could not have been kept together as Scott's were at Abbotsford.

recluse bookish men, weak-eyed and dyspeptic, shy, shrinking from, or else looking down upon, the community ; but the genial, hospitable Charles was ever forward and responsive to everyone, always in evidence, eager to know—in short, as Carlyle said, 'the good, the noble, the high-souled, ever friendly Dickens, every inch of him an honest man.'

Boz's walks were truly astonishing.   At one time of his life he used to 'do' his twenty miles a day regularly.   When we recall what we know of his ideas of the seven-league boots, of his Pickwickian walk of 'twenty-five miles before dinner,' to be undertaken by stout, elderly gentlemen, his own genial, intrepid system of walking, maintained all through his life, seems natural.   In some of my walks with him about Rochester, I must confess to being at last utterly spent and exhausted.*

And now for my introduction to the amiable, genial, and always encouraging Boz.   He had been reading in Dublin, having a most unctuous welcome.   I had been writing for him, but had never met him.   ' I

---

* As he liked to note strange things or odd things happening, how he would have been struck, as I was on this day (April 30, 1903), by noting a police case in the papers where his grandson, 'Hal' Dickens, appeared against a Mr. Budden !   It was like the father of this young counsel being once actually concerned in a case where one of the parties was named Pickwick.   Budden was a native of the Rochester district, and it was always said that the Fat Boy was drawn from him.   Long after, Captain Budden came to live at Gadshill—another coincidence.

don't know him, but I have seen him,' as Winkle once said.

There came an opportunity, as he was departing for the country next day. I find in an old diary some notes of what followed. ' I made a bold resolution,' I wrote, 'that I would go this morning and meet him at the South-Western Railway, King's Bridge. I walked over betimes and waited. I saw at last a cab arrive, with portmanteaux on the roof, labelled, in large white letters, one " C. D.," the other " A. W. S." These belonged to the immortal Boz and his aide-de-camp, Arthur W. Smith. " C. D." got out and strode away to the platform. He was in a check suit, and looked a fine, bold, well-made, sturdy Englishman, with a sort of bronzed redness—not of paint, as some of us had fancied, but of blooming health on his cheeks. I waited till I saw him standing at the carriage door, placidly reading a paper. Then, screwing up my courage, I went up to him, and said, rather nervously, "I beg your pardon, Mr. Dickens, but my name is ——." The keen eyes were looking with a sort of distorted anxiety—this was some intruder ; but when he heard the name he changed in an instant. A warm and hearty shake of a hand —up and down—from him. " And how do you *do ?*" he said. " Very glad to see you "—all spoken with a sort of metallic burr that seemed novel to me. Ego :

"I hope you will excuse me, Mr. Dickens, but I am going to Paris to-morrow morning for a couple of months, and I should have been so disappointed had I not seen you." He said he had just come from Belfast. "Tremendous houses there," he said cheerily; "curious people, though. Half Scotch."

'"I had a letter from Forster"—he knew of my interest in that doughty personage—"he's worried to death with old Land's sad business." Here he laughed, as if enjoying something. "What a pity it is, though!" "Yes," I say, "and he seems so wrong-headed, too." "Ay, ay," says Boz, in his ever prompt way; "that's the word—very wrong-headed. But there is a great deal behind. I can assure you, he is the finest and most chivalrous old fellow in the world. Lord, yes! Know him well? Lord bless you! Many years. All this business was to protect a poor governess. Is he rich or good for damages? Lord, no! Not he. He won't pay a farthing of it. He is safe in Florence this moment, and has assigned over every stick."

'Here comes up Arthur Smith—a quiet, spare, youngish man—"fit" in every way, and of inestimable value to Boz. Introduction follows. "Mr. F. tells me there is another train." "By the way," says A. Smith, "it was Mr. F. we were going to ask, wasn't it, to do that little job for us?" "So it was!" cries Boz, with that tone of rapturous alacrity

we knew so well later—" to get jaunting cars, one
for him, and one for me.   We were going to write
to you, but a friend in Belfast managed it "—this
was his friend Finlay—" much cheaper, he said,
than it could be done here.   Well, do you know,
Forster is deep in his Swift.   I tell him he will
never see it through.'   (So it proved.)

In private life he cherished, as we have seen, the
old feeling of Christmas, and delighted to gather
about him the members of his family and a few
choice friends at his Kentish house.   Gadshill
offered a good *mise en scène* and background for
such festivity, and might pass very well for a sort of
' moated grange '—certainly for a good old manor-
house, with its belfry on the roof, and its rubicund
Georgian brick, and old-fashioned and even-spread-
ing yew-trees.   Few places have seen more happy,
enjoyable days and nights.   Within there was a
notable hall of the ' well ' pattern, with a stair that
went up to the roof, and some good old chambers.
But the host was all in all, and, indeed, a host in
himself.   Visiting the place lately, I was struck
with its rather dwindled air; it seemed so much
smaller and less important than it was.   But this
was the absence of the presiding spirit—the lost
Boz—which filled and expanded every portion.   I
say advisedly there never was, and never could be,

so genial, amiable, unaffected, and untiring a person in his treatment of friends and guests. He was always eager to listen rather than to speak—to take a second or third place ; more anxious to be told, rather than to tell, an amusing story. His very presence was enough, with the bright, radiant face, the glowing, searching eyes, which had a language of their own, and the expressive mouth. You could see the gleam of a humorous thought, first twinkling there, and had a certain foretaste, and even understanding, of what was coming ; then it spread downwards — the mobile muscles of the cheek began to quiver ; then it came lower, to the expressive mouth, working under shelter of the grizzled moustache ; then finally, thus prepared for, came the humorous utterance itself !

How he enjoyed all the attendant paraphernalia of Christmas, particularly the jovial drinks which attend the season ! He would have had wassail even, had it not been an inacceptable, rather sickly compound. To hear him talk of the steaming bowl of punch, with apples 'bobbing about' merrily, of the Garrick matchless gin-punch particularly, and the anticipating zest and relish with which he compounded these mixtures, one would fancy him quaffing many a tumbler. But, alas ! how often had it been noted, to the general surprise, that his whole enjoyment was in the romantic association ! Never

was there a more abstemious bibber.   It was like
Captain Jackson, in Elia's essay, who passed round
his old rind of cheese with all the air and flourish of
its being a round of ripe Stilton.   I can never recall
any of his festivities without some special compound
of this kind figuring.   He once held a sort of village
cricket-match in his field — a diverting business,
carried out with a gravity that recalled the match
at Muggleton—where he himself 'marked' all day
long, and cheered the players with many a hearty
' Well run !' ' Well caught !'   On which occasion there
were some guests—the late Dean of Bristol and his
wife, myself, and, I think, no others.   A special
brew of borage circulated briskly, for the day was
oppressively warm.   I yielded to its seductions, it
seemed so innocent, and, as thirst grew, took yet
more of the dangerous draught.   Next morning
I had a splitting headache, and was too much over-
come to appear at breakfast.   What a sly twinkle
was in his eye, and how many a pleasant allusion to
it he made !   In vain I might have pleaded, ' It was
the salmon.'   But I think he was rather pleased than
otherwise at the implied compliment to the liquor.

Sometimes I have gone down with him for a
couple of days' stay, meeting him at the station.
This was one of the private, home-like visits.   I
was staying at the Charing Cross Hotel, and was,
bag in hand, hurrying from the side-door in the

station to catch the train, when a too zealous porter, rushing after me, put in a detainer. I suppose it had the look of 'levanting,' but the delay had nearly shipwrecked the visit. Boz, I fancy, hugely relished the contretemps. I recall playing billiards before going to bed. How many a game we had! He was a fair player.

I was at Gadshill for one or two Christmasses— not on Christmas Day, but shortly after. I remember coming down with him in the train, with his son-in-law, the faithful henchman Dolby, and some others. We walked up from the station; there was a crisp layer of snow over the fair Kent country; the air was fresh; there was a gray half-tint over everything, and we could see the red light at Gadshill afar off, twinkling through the trees. The only incident of the walk that comes back upon me was that Dolby, who was rather a brusque, rough nature, began to talk of someone having been 'bashed' by someone else. Boz caught the then rather unusual word, and began to ask for a literal explanation. Anything of this sort interested him. His sister-in-law had walked down to meet us; and so had the dogs. That night there was to be a dinner-party, and various neighbours — some from a distance — were to come in the evening. There was that agreeable sense of something exciting which is so pleasant for a guest in a country house. That night our host was to give us an experimental trial of one of his newest pieces for the readings, and he was anxious to try the effect upon a rural audience. I was looking from the window out on the wide, low-lying country, all white with the snow, and could see a carriage or two—a couple of black patches moving along the road—far off. I thought of the 'moated-grange' pictures. Here it was exactly: 'Guests arriving for the Christmas party.' They, in their turn, had their eyes on his cheerful red curtains, illuminated from within, and giving promise of the snug blazing fires, and logs, and maybe a comforting glass. One of these vehicles was the Vicar's, Mr. Hindle's. There was also the doctor, I think, then tenants of the nearest tall house, and so on. But the snow kept some away.

A delightful dinner-party it was. How many are gone now! I was beside the interesting daughter of the house—the attractive 'Mamie,' as she was called — who has herself written some most pleasing records of these joyous days. She had great personal attractions, and much of her father's observation, with a pleasant wit of her own and a certain piquancy of manner. I always admired her indomitable spirit and independence. After dinner we gathered in the cosy drawing-room, which our host had added to the old house.

The retainers came in, and Boz took his stand
at the desk and began to read ' The Boy at Mugby,'
a keen and amusing bit of satire on the then system
of railway refreshment and on the haughty damsels
who presided, and zealously served out stale sand-
wiches and scalding coffee.   He presented sketches
of their ways and doings in very amusing fashion.
But, I remember, his friend Forster, who was never
very favourable to the readings, did not quite approve
the topic.   I fancy the subject was found too local
and special for general interest—and Boz made
very little use of it in his professional readings.

A gay and hilarious night followed.   The desk
and apparatus was cleared away, and there was
proposed a series of amusing games.   Not a round
game, as at Dingley Dell, but a very remarkable
exercise of the wits, which affected one very much
as would the performance of a clever, perplexing
conjurer.   Boz himself was, of course, the central
figure.   He illuminated all with his quick, lightning
flashes and perpetual buoyancy.   There was a bright
alertness and a certain dapperness in his spare figure.
His hand was usually in his pocket, while his roguish
glances roved about.   Truly :

> ' A merrier man,
> Within the limits of becoming mirth,
> I never spent an hour's talk withal.
> His eye begets occasion for his tongue ;
> For every object that the one doth see,
> The other turns to a mirth-moving jest.'

Those who knew Dickens intimately can often trace in his writings—which others cannot—allusions to little 'pet' theories and hobbies of his. I have heard, for instance, him often dwell on the dreadfully tyrannical power of the law of average, which must be carried out. He would mention the number of persons yearly killed in the London streets—some hundreds, I think—and he would add this original suggestion : ' Now, here we are in November, and the number of such accidents is much below what it should be. So, is it not dreadful to think that before the last day of the year some forty or fifty persons *must* be killed—and killed they will be.'

How well I recall that first 'red letter' night when I was asked to meet Dickens! It was quite a gala night when I and my sister arrived at the small house at Glocester Gate. Wills, our host, his faithful friend and sub-editor, a crisp, shrewd, and perky man, but genial withal, was quite in a flutter. His clever wife was one of the Edinburgh Chambers's, sister of Mrs. Lehmann, mother of the present gifted Liza. It was Mrs. Wills who made the memorable speech that 'women's rights' were usually ' men's lefts '—a quip that de- lighted Boz. I see the scene now. The company were Boz and his daughter Mary, Wilkie Collins, Dr. Lankester, the 'Crowner,' Mrs. Lynn Linton,

Mrs. Procter, and some more whom I forget, about
ten in all. Boz seemed to glitter—he was always
' showy' on these festive occasions—and often wore
a jewelled stud with a red flower. I was 'cast' for
his daughter, of whom I must say something.

Miss Dickens was an exceedingly pretty girl,
with a bright, delicately moulded face full of
thought, and a pensive expression. This broke
occasionally into one of smiling sarcasm or raillery.
She had a pleasant tongue, was ready always with
a reply or retort. I am glad to think I was one of
her intimates ; but we had many a falling-out, and
when she grew warm she was unsparing. She disdained always the little hypocrisies of society—that
smiling agreement with all absurdities—and spoke
her true opinion in a straightforward way. Many a
time and oft I have winced under a stroke. She had
a charming taste in dress, and was always gracefully
' gowned,' as they say nowadays, her *petite* figure
showing to great advantage. She was fond of
gaiety and of a dance, and often made expeditions
from Gadshill to the Chatham balls—at this time
held under much more pretentious conditions than
was the military ball at Rochester. She was
intensely loyal to her friends, and 'would not
listen to a word' about them. There was a country
squire and his family with whom she was constantly
on visits, and whom I believe she fancied approached

perfection. I used to venture on little jests concerning these amiable people, finding imaginary
faults. How her eyes would flash, and what little
severities she would utter! So with her dog
Bouncer, a little white Pomeranian, between whom
and me there was no love lost. 'An ill-tempered
creature!' I would say, which led to a fresh burst.
She was altogether an engaging, piquant, and
delightful character, and suggested the lines :

'Thou hast so many pleasing, teasing ways about thee,
There's no living with thee or without thee.'

But, alas! those were the bright and palmy days.
Then all was luxury and enjoyment — the fair
country house, the house in town for the season,
the visits, the renowned Boz himself, whose celebrity reflected on her—his very name a *passe par
tout*. It was indeed delightful. But it only went
on for a span, a decade or so. Then came the
sudden blow of 1870, which brought a complete
change.

Years later—I suppose nearly twenty—I met her
for the last time, as it proved to be. It was at one
of Sir Henry Irving's hospitable suppers, when he
used to entertain about a hundred guests. Just
before the banquet began I met her in the crowd.
She was, alas! much changed, and had almost an
ascetic look, which was not surprising, as she lived
for good and charitable works, and gave herself

entirely to them. We could have both wished that
the places of the guests had not been arbitrarily
allotted, and a long, long talk over old times would
have been welcome. This, of course, was impossible.

But to come to our dinner-party. It went on
most pleasantly. Wilkie Collins was an almost professional diner-out, and, like Johnson, 'talked for
superiority.' This he did in a smart, ostentatious,
and voluble way, saying amusing things occasionally.
He seemed to take the lead. Boz, who liked and
admired him, listened, as his way was, smilingly
interposing sly remarks, his brilliant eyes twinkling
intensely. Who that knew him will not recall what
'Elia' styles the 'kindly engendure' of a jest in
that mobile face? It was an extraordinary exhibition. You saw it coming. The fires began to
sparkle, the eyelids to crumple; then it stole down
the face; the cheeks were drawn up in humorous
creases; the jest lurked in the corners under the
moustache; finally it came in a genial illumination.
But he never cared to lead; he preferred to listen
and to applaud.

I always thought Wilkie Collins was a rather
artificial sort of littérateur. His books seemed
manufactured. He fancied that he had a gift of
humour, but his fun was forced. He strained
after copying Boz. His was a sad fate. He

became a martyr to gout — perhaps the result of too much dining out. It settled in his eyes, which often presented a terrible spectacle, so inflamed that someone described them as 'bags of blood.' Dr. Lankester was a somewhat obstreperous talker, and held his own.

Upstairs, after dinner, I see myself standing with Boz and his friend, both good-naturedly inquiring after a certain life of 'The Unfortunate Dr. Dodd,' a work I was then busy with. I had before this issued a Life of Sterne. Boz asked in his merry, twinkling way 'How were my two disreputable parsons?' I hear him again at the end of the night, with his daughter standing before me and my sister, hospitably planning an immediate visit to Gadshill. How affectionately interested they were! No generalities, but a day instantly named. With his methodical instincts, he had his little notebook out, and was jotting down the time of trains for going and return, with various directions. He tore the scrap out, and I have carefully preserved it to this hour. The faded characters call back vividly that delightful night. Our host was a good-humoured fellow, faithful and true to his friends. He did not mind telling a joke even against himself, as when he would say, 'Did I ever tell you what Douglas Jerrold said to me?' "Wills, you would look very like a pin." " Oh, that's quite obvious!

I am so long and thin, of course." " I say you
would be, only you've not the head or the point." '
Wills always suggests a good example of how
regular correspondence has died out. Every letter
he wrote was an emanation of his mind and
feelings. He put himself into it, sometimes in
four closely-written pages, and albeit on strict
business he made it human. Nowadays there is
little or nothing of this; every word must be to the
point.

Boz lived but a mile or so from the station,
Higham. Thence, whenever he found himself
low and out of sorts, he threw himself into the
train and made the ever-exciting and romantic
journey to Paris. Who that has read his ' Flight '
will ever forget that amazing *tour de force* and
specimen of word-painting?

In a day or two the delightful expedition came
off, and I paid my first visit to Gadshill—precursor
of many others. A palace of enchantment it seemed
in its sylvan charms and greenery, with which its
cheerful rubicund tint contrasted. That was some
forty years ago! *Eheu fugaces!* How complete,
how compact was everything, and what an abode
of bliss! There was only the household, his sister-
in-law, and the son-in-law, the gentle 'Charley
Collins,' who 'enjoyed,' as it is called, the most
appalling health. He was indeed sorely tried, but

ever patient.　He had an ardent longing to have
a reputation like his brother, but was slow-moving,
and his notions of humour were light enough.　His
novel ' Brought up to the Bar' was ponderous.　I
recall his father-in-law bringing me into a room to
pass judgment on a huge yellow poster, some four
or five feet long, laid out on the floor 'to see how it
would strike me.'　'The Cruise upon Wheels,' an
account of a horse and gig journey through France,
was too much beaten out and too laboriously funny.
The trivialities of thought revealed are most curious.
He had conceived a sort of romantic ideal of such
a journey, which completely vanished in the performance.

On that day the whole of this amiable family
were lavish in their hospitality.　I see Dickens now
reposing on the grass, now at croquet, or walking
in the woods, and then at the delightful dinner.
Boz's dinners were always of the best.　I have
many of the menus, written on the favourite blue
paper with blue ink.

Boz himself had a wit of his own, and was always
ready to season talk with some lively and ready
allusion.　My friend Mr. Birrell told me that he
was once present when Dickens was giving prizes
to some schoolgirls—at Birmingham, I think—when
a girl came up whose name was Weller.　There
was loud laughter from the audience.　' You see,

my dear,' said the pleasant Boz to her, ' you will have to change your name at once.'

When Scrooge was taken by the spirit to Scrooge's nephew's Christmas festivities, a number of drawing-room games are described, notably one called ' Yes or No,' wherein Scrooge's nephew had to think of something, and ' the rest must find out what. There was a brisk fire of questions in which it was elicited from him that he was thinking of an ' animal, a live animal, a rather disagreeable animal . . . that wasn't made a show of, and wasn't led by anybody—which didn't live in a menagerie and was neither a horse or an ass, a cow, a bull or a tiger, etc.,' and so on. In this particular game Boz himself excelled, carrying it on with the most brilliant spirit and animation. I have so seen him play it—on this night at Gadshill ; when, however, he would reverse the process, going out of the room while we fixed on some subject. Then he came back and plied us with a shower of inquiries until he actually *forced* his way to the solution ; so brilliant a being he was in all that he did.

If we look round our acquaintance at, say, some paterfamilias—a writer, a senator, 'celebrated person' —in the bosom of his family, what do we find ? A reserved and stately personage, seated in his chair, looking on indulgently at his daughters, whom he thinks foolish girls enough, but will tolerate.

He is resting after the hard exertion of his talents, but he has nothing to do with 'the young people' (and does not care to have to do with them) and their noisy pastimes. Or else this great gentleman is not there at all, but in his study or at the club. Something after this kind is a usually accepted pattern. But Dickens! between his two bright daughters, and he the brightest of the trio — his trim, well-made figure in motion; his keen, ever-glancing face and laughing eyes; his gay, showy dress—velvet collar, red carnation (invariable as Mr. Chamberlain's orchid); his general showy, gleaming air, bringing light and quicksilver wherever he was; his gay, cheerful talk; hearty laugh; every-thing kept moving by *him;* good-natured and kindly; in all corners, and bringing genial fun and frolic—what an amazing man this was! And yet all the time one of the most famous men in England! And his modesty and retirement — never obtruding, always wishful to listen and not to speak himself, to be second while others were first, to laugh and not to cause laughs. 'I vow and protest,' so Thackeray used to begin one of his moralizings, there seems to have been no one ever like or approaching to this wonderful and most engaging man. And for how much that is admirable and sympathetic in his writing does this character and personality account for? It was surely another

motor force of an unusual kind. Affection, good-
humour, domestic enjoyments—these things were
next his heart. So when he wrote the same qualities
were displayed. Thus the happy jovialities of the
'Christmas Carol' were quite real.

The group of those who knew Boz intimately is
dwindling rapidly at this moment. Outside his own
family there are but few left of his friends—not a
dozen, I fancy, 'all told.' A few years hence they
will be counted on the fingers of one hand, and then
some feeble, decrepit personage will be pointed out
with curiosity : ' There goes the last man that knew
Boz !' It was remarkable that some of his fastest
friends were Roman Catholics, as, indeed, he told
the world in his preface to ' Barnaby Rudge.'
Perhaps, of all his friends, the one for whom he had
the warmest and most tender affection was Stanfield,
the great sea-painter—the always ' Stanny ' of those
times—and who, indeed, seems to have been a most
engaging person ; and Stanfield was a Roman
Catholic. Remarkable, too, for his faithful service,
admiration, and constancy was Charles Kent, who
died lately, a warm-hearted creature who showed
him an almost terrier-like devotion ; he also was
a Roman Catholic. Dickens always reciprocated
this attachment in the most affectionate way, and,
by a curious chance, the last letter he wrote was to
Kent. In it occurs a pleasant allusion to his friend's

creed : 'It was, I believe, a divine of your Church who said that these violent delights have violent endings,' etc.   I have heard Dickens, speaking of him, quote from ' King Lear,' where, as we know, there is another faithful Kent, and apply to him the old King's praise of the trusty follower that would strike hard and home for his master.   I may say here that nothing was more striking than Boz's familiarity with Shakespeare and the English classics, or more apropos than his quotations ; and these he always used in a very novel and engaging way.   I once, when staying at Folkestone—newly married— wrote to him to ask him—more for the sake of an excuse for writing than for actual need of his aid—to direct his favourite purveyors, Fortnum and Mason (he used to say he could get everything that was good at that house) to send down some wine.   He good-naturedly did so, adding slyly the quotation from Gray : ' Ah, the little victims play !'

The story of Boz's Italian apparition, I may say, I often heard told by Kent, who had it from Dickens himself, with some little additions. He said there was a statue of the Madonna in his room.   ' Do tell me, is the Catholic Church the true one ?' he asked.   ' Yes,' she said—' it is, for *you.*'   The curious part is not so much the vision, as that it should have so deeply impressed him.

Kent described also another friend and patron

of his—the first Lord Lytton—visiting a French cathedral with him. Kent was astonished to see him dip his finger into the holy water, on which he asked him, ' Did you ever hear the Mass ?' ' Never,' he answered, ' I dared not ; it would be too awful '— or something of the kind. This we might expect from him. His son, the first Earl, one day passing across the lawn at Knebworth to the fishing-hut, suddenly put his arm on his (Kent's) shoulder, and said, apropos of nothing : ' If there *be* a true Church, I am convinced yours is the one.'

Charles Kent once told me a pretty story of his great friend, which he told well. He met him at the corner of some street, and began to relate to him what he knew would please him, how a certain fanatical Pickwickian—whose name, I think, was Amcott—used to have the book steadily read to him every night until completed, and then ordered it to be begun again all afresh. It took about three months to get through : so there were four readings in the year. Boz was chuckling over his admirer's enthusiasm, when a miserable unfortunate, with the usual baby, drew near, and begged of Kent, who, being at the critical part of his story, motioned her away. And Boz appeared also to deprecate the interruption. Turning for a moment from Boz's expressive face, who was still relishing the jest, adding a comic touch of his own, he saw his hand gliding behind his back, and a half-crown drop softly in the woman's hand !

Dickens was fond of songs, and could troll them well. He knew all the familiar ones which people of his day were chanting—also all the old lilts, and knew how to jest on these time-worn favourites. I have constantly heard him allude to them in his airy, pleasant fashion, and burlesque them. As in the case of 'When the wind blows,' at the opening of the 'Miller and his Men,' that venerable melodrama 'More Sacks to the Mill.' (When it was revived he brought it me to see it.) Naturally, therefore, we find all his stories full of lively allusions to old songs. What could be more humorous than Micawber's treatment of 'Auld Lang Syne' and the 'Gowans fine'? He often quoted 'The Woodpecker tapping'—*i.e.*, the 'Hollow Beech-Tree,' the 'All's Well,' which begins so solemnly : 'Deserted by the waning moon.' He took a genuine delight in Moore's melodies, and as a matter of course we find constant allusions to these lyrics. They are bound up humorously with Swiveller, whose adaptations are truly grotesque and original. When Rosa Dartle is in one of her 'fits,' he makes Steerforth beg for an Irish melody, just as he himself would ask his daughter for one at Gadshill.

I doubt if there be anyone now alive except myself who can say that he had the priceless

advantage of Dickens's aid and advice in the
correction and construction of his stories. This he
gave generously. I remember once consulting him
as to the wind-up of a novel I was writing for him,
and where there was a sort of entanglement. His
fine power of construction was at once brought out.
An innocent lady was under suspicion as to the
death of her husband, who had died in some strange
way, and in a flash he suggested the following extri-
cation :

'What do you think of the pursuing relation so
dying at last of the same disorder as the Baronet's
daughter, and under such circumstances as to make
out the case of the clergyman's daughter and clear
the story ? As for example : Suppose the husband
himself does almost the same thing in going for
help when this man is dying ? I think I see a fine
story here. There is something very brilliant and
original in this.'

I ventured often thus to ask his counsel. Of
another novel—'Never Forgotten'—he wrote to me :

'The only suggestion that I have to make is that
Captain Fermor wants relief. It is a disagreeable
character, as you mean it to be. And I should be
afraid to do too much with him, if he were mine,
without taking the taste of him here and there out
of the reader's mouth. It is remarkable that if you
do not administer a disagreeable character carefully

the public has a decided tendency to think that the
story is disagreeable, and not merely a fiction.' Most
judicious advice. So I might fairly say I was in
some measure a pupil of Dickens in the art of novel-
writing.

Boz, as I have said, had quaint pet theories as
to a sort of fatalism that obtains in social matters,
and on which it was interesting for his friends to
hear him expatiate. Some will recall the following,
in which he dwells on the compelling power of
events : 'Which of the vast multitude of travellers,
under the sun and the stars, climbing the dusty hills
and toiling along the weary plains, journeying by
land and journeying by sea, coming and going so
strangely, to act and react on one another—which of
the host may, *with no suspicion of the journey's end,
be travelling surely hither*—that is, to the spot that
must be come to—none shall show us.'

A fine idea and finely expressed. This he would
develop, and it would lead on to his favourite theory
of the world being so small that utter strangers, who
meet, are sure to find that they have been connected
in some fashion. This last was the most favourite of
all his latter theories, and I have heard him illustrate
it again and again, as when Mr. Moore, the philan-
thropist, was with him, and I had named someone who
turned out to be known to us both : 'There again!'
he cried out : 'you see how small the world is!'

Boz once recommended me to read two books as being the best of their class, and his excellent judgment will be endorsed by all. These were Poole's 'Little Pedlington' and Dana's 'Two Years before the Mast.' I have read them again and again since, and with increasing admiration. No modern sea-book can be compared with Dana's. He told me a vast deal about this Poole, author of 'Paul Pry,' a fellow of infinite jest, for whom he got a pension.

Once when he had engaged me to write him a novel, it came to his ears that I was actively busy with two other novels at the same moment, making three in all. But those were extraordinary times of production. He was not pleased, and wrote me a gentle reproof, or, rather, remonstrance — the only letter of the kind out of the fifty or so I received from him : 'You make me very uneasy by your amount of writing in all directions.' He said it was impossible to do justice under such conditions to his story. Could anything be more indulgent? I felt, and I feel now, deeply for so trying his good-nature. He said of this business to his friend Forster, who told it to me : 'I gave him a severe rating, and I really believe I am the only person he would have taken it from.' Admirable, good Boz! Any other editor would have remarked : 'He be hanged! Let him take it or leave it. What do I care?'

Once at the railway-station in Belfast—it was in the morning, and I was travelling with him—there was a little incident that amused him. Of course, his figure always excited a good deal of attention ; everyone knew him from the prints or description. He was always quite unconcerned at the staring and whispering. He was so unaffected ; he behaved just as though he were alone. I see him as the stationmaster comes up obsequiously to make a request. We had noted a smug, burly man, in a white waistcoat and heavy gold chain, who was standing by smiling on us with affability. It was he who had deputed the stationmaster : ' That yonder was Mr. (say) McKillan, one of the great local flax-spinners. He would like—if Mr. Dickens had no objection—to join him in his coupé for the journey.' The spinner still kept smiling on at us, quite confident that he was suitable company. Genuine alarm came into Boz's face. He dreaded these sort of intrusions. But I noticed how carefully he worded his refusal. I fancy the white-waistcoated one expected at the least to be called up and introduced ; but Boz turned off summarily and gained the coupé the company had given him.

On this journey we were to have an adventure, and really a narrow escape from death or injury. We were somewhere between Belfast and Porta-down, and our coupé was next the engine, with a fine view of a not very interesting manufacturing country. Dickens was in the middle, his sister-in-law next him, I and Dolby, the henchman, next the windows. Suddenly came a sort of crash or thud overhead, and we next saw the engine-driver struggling in great agitation with his brake. There was a grinding and hissing and jolting, and a few seconds later the train was brought to a standstill. Dickens was agitated, I saw, though he strove to conceal it ; for the accident at Staplehurst, as is well known, had shaken his nerves considerably.

The next moment all the passengers were out on the line and crowded round Dickens ; they did not know who he was who was quietly talking to the driver. The latter, in his quaint Northern accent, was explaining about 'her' and 'her gudgeons.' It seems the tire of the great driving-wheel had been fractured and the fragments shot into the air. One of these had struck the top of our coupé and caused the great thud. A little lower it had been among us, and we would all have perished. I see the scene perfectly : Boz's cheery and commanding figure dominating all ; I feel the smell of the engine and of the water on the fire.

Dickens, who gave us in his works so many fine specimens of heroism and fortitude displayed at a crisis, was destined to furnish in his own person an example of calm courage, which is, indeed, just what we might expect from such a man. Did he write nobly of what duty requires us to do for each other, he showed in one signal act that he could practise as well as preach. This he did in the terrible and bloody Staplehurst accident on his favourite line —the South-Eastern—in which he had an almost miraculous escape of his life. It occurred on June 9, 1865. He had been spending one of his happy flying holidays in Paris, and was returning full of spirits, when this dreadful catastrophe occurred, in which many were cruelly injured and half a dozen killed. The train was thrown over a viaduct into the water. The carriage in which he sat was next the engine, and was following the rest, when by some chance it was checked, and hung suspended by the couplings. He has described the whole scene very vividly. He received a violent shock and shake, the results of which he felt ‘off and on’ during the rest of his life. With his sensitive brain and nervous, highly-strung system, some fibres were likely to have been affected ; yet, on recovering, he only thought of giving assistance to his companions and to those who were suffering. A passenger who, like Dickens, had a narrow escape from death has described the scene and all he saw of Dickens's exertions, who had climbed out of the window and got down to the wreck. Here is what he says :

'When we crossed the Channel for England in the afternoon, nothing could be more beautiful than the scene on board the passage-boat. All seemed happy and delighted, and although I have performed the journey on many occasions, I don't think I ever had a more delightful trip, as the sun shone out brilliantly the whole of the time we were afloat, and the sea was without a ripple. We entered the train in waiting at Folkestone, and in a few minutes we were on our road to the Metropolis. Just as the train arrived at Staplehurst, and while I was reading the severe comments made in one of the morning papers on the railway accident at Shrewsbury, I and my fellow-passengers were startled by a deep and heavy-sounding noise ; then followed two terrible jolts or bumps, and in an instant afterwards from bright sunshine all became darkness, and to me chaos. In a second or two I found myself enveloped in moisture, and then, in the terrible din, I became conscious that an accident had happened to the train in which I was a passenger. I found myself afterwards up to my knees in water, in the middle of a heap of broken carriages, amidst which the whole of the party I had seen but a short time ago on board the steamer were lying. The carriages, with one exception, I now discovered had been thrown from the bridge over which the trains pass at Staplehurst, into the

water below, and death and destruction reigned
around. The remains of the shattered carriages
were projecting wheels upwards from the water, and
the screams of the sufferers were heart-rending.
Immediately I could relieve myself from the
perilous position, I, with some other gentlemen
who fortunately escaped with a few bruises and
a plunge in the water, endeavoured to extricate
some of our less-fortunate fellow-passengers. We
succeeded after great difficulty in getting a female
from the muddy bed of the river, all but dead, and
as we were assisting another sufferer, Mr. Charles
Dickens, the world-renowned novelist, who was a
passenger, came upon the scene. He, it appeared,
had occupied a seat in the only carriage that did not
go over the bridge, although the chance that it did
not do so was the slightest in the world. This
carriage, which was the first from the engine, had
held firm by the coupling-iron to the tender, and
thus it was prevented sharing the fate of the others,
although it literally hung half upon the line, half
down bank, and high above the terrible confusion
below. Mr. Dickens was most energetic in the
assistance he rendered to his fellow-passengers. I
heard this gentleman call for brandy for some of the
wounded persons, but, unfortunately, none was at
hand, it being with the luggage, or else in the
possession of those who were struggling in the

river.   As brandy was not to be had, Mr. Dickens
took off his hat, and, having filled it with water,
I saw him running about with it and doing his
best to revive and comfort every poor creature he
met who had sustained serious injury.   Another
gentleman, whom I afterwards discovered to be
Mr. Samuel Reed, a gentleman connected with the
Illustrated London News, acted in a praiseworthy
manner; for although he had a narrow escape from
a terrible death, he, with great nerve, assisted in
extricating those imploring help from beneath the
carriages.   One lady, whom I had particularly
noticed on board the steamer as being a very fine
and handsome person, I saw taken from the water.
She had been actually crushed to death, and, as
she was laid on the bank, her husband, who had
been previously frantically running about, exclaim-
ing, 'My wife! my wife!' came up, and when he
discovered that the mangled and disfigured corpse
was that of her he was in search of, he sat down
by the side of the body, a figure of utter despair.
I cannot dwell upon the terrible scene.   It is too
much for human nature.   Nine or ten persons had
been killed, and God knows how many wounded.'

This dreadful accident caused a great sensation all
over the kingdom, partly, no doubt, owing to the
narrow escape of so distinguished a man.   Narrow
indeed it was.   But it was long a question among

his friends whether the serious shock had not left
permanent impression on his nervous system and
constitution. Specialists were inclined to think
that it did. My old friend Mr. Hollingshead once
described to me how Boz used to give a sort of
pantomimic reproduction of the scene, lying down
under the table, and enacting the whole in most
dramatic manner. A letter to Mrs. Sartoris of
June 14, 1865, written shortly after the accident, he
had to dictate to an amanuensis. He was too much
overset to write. ' This,' he said, ' is not all in my
own hand, because I am too much shaken to write
many notes : not by the beating and dragging of
the carriage in which I was—it did not go over,
but was caught on the turn among the ruins of the
bridge—but by the work after, to get out the dying
and the dead, which was terrible.' He told his
readers that he had thought nervously of the new
portion of his story, which was in his pocket, and
which thus had also a narrow escape. As this
occurred not five years before his death, it may have
contributed to that nervous break-up which was perceptible to his friends. I remember being with him
and his family at night-time in a train which stopped
suddenly and for some time, and noticed the silence
and uneasiness that came on him. I was told that
he was often thus affected.

A great railway, with all its incidents, had for

him something of the charm of romance, and he invested it with romance. How much it is bound up with his later writing, just as the coaches were with his earlier! He went deep down to the poetry of the thing. As in the stirring passages, 'Away with a shriek, a rattle, and a roar'; the 'Flight' to Paris; 'the Mugby Junction'; Carker's death; and many other vivid episodes. The South-Eastern to Folkestone he looked on as his own special line, where he was known to every guard, porter, and station-master, who could be seen flying to open the door for him.

CHAPTER IX

JOHN FORSTER

ONE of the most robust, striking, and many-sided characters of his time was Dickens's trusty friend John Forster, a rough, uncompromising personage who, from small and obscure beginnings, shouldered his way to the front until he came to be looked on by all as guide, friend, and arbiter. Without knowing Forster we can hardly know Dickens. As I look back, I can never call up the image of Dickens without seeing Forster beside him : Forster seems always to interpose his burly form. He was ever bustling round his friend, interpreting and explaining him. He had a fortunate career. From a struggling newspaper man he emerged into handsome chambers in Lincoln's Inn Fields ; from thence to a snug house in Montague Square, ending in a handsome stone mansion which he built for himself at Palace Gate, Kensington, with its beautiful library-room at the back, and every luxury of 'lettered ease.'

If anyone desired to know what Dr. Johnson was like, he could have found him in Forster. There was the same social intolerance; the same ' dispersion of humbug '; the same loud voice, attuned to a mellifluous softness on occasion, especially with ladies or persons of rank; the love of 'talk' in which he assumed the lead, and kept it, too; with the contemptuous scorn of what he did not approve. But, then, all this was backed by admirable training and full knowledge. He was a deeply-read, cultivated man, a fine critic, and, with all his arrogance, despotism, and rough 'ways,' a most interesting, original, delightful person—for those he liked, that is, and those he had made his own. His very 'build' and appearance was also that of the redoubtable Doctor; so was his loud and hearty laugh. Woe betide the man on whom he chose to 'wipe his shoes' (Browning's phrase), for he could wipe them with a will. He would thus roar you down : it was ' in*tol*-er-able '—everything was ' *in-tol-erable !*'—it is difficult to describe the fashion in which he rolled forth the syllables. Other things were ' All stuff!' ' Monstrous !' ' Incredible !' ' Don't tell me !' Indeed, I, with many, could find a parallel in the great old Doctor for almost everything he said.

Forster's life was indeed a striking and encouraging one for those who believe in the example of ' self-made men.' His moderate aspiration was to reach to the foremost rank of the literary world; and he succeeded. He secured for himself an excellent education, never spared himself for study or work, and never rested till he had built himself that fine mansion at Kensington of which I have spoken, furnished with books, pictures, and rare things. It is astonishing what a circle he had gathered round him here, and how intimate he was with all: political men, such as Brougham, Guizot, Gladstone, Cornwall Lewis (Disraeli he abhorred); Maclise, Landseer, Frith, and Stanfield, with dozens of other painters; every writer of the day, almost without exception. With novelists like Anthony Trollope and Reade he was on the friendliest terms, though he did not 'grapple them to him with hooks of steel.' With the Bar it was the same: he was intimate with the brilliant and agreeable Cockburn; with Lord Coleridge (then plain Mr. Coleridge), who found a knife and a fork laid for him any day that he chose to drop in, which he did pretty often. The truth was that in any company his marked personality, both physical and mental, his magisterial face, loud, decided voice, and his reputation of judge and arbiter, at once impressed and commanded attention. People felt that they ought to know this personage at once.

It is extraordinary what perseverance and a certain power of will, and that of not being denied, will do in this way. His broad face and burly person were not made for rebuffs. He seized on persons he wished to know, and made them know him at once. As Johnson was said to toss and gore his company, so Forster trampled on those he condemned. I remember he had a special dislike to one of Boz's useful henchmen. An amusing story was told, that after some meeting to arrange matters with Bradbury and Evans, the printers, Boz, ever charitable, was glad to report to Forster some hearty praise by this person of the ability with which he (Forster) had arranged matters, thus amiably wishing to propitiate the autocrat in his friend's interest. 'But,' said the uncompromising Forster, 'I am truly sorry, my dear Dickens, that I cannot reciprocate your friend's compliment; for *a damnder ass I never encountered in the whole course of my life!*' A comparative that is novel, and will be admired.

It was something to talk to one who had been intimate with Charles Lamb, and of whom he once spoke to me, with tears running down his cheeks, 'Ah! poor dear Charles Lamb!' The next day he had summoned his faithful clerk, instructing him to look out among his papers—such was his way—for all the Lamb letters, which were then lent to me. And most interesting they were. In one Elia calls him '*Fooster*'—I fancy taking off Carlyle's pronunciation.

At this time the intimacy between Boz and the young writer—two young men; for they were only thirty-six—was of the closest. Dickens's admiration of his friend's book, 'The Life of Goldsmith,' was unbounded. He read it with delight, and expressed his admiration with an affectionate enthusiasm. It was no wonder that in 'gentle Goldsmith's life' thus unfolded he found a replica of his own sore struggles. No one knew better the 'fiercer crowded misery in garret toil and London loneliness' than he did. Forster addressed to him this sonnet:

To Charles Dickens.

Genius and its rewards are briefly told:
 A liberal nature and a niggard doom,
 A difficult journey to a splendid tomb.
New writ, nor lightly weighed, that story old
In gentle Goldsmith's life I here unfold;
 Thro' other than lone wild or desert gloom,
 In its mere joy and pain, its blight and bloom,
Adventurous.   Come with me and behold,
O friend with heart as gentle for distress,
 As resolute with fine wise thoughts to bind
 The happiest to the unhappiest of our kind,
That there is fiercer crowded misery
In garret toil and London loneliness
Than in cruel islands mid the far-off sea.

JOHN FORSTER.

March, 1848.

It will be noted what a warmth of affection is shown in these pleasing lines. Some of the verses linger in the memory, the last three especially. The allusion to Dickens is as truthful as it is charming. The 'cruel islands mid the far-off sea' were often quoted, though there were sometimes sarcastic appeals to the author to name his locality.

Later Forster lost this agreeable touch, and issued a series of ponderous historical treatises, enlargements of his old 'Statesmen.' I must say these were dreary things—pedantic, solemn, and heavy ; they might have been by the worthy Rollin himself. Such was the 'Life of Sir John Eliot,' the 'Arrest of the Five Members,' and others.

Forster, however, more than redeemed himself when he issued his well-known 'Life of Dickens,' a work that was a perfect delight to the world and to his friends. For here is the proper lightness of touch. The complete familiarity with every detail in the course of the man of whose life his had been a portion, and the quiet air of authority which he could assume in consequence, gave the work an attraction that was beyond dispute. All the fifteen or sixteen official Lives issued since the writer's death have been written 'from outside,' as it were, and it is extraordinary what a different man each presents. But hardly sufficient credit has been given to him for the finished style which only a true and well-trained critic could have brought, the easy touch, the appropriate treatment of trifles, the mere indication, as it were, the correct passing by or gliding over

of matters that should not be touched.   All this im-
parted a dignity of treatment, and, though familiar,
the whole was gay and bright.   True, occasionally
he lapsed into his favourite autocracy and pompous-
ness, but this made the work more characteristic
of the man.   Nothing could have been in better
taste than his treatment of certain passages in the
author's life, as to which, he showed, the public were
not entitled to demand more than a mere historical
mention of the facts.   When he was writing this
Life it was amusing to find how sturdily independent
he became.   The 'Blacking episode' could not have
been acceptable, but Forster was stern, and would
not bate a line.   The true reason, by the way,
of the uproar raised against the writer was that
it was too much of a close borough, no one but
Boz and his Bear-leader being allowed upon the
stage.   Numbers had their little letters from the
great man with many compliments and favours
which would look well in print.   Many, like Wilkie
Collins or Edmund Yates, had a whole collection.
I myself had some forty or fifty.   Some of these
personages were highly indignant, for were they not
characters in the drama?

No doubt the subject inspired.   The ever gay
and lively Boz called up for him many a happy
scene, and gave the pen a certain airiness and
nimbleness.   There is little that is official or magis-

terial about the volumes. Everything is pleasant
and interesting, put together—though there is a
crowd of details—with extraordinary art and finish.
It furnishes a most truthful and accurate picture of
the 'inimitable,' recognisable in every page. It was
only in the third volume, when scared by the per-
sistent clamours of the disappointed and the envious,
protesting that there was 'too much Forster,' that
it was virtually a 'Life of John Forster, with recollections of Charles Dickens,' that he became of
a sudden official, and allowed others to come too
much on the scene, with loss of effect. That
third volume, which ought to have been most
interesting, is the dull one. We have Boz described
as he would be in an encyclopædia, instead of
through Forster, acting as his interpreter, and much
was lost by this treatment. Considering the homeli-
ness and everyday character of the incidents, it is
astonishing how he contrived to dignify them.
He knew from early training what was valuable and
significant and what should be rejected.

Granting the objections—and faults—of the book,
it may be asked, Who else in the seventies was, not *so*
fitted, but fitted at all to produce a Life of Dickens ?
Every eye looked on, every finger pointed to,
Forster : the worker, patron, and disciple ; confidant,
adviser, corrector, admirer, the trained man of
letters, a school in which Boz had been trained, who

had known everyone of that era. No one else could have been thought of. And as we now read the book, and contrast it with those ordered or commissioned biographies so common now, and perhaps better wrought, we see at once the difference. The success was extraordinary. Edition after edition was issued, and that so rapidly that the author had no opportunity of making the necessary corrections or of adding new information. He contented himself with a leaf or two at the end, in which, in his own imperial style, he simply took note of the information. I believe his profit was about £10,000.

A wonderful feature was the extraordinary amount of Dickens's letters that was worked into it. To save time and trouble—and this I was told by Mrs. Forster—he would cut out the passages he wanted with a pair of scissors and paste them on his MS.! As the portion written on the back was thus lost, the rest became valueless. I can fancy the American collector tearing his hair as he reads of this desecration. But it was a rash act and a terrible loss of money. Each letter might have later been worth, say, from £5 to £10.

It has been often noted how a mere trifle will, in an extraordinary way, determine or change the whole course of a life. I can illustrate this by my own case. I was plodding on contentedly at the Bar without getting 'no forrarder,' with slender, meagre prospects, but with a hankering after 'writing,' when I came to read Forster's 'Life of Goldsmith' before described, and which filled me with admiration. The author was at the moment gathering materials for his 'Life of Swift,' when it occurred to me that I might be useful to him in getting up all the local Swiftian relics, traditions, etc. I set to work, obtained them, made sketches, and sent them to him. He was supremely grateful, and never forgot the service. These trifles are now at Kensington. To it I owe a host of literary friends and acquaintance with Dickens, Carlyle, and the rest ; and when I ventured to try my prentice pen, it was Forster who took personal charge of the venture. It was long remembered at the *Household Words* office how he stalked in one morning, stick in hand, and, flinging down the paper, called out, 'Now, mind, no nonsense about it, no humbug, no returning it with a polite circular, and all that ; see that it is read and duly considered.' *That* was the turning-point. To that blunt declaration I owe some forty years of enjoyment and em-ployment—for there is no enjoyment like that of writing—to say nothing of money in abundance.

It would be difficult to give an idea of Forster's overflowing kindness on the occasion of the coming of friends to town. Perpetual hospitality was the order of the day, and, like so many older Londoners, he took special delight in hearing accounts of the strange out-of-the-way things a visitor will discover, and with which he will even surprise the resident. He enjoyed what he called 'hearing your adventures.' I never met anyone with so boisterous and exuberant a laugh. Something would tickle him, and, like Johnson in Fleet Street, he would roar and roar again.

At the head of his table, with a number of agreeable and clever guests around him, Forster was at his best. He seemed altogether changed. Beaming smiles, a gentle, encouraging voice, and a tenderness verging on gallantry to the ladies, took the place of the old, rough fashion. He talked ostentatiously, he *led* the talk, told most apropos anecdotes of the remarkable men he had met, and was fond of fortifying his own views by adding, 'As Gladstone, or Guizot, or Palmerston said to me in this room,' etc. But you could not but be struck by the finished shapes in which his sentences ran. There was a weight, a power of illustration, and a dramatic colouring that could only have come of long practice. He was gay, sarcastic, humorous, and it was impossible not to recognise that here was a clever man and a man of power.

Forster's ideal of hospitality was not reciprocity, but was bounded by *his* entertaining everybody. Not that he did not enjoy a friendly quiet dinner at your table. Was he on his travels at a strange place? *You* must dine with him at his hotel. In town you must dine with him. He might dine with you, but this dining with you must be according to his programme. When he was in the vein and inclined for a social domestic night he would let himself out.

Maclise's happy power of realizing character is shown inimitably in the picture of Forster at the reading of the 'Christmas Carol,' seated forward in his chair, with a solemn air of grave judgment. There is an air of distrust, or of being on his guard, as who should say, 'It is fine, very fine, but I hold my opinion in suspense till the close. I am not to be caught, as you are, by mere flowers.' He was, in fact, distinct from the rest, all under the influence of emotion. Harness is shown weeping, Jerrold softened, etc. These rooms, as is well known, were Mr. Tulkinghorn's in the novel, and over Forster's head, as he wrote, was the floridly-painted ceiling, after the fashion of Verrio, with the Roman pointing. This was effaced many years ago, but I do not know when or why.

By all his friends Forster was thought of as a sort of permanent bachelor. His configuration and air were entirely suited to life in chambers : he was thoroughly literary ; his friends were literary ; there he gave his dinners ; married life with him was inconceivable. He had lately secured an important official post—that of Secretary to the Lunacy Commissioners—which he gained owing to his useful services when editing the *Examiner*. This later led to the Commissionership, which was worth a good deal more. Nowadays we do not find the editors of the smaller papers securing such prizes. I remember, when he was encouraging me to 'push my way,' he illustrated his advice by his own example : 'I never let old Brougham go. I came back again and again until I wore him out. I forced 'em to give me this.' I could quite imagine it. Forster was a troublesome customer, 'a harbitrary cove,' and not to be put off, except for a time. It was an excellent business appointment, and he was admitted to be an admirable official.

In one of Dickens's letters, published by his children, there is a grotesque outburst at some astounding piece of news—an event impending which seemed to have taken his breath away. It clearly refers to his friend's marriage. Boz was so tickled at this wonderful news that he wrote : 'Tell Catherine that I have the most prodigious, overwhelming, crushing, astounding, blinding, deafening, pulverizing, scarifying secret, of which Forster is the hero, imaginable, by the whole efforts of the whole British population. It is a thing of the kind that, after I knew it (from himself) this morning, I

lay down flat as if an engine and tender had fallen
upon me.'   This pleasantly boisterous humour is in
no wise exaggerated.   I fancy it affected all Forster's
friends much in the same way, and as an exquisitely
funny and expected thing.   How many pictures did
Boz see before him ?   Forster proposing to the
widow in his sweetest accents, his deportment at
the church, etc.   There was not much sentiment
in the business, though the bride was a gentle,
charming woman, as will be seen, too gentle for
that tempestuous spirit.   She was a widow—'Yes,
gentlemen, the plaintiff is a widow'—widow of
Colburn, the publisher, a quiet little man, who
worshipped her.   She was well endowed, inheriting
much of his property, even to his papers, etc.   She
had also a most comfortable house in Montague
Square, where, as the saying is, Forster had only to
move in and 'hang up his hat.'

Mrs. Forster, as her friends knew well, was one
of the sweetest women 'under the sun'—a sweet-
ness brought out by contrast with the obstreperous
ways of her tempestuous mate.   Often, when something went wrong—rather, did not go with an almost
ideal smoothness—at one of his many banquets (and
there never was a more generously hospitable man),
it was piteous to see her trying to smooth away the
incident, with the certainty of inflaming the dictator
and turning his wrath upon herself.

But she knew well that not he, but his health, was accountable. She believed from her heart in this duality of Forster. There was a hapless page-boy whose very presence and assumed stupidity used to inflame his master to perfect berserker fits of rage. The scenes were exquisitely ludicrous, if painful ; the contrast between the giant and the object of his wrath, scared out of his life with terror, was absolutely diverting. Thus, the host would murmur ' Biscuits !' which was not heard or not heeded ; then louder and more sharply, ' BISCUITS !' then a roar that made all start, ' BIScuits !' Poor Mrs. Forster's agitation was sad to see, and between her and the butler the luckless lad was somehow got from the room. This attendant was an admirable comedy character, and in his way a typical servant, stolid and reserved. No one could have been so portentously sagacious as *he* looked. It was admirable to see his unruffled calm during his master's outbursts when something had gone wrong during the dinner. No violence could betray him into anything but the most placid and correct replies. There was something fine and pathetic in this, for it showed that he also recognised that it was not his true master that was thus raging. I recall talking with him shortly after his master's death. After paying his character a fine tribute, he spoke of his illness. ' You see, sir,' he said at last, ' what was

at the bottom of it all was he 'ad no *staminer, no
staminer*—NO STAMINER, sir.'   And he repeated the
word many times with enjoyment.   I have no doubt
he picked it up at Forster's table, and it had struck
him as a good effective English word, spelled as he
pronounced it.

With all his roughness and bluntness, Forster had
a very soft heart, and was a great appreciator of the
sex.   He had some little 'affairs of the heart,' which,
however, led to no result.   He was actually engaged
to the interesting L. E. L. (Letitia Landon), whom
he had no doubt pushed well forward in the *Examiner;* for the fair poetess generally contrived to
enlist the affections of her editors, as she did those
of Jerdan, director of the once powerful *Literary
Gazette.*   We can see by his memoirs how attracted
he was by her.   The engagement was broken off, it
is believed, through the arts of Dr. Maginn, and it
is said that Forster behaved exceedingly well in the
transaction.   Later he became attached to another
lady, still alive, who had several suitors of distinction,
but she was not disposed to entrust herself to him.

No one so heartily relished his Forster, his ways
and oddities, as Boz; albeit the sage was his faithful
friend, counsellor, and ally.   He had an exquisite
sense for touches of character, especially for the
little weaknesses so often exhibited by sturdy,
boisterous natures.   We again recall that disposition

of Johnson, with his ' bow to an Archbishop,' listening with entranced attention to a dull story told by
a foreign ' diplomatist.' ' *The ambassador says well*,'
would the sage repeat many times, which, as Bozzy
tells, became a favourite form in the coterie for
ironical approbation. There was much of this in our
great man, whose voice sank into the sweetest and
most mellifluous key as he bent before a peer.
' Lord ——,' he would add gently, and turning to
the company, ' has been saying, with much force,' etc.

I recall the Guild fête down at Knebworth, where
Forster was on a visit to its noble owner, Lord
Lytton, and was deputed to receive and marshal the
guests at the station, an office of dread importance,
and large writ over his rather burly person. His
face was momentous as he patrolled the platform.
I remember coming up to him in the crowd, but he
looked over and beyond me, big with unutterable
things. Mentioning this later to Boz, he laughed
his cheerful laugh. ' Exactly !' he cried. ' Why, I
assure you, Forster would not see *me* !' He was
busy pointing out the vehicles, the proper persons
to sit in them, according to their dignity. All
through that delightful day, as I roamed through
the fine old halls, I would encounter him passing by,
still in his lofty dream, still controlling all, with a
weight of delegated authority on his broad shoulders.
Only at the very close did he vouchsafe a few digni-

fied, encouraging words, and then passed on. He
reminded me much of Elia's description of Bensley's
Malvolio.

There was nothing ill-natured in Boz's relish of
these things; he heartily loved his friend. It was
the pure love of fun. Podsnap has many touches of
Forster, but the writer dared not 'let himself go'
in that character as he might have longed to do.
When Podsnap is referred to for his opinion, he
delivers it as follows, much flushed and extremely
angry : 'Don't ask me! I desire to take no part in
the discussion of these people's affairs. I abhor the
subject! It is an odious subject, an offensive subject *that makes me sick*, and I——' with his favourite
right-arm flourish which sweeps away everything
and settles it for ever, etc. These very words
might Forster have used. It may be thought that
Boz would not be so daring as to introduce his
friend into his stories, 'under his very nose,' as it
were, submitting the proofs, etc., with the certainty
that the portrait would be recognised. But this, as
we know, is the last thing that could have occurred,
or the last thing that would have occurred to Forster.
It was like enough someone else, but not he.

'Mr. Podsnap was well to do, and stood very
high in Mr. Podsnap's opinion.' 'He was quite
satisfied. He never could make out why everybody
was not quite satisfied, and he felt conscious that he

set a brilliant social example in being particularly well satisfied with most things and with himself.' 'Mr. Podsnap settled that whatever he put behind him he put out of existence.' 'I don't want to know about it; I don't desire to discover it.' 'He had, however, acquired a peculiar flourish of his right arm in the clearing the world of its difficulties.' 'As so eminently respectable a man, Mr. Podsnap was sensible of its being required of him to take Providence under his protection. Consequently he always knew exactly what Providence intended.'

These touches any friend of Forster's would recognise. He could be very engaging, and was at his best when enjoying what he called a shoe-maker's holiday—that is, when away from town at some watering-place with friends. He was then really delightful, because happy, having left all his solemnities and ways in London.

Once, travelling round with Boz on one of his reading tours, we came to Belfast, where the huge Ulster Hall was filled to the door by ardent and enthusiastic Northerners. I recall how we walked round the rather grim town, with its harsh red streets, the honest workers staring at him hard. We put up at an old-fashioned hotel, the best—the Royal it was called—where there was much curiosity on the part of the ladies to get sly peeps at the eminent man. They generally contrived to be on the stairs when he emerged.   Boz always appeared, even in the streets, somewhat carefully 'made up.' The velvet collar, the blue coat, the heavy gold pin, added to the effect.

It was at this hotel, when the show was over, and our agreeable supper cleared away, that I saw the pleasant Boz lying on the sofa somewhat tired by his exertions—not so much on the boards as in that very room ; for he was fond of certain parlour gymnastics, in which he contended with his aide-de-camp Dolby.   Well, as I said, he was on his sofa somewhat fatigued with his night's work, in a most placid, enjoying frame of mind, laughing with his twinkling eyes, as he often did, squeezing and puckering them up when our talk fell on Forster, whom he was in the vein for enjoying.   It had so fallen out that, only a few weeks before, Trinity College, Dublin, had invited Forster to receive an honorary degree, a compliment that much gratified him.   I was living there at the time, and he came and stayed with me in the best of humours, thoroughly enjoying it all. Boz, learning that I had been with him, insisted on my telling him *everything*, as by instinct he knew that his friend would have been at his best.   The scenes we passed through together were indeed of the richest comedy.   First I see him in highest spirits trying on a Doctor's scarlet robe, to be had on hire.   On this day he did everything in state, in

his special 'high' manner.   Thus he addressed the
tailor in rolling periods : 'Sir, the University has
been good enough to confer a degree on me, and I
have come over to receive it.   My name is John
Forster.'   (I doubt if his fame had reached the
tailor.)   'Certainly, sir.'   And my friend was duly
invested with the robe.   He walked up and down
before a pier-glass.   'Hey, what now ?   Do you
know, my dear friend, I really think I must *buy* this
dress.   It would do very well to go to Court in,
hey ?'   He indulged his fancy.   'Why, I could
wear it on many occasions.   A most effective dress.'

But it was time now to wait on 'the senior Bursar,'
or some such functionary.   This was one Doctor
L——, a rough, even uncouth, old don, who was
for the nonce holding a sort of rude class, surrounded
by a crowd of 'undergrads.'   Never shall I forget
that scene.   Forster went forward, with a mixture
of gracious dignity and softness, and was beginning,
'Doc-tor L——'   Here the turbulent boys round
him interrupted.   'Now see here,' said the irate
Bursar, 'it's no use all of yes talking together.   Sir,
I can't attend to you now.'   Again Forster began
with a gracious bow : 'Doctor L——, I have come
over at the invitation of the University, who have
been good enough to offer me an honorary degree,
and——'

'Now, see here,' said the doctor, 'there's no use

talking to me now. I can't attend to yes. All o' yes come back here in an hour and take the oath—all together, mind.'

' I merely wished to state, Dr. L——,' began the wondering Forster.

' Sir, I tell yes I can't attend to yes now. You must come again,' and he was gone.

I was at the back of the room when my friend joined me, very ruminative and serious. ' Very odd all this,' he said ; ' but I suppose when we *do* come back it will be all right ?'

' Oh yes ; he is noted as an odd man,' I said.

' I don't at all understand him, but I suppose it *is* all right. Well, come along, my dear friend.' I then left him for a while. After the hour's interval I returned. The next thing I saw from the back of the room was my burly friend in the front row of a number of irreverent youngsters of juvenile age, some of whom, close by me, were saying, ' Who's the stout old bloke ? What's he doing here ?'

' Now,' said the Bursar and senior Fellow, 'take these Testaments in your hands, all o' yes.' And then I saw my venerable friend, for so he looked in comparison, with three youths, sharing his Testament with them ! But he was most serious. For here was a solemn duty before him. ' Now repeat after me, all o' yes : " *Ego* "—a shout—" *Joannes, Carolus*," as the case might be, " *juro solemniter*," etc. Forster might have been in a chuich going through a marriage ceremony, so reverently did he repeat the formula. The lads were making a joke of it.

Forster, as I said, was indeed a man of the old fashion of gallantry, making his approaches where he admired *sans cérémonie*, and advancing boldly to capture the fort. I remember a dinner, with a young lady who had a lovely voice, and who sang after the dinner to the general admiration. Forster had never seen her before; but when she was pressed to sing again and again, and refused positively, I was amazed to see him triumphantly passing through the crowded room, the fair one on his arm, he patting one of her small hands which he held in his own. She was flattered immensely and unresisting; the gallant Forster had carried all before him. This was his way; never would he be second fiddle anywhere if he could help it. Not a bad principle for anyone, if they can only manage it.

I remember one night, when he was in his gallant mood laying his commands on a group of ladies, to sing or do something agreeable, he broke out: 'You know I am a despot, and must have my way, I'm such a harbitrary cove.' The dames stared at this speech, and I fancy took it literally, for they had not heard the story. The story referred to was that of the cabman who summoned Forster for giving him a too strictly-measured fare, and when defeated said 'it warn't the fare, but he was determined to bring him there, for he was such a harbitrary cove.' No story about Forster gave such delight to his friends as this ; he himself was half flattered. There is also another version.

Forster liked to be with people of high degree— as, perhaps, most of us do. At one time he was infinitely flattered by the attentions of Count d'Orsay, who, no doubt, considered him a personage. This odd combination was the cause of great amusement to his friends, who were, of course, on the look-out for droll incidents. There was many a story in circulation. One was that Forster, expecting a promised visit from 'the Count,' received a sudden call from his printers. With all solemnity he impressed the situation on his man. ' Now,' he said, ' you will tell the Count that I have only just gone round to call on Messrs. Spottiswoode, the printers —you will observe, Messrs. Spott-is-woode,' added he, articulating the words in his impressive way. The next time Forster met the Count the former gravely began to explain to him the reason of his absence. 'Ah! I know,' said the gay Count: 'you had just gone round to ze *Spotted Dog*—I understand,' as though he could make allowance for the ways of literary men. Once Forster had the Count to dinner—a great solemnity. When the fish was

' on,' the host was troubled to note that the sauce had not yet reached his guest. In an agitated, deep *sotto voce*, he muttered, ' Sauce to the Count!' The ' aside' was unheard. He repeated it in louder but more agitated tones, ' *Sauce* to the Count!' This, too, was unnoticed ; when, louder still, the guests heard, ' *Sauce for the flounders of the Count !*' This gave infinite delight to the friends, and the phrase became almost a proverb. Forster learning to dance in secret, in preparation for some festivity, was another enjoyment, and his appearance on the scene carefully executing the steps, his hands on the shoulders of a little girl, caused much hilarity.

There now comes back on me a pleasant comedy scene in which Boz figured, and which even at this long distance of time raises a smile. When I had come to town, having taken a house, etc., with a young and pretty wife, Dickens looked on encouragingly ; but at times shaking his head humorously, as the too sanguine plans were broached, ' Ah, *the little victims play*,' he would quote. Early in the venture he good-naturedly came to dine *en famille* with his amiable and interesting sister-in-law. He was in a delightful mood, and seemed to be applying all the points of his own Dora's attempts at housekeeping with a pleasant slyness, the more so as the little lady of the house was the very replica of that piquant and fascinating heroine. She was destined, alas! to but a short enjoyment of her little rule, but she gained all hearts and sympathies by her very taking ways. Among others, the redoubtable John Forster professed to be completely 'captured,' and was her most obstreperous slave. He, too, was to have been of the party, but was prevented by one of his troublesome chest attacks. Scarcely had Boz entered, when he drew out a letter—I see him now standing at the fire, a twinkle in his brilliant eyes. 'What *is* coming over Forster?' he said, ruminating; 'I cannot make him out. Just as I was leaving the house I received this;' and he read aloud: 'I can't join you to-day. But mark you this, sir! No tampering, no poaching on *my* grounds; for I won't have it. Recollect *Codlin's the friend not Short!*' With a wondering look Boz kept repeating in a low voice: ' " Codlin's the friend not Short." What *can* he mean? What do you make of it?' I knew perfectly, as did also the little lady who stood there smiling and fluttered, but it was awkward to explain. But he played with the thing and, it could only be agreed that Forster at times was perfectly 'amazing' or 'a little off his head.'

And what a dinner it was! What an amusing failure, too, as a first attempt! Suddenly, towards the end of the dinner, a loud, strange sound was heard, as of falling or rushing waters ; it was truly alarming. I ran out and found a full tide streaming down the stairs. The cook in her engrossment had forgotten to turn a cock. 'Ah, the little victims play!' and Boz's eyes twinkled. A loud-voiced cuckoo and quail were sounding their notes, which prompted me to describe a wonderful clock of the kind I had seen, with two trumpeters who issued forth at the hour and gave a prolonged flourish before striking, then retired, their doors closing with a smart clap. This set off Boz in his most humorous vein. He imagined the door sticking fast or only half opening, the poor trumpeter behind pushing with his shoulder to get out, then giving a feeble, gasping tootle with much 'whirring' and internal agonies ; then the rest silence.

On another occasion came Forster himself and lady, for a little family dinner ; the same cook insisted on having in her husband, 'a dear broth of a boy,' to assist her. Forster arriving before he was expected—he was ever *more* than punctual—the tailor rushed up eagerly to admit him, forgetting, however, to put on his coat! As he threw open the door, he must have been astonished at Forster's greeting, ' No, no, my good friend, I altogether decline. I am *not* your match in age, weight, or size '—a touch of his pleasant humour and good spirits.

Forster of course deeply felt the death of his old friend and comrade, the amiable, noble-hearted Dickens. He was the great central figure in all the dismal ceremonial that followed ; he arranged everything admirably, he was executor with Miss Hogarth, and I could not but think how exactly he reproduced his great prototype, Johnson, in a similar situation, who was seen hurrying about with a pen in his hand and dealing with the effects, and talking of the potentiality of growing rich beyond the dreams of avarice. So was Forster busy, appraising copyrights and realizing assets, all which work he performed in a most business-like fashion. That bequest in the will of the gold watch to his 'trusty friend, John Forster,' I always thought admirably summarized the relations of the two friends. I myself received under his will one of his ivory paper-knives, and a paper-weight marked ' C. D.' in golden letters, which was made for and presented to him at one of the pottery works.

One of the most delightful little dinners I had was an impromptu one at Forster's house, the party being himself, myself, and Boz. The presence of a third, not a stranger yet not an intimate, prompted both to be more free than had they been *tête-à-tête*. Boz was what might best be called 'gay.' His fashion of talk was to present things that happened in a pleasantly humorous light. On this occasion he told

us a good deal about that strange being, Chauncey
Hare Townshend, from whom he may have drawn
Twemlow in 'Our Mutual Friend.' Every touch in
that sketch reminds me of him ; he, too, had a shy,
shrinking manner, a soft voice, but in his appearance most of all was Twemlow ; he had a rather
overdone worship of Dickens, wishing 'not to in-
trude,' etc. ; he was a delicate, unhealthy-looking
person, rather carefully made up. Boz was specially
pleasant this day on an odd bequest of his, for poor
Twemlow had died, and he (Boz) was implored to
edit his religious writings—rather, a compendium of
his religious opinions to be collected from a mass
of papers in a trunk, for which service £1,000 was
bequeathed. Boz was very humorous on his first
despair at being appointed to such an office ; then
described his hopeless attempts 'to make head or
tail' of the papers. 'Are they worth anything as
religious views ?' I asked. 'Nothing whatever, I
should say,' he said, with a humorous twinkle in his
eye ; 'I must only piece them together somehow.'
And so he did, I forget under what title—I think,
'Religious Remains of the late C. H. T.' There
was probably some joking on this description. It is
fair to say that Boz had to put up with a vast deal
of this admiring worship, generally from retiring
creatures whom his delicate good-nature would not
let him offend.

Forster's large sincerity was remarkable, as was his generous style, which often carried him to extra- ordinary lengths. They were such as one would only find in books. I remember once coming to London without giving him due notice, which he always imperatively required to be done. When I went off to his house at Palace Gate, presenting myself about five o'clock, he was delighted to see me, as he always was, but I saw he was very un- comfortable and distressed. ' *Why* didn't you tell me,' he said testily, 'a day or two would have done ? But *now*, my dear fellow, *the table's full*— it's impossible.' ' What ?' I asked, yet not without a suspicion of the truth—for I knew him. ' Why, I have a dinner-party to-day ! De Mussy, the doctor of the Orleans family, and some others are coming, and here you arrive at this hour ! Just look at the clock—I tell you it can't be done.' In vain I pro- tested ; though I could not say it was ' no matter,' for it was a serious business. ' Come with me into the dining-room, and you'll see for yourself.' There we went round the table, and ' The table's full,' he repeated from ' Macbeth.'

There was something truly original in the im- plied premise that his friend was *entitled* of right to have a place at his table, and that the sole dispensing cause to be allowed was absence of space or a physical impossibility. It seems to me that this was a very genuine, if rare, shape of hospitality.

Forster was the envied possessor of nearly every one of Boz's MSS.—a treasure at the time not thought very much of, even by Dickens himself, but since his death become of extraordinary value. I should say that each was now worth some £2,000 or £3,000 at the least. How amazing has been this appreciation of what dealers call 'the Dickens stuff' during these years! It is almost incredible. I mind the day when a Dickens book, a Dickens letter, was taken tranquilly. The original 'Pickwick'—that is, bound from the numbers—is indeed a nugget of old gold. I remember once asking Wills, his sub-editor, could I be allowed to have the original MSS. of some of Boz's old stories? He said, 'To be sure,' that nothing was more easy than to ask him, for the printer sent each back to him after use, carefully sealed up. What became of all these papers I cannot tell, but I doubt if anyone was then *very* eager about them.

Lately, turning over some old letters, I came upon a large bundle of proof 'slips' of a story I had written for *All the Year Round*. It was called 'Howard's Son.' To my surprise and pleasure, I found that they had passed through Boz's own hands, and had been corrected throughout in his own careful and elaborate fashion, whole passages written in, others deleted, the punctuation altered and improved. Here was a *trouvaille*. These slips, I may add, have extraordinary value, and in the States would fetch a considerable sum. It was extraordinary what pains Boz took with the papers of his contributors, and how diligently and laboriously he improved and polished them.

Forster's latter days—that is, I suppose, for some seven or eight years—were an appalling state of martyrdom; no words could paint it. It was gout in its most terrible form—that is, on the chest. This malady was due, in the first place, to his early hard life, when rest and hours of sleep were neglected or set at naught. Too good living also was accountable. He loved good cheer, and had an excellent taste in wines, fine clarets, etc. Such things were fatal to his complaint. This gout took the shape of an almost eternal cough, which scarcely ever left him. It began invariably with the night, and kept him awake, the waters rising on his chest and overpowering him. I have seen him on the following day, lying spent and exhausted on a sofa, and struggling to get some snatches of sleep if he could. But as seven o'clock drew near a change came. There was a dinner-party; he 'pulled himself together'—began another jovial night, and in good spirits. But he could not resist the tempting wines, etc., and, of course, had his usual 'bad' night.

Once dining with me, he, as usual, brought his
Vichy bottle with him, and held forth on the
necessity of 'putting on the muzzle,' restraint, etc.
He 'lectured' us all in a very suitable way, and
maintained his restraint during dinner.   There was
a bottle of good Corton gently warming at the fire,
about which he made inquiries, but which now,
alas! need not be opened.   When the ladies were
gone, he became very pressing on this topic.   'My
dear fellow, you must *not* let me be a kill-joy ; you
must really open the bottle for yourself.   Why
should you deny yourself for me ?   Nonsense!'   It
suggested Winkle going to fight a duel, saying to
his friend, ' Do *not* give information to the police.'
But I was inhospitably inflexible.   These little
touches were Forster all over.   One would have
given anything to let him have his two or three
glasses, but one had to be cruel to be kind.   Good
Samuel Johnson was of the same pattern, and could
not resist a dinner-party, even when in serious
plight.   He certainly precipitated his death by his
greed.

On one occasion a London bookseller sent me
the two large quartos of Garrick's letters, with
Forster's bookplate, which I mentioned to their late
owner as a coincidence.   The way he took it was
characteristic.   I had to go at once into the dock.
' How did you suppose this bookseller got 'em ?'

'Oh, really—I really can't say.' 'You don't suppose
that I am in the habit of selling my books in this
way?' 'Dear me, no.' 'Well, then, how do you
account for it? I beg'—*i.e.*, insist—'that you
tell : you must have had an opinion.' I feebly said
something about 'exchanging,' but he continued
resolutely to press me. He at last explained that
he had lent them to that thirsty littérateur C——.
This was Forster all over, actually asserting a right
to know your very thoughts.

I look back to another of Forster's visits to
Dublin, when he came in quest of materials for his
'Life of Swift.' He was in the gayest and best of
his humours, and behaved much as the redoubtable
Doctor Johnson did on his visit to Edinburgh. I see
him seated in the library at Trinity College, making
his notes, surrounded by the dons. Dining with
him at his hotel—for even here he must entertain
his host—he lit his cigar after dinner, when an aged
waiter of the old school interrupted : ' Ah, sor, you
mustn't do that. It's agin the rules and forbidden.'
He little knew his Forster. What a storm broke on
his head! ' Leave the room, you scoundrel! How
dare you, sir, interfere with me! Get out, sir !' with
much more. The scared waiter fled. ' One of the
pleasantest episodes in my life,' I wrote in a diary,
' has just closed. John Forster come and gone,
after his visit here (*i.e.*, to Dublin). Don't know

when I liked a man more. He was most genial
and satisfactory to talk with. His amiable and
agreeable wife with him. She told a great deal of
Boz and his life at home, giving a delightful picture
of his ordinary day. He would write all the
morning till one o'clock, and no one was allowed
to see or interrupt him. Then came lunch; then
a long hearty walk until dinner-time. During the
evening he would read in his own room, but the
door was kept open so that he might hear the girls
playing—an amiable touch. At Christmas time,
when they would go down on a visit, he would
entertain them by reading aloud his proofs and
passages not yet published. She described to us
" Boffin," out of " Our Mutual Friend," as admirable.
He shows all to Forster beforehand, and consults
him as to plot, characters, etc. He has a humorous
fashion of giving his little boys comic names—later
to appear in his stories. Thus, one is known as
" Plorn," which later appeared as " Plornish."
This is a pleasant picture of the great writer's
domestic life, and it gives also a faint " adumbration "
of what is now forgotten : the intense curiosity and
eager anticipation that was abroad as to what he
was doing or preparing. Hints of his characters
got known ; their movements and developments
were discussed, and the incidents of his story were
like public events. We have nothing of this nowa-

days, for no writer or story rouses the same interest. Forster also told us a good deal about Carlyle, whose proof-sheets, from the abundant corrections, cost three or four times what the original "setting" did.' Thus the diary.

Once, on a Sunday in Dublin, I brought Forster to the Cathedral in Marlborough Street to hear the High Mass, at which Cardinal Cullen officiated. He sat it out very patiently, and I remember, on coming out, drew a deep sigh, or gasp, with the remark, 'Well, I suppose'—long pause—'it's all right.'

Forster, whatever might be said of his sire's calling, was at least of a good old Newcastle Border stock of fine 'grit,' and sturdily independent. A notable instance was his imbroglio with the clever and amiable Frederick Locker, who had incautiously included some verses of Landor's in his 'Lyra.' This was Forster's copyright, who threatened law and all its pains and penalties. He presently found that a copy had been presented to the Athenæum Club library, that the usual stamp, inscription and Minerva's head of the club had been added. Forster went to the library, put the book *sans façon* into his pocket, and took it away home—confiscated it, in fact. There was a great hubbub. The committee met, determined that their property had been removed, and demanded that it should be brought

back.   Forster flatly refused ; defied the club to do
its worst.   Secretary, solicitors, and every means
were used to bring him to reason.   It actually
ended in his retaining the book, the club shrinking
from entering into public contest with so redoubtable
an antagonist.

Forster was sumptuous in his tastes, always liking
to have the best.   When he wanted a thing, con-
siderations of expense would not stand in the way
When he heard that Lord Lytton was going to India,
he gave Millais a commission to paint a portrait of
the new Viceroy.   Millais used good-humouredly to
relate the lofty, condescending style in which it was
announced.   ' It gives me, I assure you, great
pleasure to learn that you are so advancing in your
profession.   I think highly of your abilities'—or
something to that effect.   Millais at this time was
at the very top of his profession, as, indeed, Forster
knew well ; but the state and grandeur of the subject,
and his position in expending so large a sum—I
suppose 1,000 guineas, for it was a three-quarter
length—lifted my old friend into one of his dreams.
The portrait was a richly-coloured and effective
one, giving the staring, owl-like eyes of the poet-
diplomatist.   Another of Forster's purchases was
Maclise's huge picture of Caxton showing his first
printed book to the King.

It was a treat and an education to go round

a picture-gallery with him, so excellent and to the point were his criticisms. He seized on the *essential* merit of each. I remember going with him to see the collected works of his old friend Leslie, R.A., when he frankly confessed his disappointment at the general *thinness* of the colour and style, brought out conspicuously when the works were all gathered together. At the Dublin Exhibition he was greatly struck by a little cabinet picture by an Anglo-German artist, one Webb, and was eager to secure it, though he objected to the price. However, on the morning of his departure the secretary drove up on an outside car to announce that the artist would take £50, which Forster gave. This was 'The Chess-players,' which now hangs at South Kensington.

He had deep feeling and hesitation even as to putting anything into print without due pause and preparation. Print had not then become what it is now, with telephone, typewriting, and other aids, a mere expression of conversation and of whatever floating ideas are passing through the mind. I was present when a young fellow, to whom he had given some of his papers, brought him the proofs in which the whole was printed off without revision or restraint. He gave him a severe rebuke. 'Sir, you seem to have no idea of the *sacredness* of the Press; you *pitch in*

everything, as if into a bucket. Such carelessness
is inexcusable.' Among them was a letter from
Colburn, the former husband of his wife. ' I am
perfectly *astounded* at you! Have you not the
tact to see that such a thing as that should not
appear?' And he drew his pen indignantly across
it. That was a good lesson for the youth. In
such matters, however, he did not spare friend or
stranger.

It is curious, considering how sturdy a pattern
of Englishman was Forster, that his oldest friends
were Irishmen : such as Maclise, Emerson Tennent,
Whiteside, Macready, Quain, Foley, Mulready, and
many more. For all these he had almost an affection, and he cherished their old and early intimacy.
He liked especially the good-natured, impulsive type
of the Goldy pattern ; for such he had interest and
sympathy. As a young man, when studying for the
Bar, he had been in Chitty's office, where he had
for companions Whiteside and Tennent, afterwards
Sir Emerson. Whiteside became the brilliant
Parliamentary orator and Chief Justice ; Tennent
a Baronet and Governor of Ceylon ; and Forster
himself the distinguished writer and critic, the friend
and biographer of Dickens. It was a remarkable
trio, certainly. Chitty, the veteran conveyancer, his
old master, he never forgot, and was always delighted
to have him to dinner, to do him honour in every

way. His son, the Judge, was a favourite protégé,
and became his executor. He had a warm regard
for Sir Richard Quain, who attended Lord Beacons-
field *in extremis*, who literally knew everyone
that ought to be known, and who would visit a
comparatively humble patient with equal interest.
Quain was thoroughly good-natured, ever friendly,
and even affectionate. Forster's belief in him was
supreme. He was not only physician-in-ordinary,
but the warm and devoted friend, official consultant,
as he was of the whole coterie. For a long course
of years he had charge of his friend's health, if
health it could be called, where all was disease
and misery; and it was his fate to see him affectionately through the great crisis at the last.
There was a deal of this affection in Quain; he
was eminently good-natured. Good, true-hearted
Quain!

After all, that must have been an almost joyous
moment that brought poor Forster his release from
those awful and intolerable days and nights of
agony, borne with a fortitude of which the world
had no conception — eternal frightful spasms of
coughing day and night, together with other maladies
of the most serious kind. And yet on the slightest
respite this man of wonderful fortitude would turn
gay and festive, recover his spirits, and look forward

to some enjoyment, a dinner it might be, where he
was the old Forster once more, smiling enticingly
on his favourite ladies, and unflinchingly prepared
to go back to the night of horrors that awaited
him!

BOOK SECOND

PICTURED PLACES IN TOWN AND COUNTRY

CHAPTER X

BOZ AND BATH

WHEN Dickens was giving his famous readings, he always appeared before a violet screen, which threw out most effectively his showy and brilliant figure. This is symbolical of his literary methods, for he generally showed with most effect on a background of some favourite city for which he had a deep sympathy or which was bound up with his recollections. There were four cities which were thus near to his heart, all save one being Pickwickian. And no mean recommendation this! These were Rochester, Canterbury, Ipswich, and Bath. No one knew their physiognomy and anatomy so well; they were bone of his bone; they had grown up with him. And it is curious how reciprocal were the advantages of his treatment. The city thus treated gained enormously by his interpretation—was galvanized into life, romance, and humour; it attained a world-wide celebrity. Every building and every stone are registered, drawn again

and again, and described until they have become
sacred things. Pilgrimages are made, and tourists
come in shoals. In return, his pen was stimulated,
the old town imparting life, force, and vivacity to his
pen, calling up bygone visions, dreams, adventures,
and recollections of his childhood, all put forward
with a living vividness.

It has been often repeated that Boz was not very
partial to Bath, and did not admire it. His liken-
ing it to a city of gravestones might seem to support
this view ; but we have also on record his genuine
and very handsome compliment paid to the city
when he first saw it. In his version of the Bladud
story he says :

‘ There was no city where Bath stands then.
There was no vestige of human habitation ; but
there was the same noble country, the same broad
expanse of hill and dale, the same beautiful channel
stealing on far away, the same lofty mountains
which, like the troubles of life, viewed at a distance,
and partially obscured by the bright mists of the
morning, lose their ruggedness and asperity, and
seem all ease and softness. Moved by the beauty
of the scene,’ etc.

There may have been a reference here to his own
recent heavy trouble, which had caused the interruption of his story, and which he could now look back
to more calmly. Thus, we see, however tender and

romantic and amiable, he loved to associate objects about him that gave him pleasure with his own feelings, whether joyous or sorrowful.

Ardent Pickwickians, full of enthusiasm, it strikes with something of a chill to discover Boz's later indifference to such cherished places as the Bull at Rochester, the Angel at Bury, or the great White Horse, where he put up on his reading tours. We do not find a word or a recollection. It is so with Bath, which he also visited. We might have expected some fond retrospection. Could the amiable Boz have dreamed, or could I have dreamed, as he walked and talked and wrung my hand in his hearty way, that some thirty years after his death that hand should, on one fair day in the Bath streets, be drawing aside a cloth covering up his own image in bronze ; and that this act was to be acclaimed by a large crowd gathered before it and responsive to the earnest words of his old friend and admirer ?

Mr. Pickwick, as we know, after his disastrous experience of the Law Courts, carried his ' followers ' with him to Bath for a sort of holiday, and a very enjoyable one they had. They found themselves at the White Horse Cellars in Piccadilly at about seven o'clock one morning, going down by the Bath coach. I well recall the White Horse Cellars through all its vicissitudes. I can go back even to the fifties, little more than ten years after Boz described it.

I lived at Richmond then, and convenient omnibuses used to jog along all the way—fare one shilling. Even up to the late years, before its fall—that is, in the eighties — was exactly as Boz described : almost a roadside inn, with rude benches and sanded floor. It flashed up a little before its final destruction, just at the time when the new coaching mania set in, when it was really exhilarating, between six and seven o'clock in the evening, to hear horns winding and coach after coach rattling up—all up to time— at the ' Whyteorsesellar '—as Boz used comically to spell it. When a school boy, how often had I been left—left till called for—in this very sanded parlour of the Cellars, while the family spent the day a-shopping ! When we returned all went down again together by the stage. And forty years later, on the eve of its extinction, it was in no better state. Now there are the Cellars left, strictly speaking, fashioned into a restaurant. I always call up the image of the brilliant young fellow as he was then— full of animation, energy, and quicksilver—entering the coach offices at the early hours, as he has described them in one of his ' Sketches,' a pale, not overstrong, young man.

Twelve hours was the ' regulation ' time from London to Bath. Twelve hours of jogging and jolting and swerving round corners, with hard bits of road and soft bits ; and yet our travellers

seem to have taken it all lightly enough, for we are
told so. Yet these coach journeys must have been
serious, fatiguing things. There was no getting
down for a moment even at the change of horses,
as it has been described to me by 'old stagers,' for
the change of horses was like a flash of lightning.
The outgoing animals were taken off in an instant—
there were so many hands—and the fresh ones
attached as speedily. In some of Mr. Pickwick's
journeys we are told how he and his friend Tupman
used to get down 'for a glass,' and when the coach
was ready to start were seen rushing from the bar,
to the indignation of the coachman. But these
were easy-going stage vehicles, and not 'mails,' on
the mains roads, like the Bath Road.

The Pickwickians on their journey down might
have been even more amused than they really were
at Sam's wonderful discovery of his master's name
on the coach door. When they found themselves
drawing near to Bath, they passed through a village
which the guard could have told them was called
Pickwick! Here was a fresh surprise. Nay, he
would have pointed out to them various gentlemen's
houses of the same name :

'See ! yon be Squoire Loscombe's—Pickwick
Hoose ; and thot be Squoire Fenton's—the Captain,
ye know—Pickwick Lodge.' By a curious coincidence, we find in Pierce Egan's ' Life in London '

the Fat Knight stopping at this very Pickwick Lodge. Mr. Pickwick, through his circular spectacles, would have regarded these objects with mild surprise. What has now become of those places? 'Wick' was a local term, and there is Bathwick now. And, again, what must he have thought later when he found himself under his namesake's roof, with, probably, an inscription over the door in small letters :

> ELEAZAR PICKWICK,
> *Licensed to sell*
> *Beer and Spirits.*

For Eleazar kept the hotel, dying some eleven years after the Pickwickian arrival on December 8, 1838.

One of the many associations on which Bath may plume itself is the having supplied this glorious and immortal name of Pickwick to the world. ' Pickvick and Principle!' cried Sam. And so cry we all. ' Pickvick and Principle—and Bath!' we may add. This happy name—a boon and a blessing to men— was truly appropriate, for no other would have done so well. Only conceive that by some chance Boz had never gone down to Bath, and had to devise some other say—Clutterbuck! We should have had —' The Perambulations of the Clutterbuck Club, with the Clutterbuckians.' And what a unique name it is! No one could bear it without finding

his social life impossible.   Imagine a dinner-party,
and the servant announcing 'Mr. Pickwick!' There
would be a general titter, if not a burst of laughter.
Every eye would settle on the hapless man.   Many
years ago a gentleman found the burden unendur-
able, and people read in the *Times* with much
amusement of his application to the Crown for
leave to change it.   There is a Pickwick or two
about, but not one in the 'London Directory.'   I
suppose there is not a single English name that
can compare with it in notoriety, or for suggestion
of comic and pleasant associations.   The name
seems to have lain long dormant in Boz's mind,
until, when casting about for a suitable one for his
hero, it recurred to him.   Rushing into Chapman's
shop in the Strand, he called out triumphantly, 'I
have got it!   Pickwick!'*

* We find in the books, Annual Registers, etc., various references to the family.   Thus, 'In October, 1807, a casualty occurred
to the driver of Pickwick's coach from Southampton to Bath,
George Hawkins, who was taken suddenly and very alarmingly ill
on Standerwick Common.   The honest fellow showed much fortitude, and refused to be taken from his coach to a neighbouring
cottage, and at his own desire was placed inside, and thus pur-
sued his journey to Bath.   (But who drove?) Just before having
reached the city he expired.'   This story might have been related
by the elder Mr. Weller, and shows that there was among the class
a sort of heroism akin to that displayed by the later engine-drivers.

There is every probability that the legend is true which relates
that Moses Pickwick, the coach proprietor, was a foundling, and
owed his name to the fact of his having been discovered in the
locality so named.

Boz is very silent as to the merits or shortcomings of the White Hart, contenting himself with a single remark on the waiters, 'who from their costume might be mistaken for Westminster boys, only they destroy the illusion by behaving themselves much better.' Here was an actual compliment. The late Mr. Peach, the antiquarian and bookseller of Bath, told me that he perfectly remembered this unusual dress, and added that the chambermaids also had their uniform.

Boz's first visit to Bath was in 1835, at which time he was the clever, enterprising young reporter on the *Chronicle*, under Mr. Black. Forster has well described the energy and capacity of the young fellow, then only twenty-three. He seems to have the same versatile talent of getting his business

Pickwick (the living one) was at the White Hart so far back as 1795, and flourished so well that he could send his son, Mr. William Pickwick, to Oxford. The young man had been there a short time when he broke a bloodvessel, which 'impaired a constitution naturally good, and terminated in depriving society of a valuable young man, and his distressed parents of an only child, as amiable in manners as his genius was surprising.' We like 'a valuable young man.'

In the year 1843 we find a Captain Pickwick serving in the 6th Dragoons, and promoted to be Major. The coaching family, however, had its members in all the professions. The Rev. Charles Pickwick, 'late of Worcester College,' held a living at Beckington, Somerset. He died in March, 1835, and was a nephew of 'E. Pickwick, Esq., of Queen's Square, Bath.' He left a son behind him, born in May, 1831.

'through' that our modern war-correspondents have,
being ever ready and fertile in resource and in
planning his 'expresses.' Mr. Black had the greatest confidence in him, and could rely on him in any
difficult matter, which was sure to be attended to—
as he said in his 'Pickwick,' recalling his own advice
to his employer, ' Pay the bearer half a crown extra
for instant delivery, which was surer still.' Thus
did Boz always incorporate his own little experiences
with his writing, not only adding a feeling of reality,
but pleasing himself by the reminiscence.

It is clear, however, that on this visit to Bath he
could not have an opportunity to see anything of
Bath or its entertainments. But at what period was
he staying at that curious little old inn in Walcot,
where traditions of him used to be preserved and, I
believe, his chair and other relics were shown? Used
to be, alas! The traditions alluded to were all in
favour of the young fellow's good-humour and high
popularity. There were stories about a lighted
candle, and his going up the open-air staircase—I
forget the precise form of the tale. On a late visit
I was grieved to find that this very picturesque
memorial, with its curious yard and outside stone
staircase, had been turned into shops. It always
reminded me of the inn at Edinburgh, 'the White
Horse,' where Dr. Johnson put up at on his famous
tour with Bozzy. I always, by the way, see a

fanciful likeness in the Pickwickian tour to this
pilgrimage, and it is not very far-fetched, for
Dickens knew and admired the tour, and took
incidents out of it for his book. There is a quaint
suggestion even in the names Boz and Bozzy, and
Mr. Pickwick had a good deal of the sage's tyrannical domination. I once, indeed, read a paper
on this very topic at one of the Johnson Club
dinners.

Boz, when actively engaged in writing his book,
would often start off on a journey specially to inspect
some locality that he had selected for treatment. In
this fashion he visited Yorkshire and the Yorkshire schools, Kenilworth, and Warwick Castle.
Even in London he tells us how he was 'just going
out to select a house for Sampson Brass.' The
sight of the building or the place seemed to inspire
him and to furnish him with ideas.

With this view, after he had tried and sentenced
his hero in ' that 'ere conviction,' he resolved to
bring his travellers to Bath ; but certainly first
visited the place to survey the ground and see what
was going on.

In May, 1835, he had been sent to Bristol to
' take ' a speech of Lord John Russell's, who was on
a canvassing tour in Devonshire. He had come
from the *Chronicle* in company with another reporter,
Beard. Nothing more business-like or efficient can

be conceived than his arrangements, as he planned
them for his principal, Mr. Black. He was to
forward the 'conclusion of Russell's dinner' by
Cooper's coach leaving the Bush at half-past six
next morning. He would go on to Bath to take
another speech, which would be forwarded on the
Thursday morning by the first Ball's coach, en-
dorsing the parcel for immediate delivery, paying
porters, etc. We may feel a little surprised that he
did not use one of Moses Pickwick's vehicles, but I
fancy these were not mail-coaches. His companion
was to go to Bath next morning, while he himself
would write out his notes while travelling to Marlborough. It will be seen from this that they had
had to sit up for two nights running to decipher
their notes, and which he calls ' sharp work for both
of us.' They would send on saddle-horses with the
despatches from Marlborough, and after a few hours'
sleep would then return. This energetic, careful
young fellow who thought of everything hoped he
would be forgiven for waiting here and there to pay
moneys and express satisfaction to those who had
helped them. No wonder his chief was delighted
with him and his intelligent exertions. To these
flying visits we owe the delightful Bath and Bristol
scenes, to be written two years later when they were
still fresh in his recollections.

In the old palmy days of Bath, when the White

Hart was standing, and Pickwick's coaches arriving
and departing in gallant style, the scene opposite the
Pump Room must have been an animated one—
all the flagged pavement, crowded with fashionable
water-drinkers, the Bath and Sedan chairs, the hum
of voices. What stir and bustle! Miss Austen,
who wrote nearly twenty years before, describes the
scene before the White Hart in her pleasant style.

'Half a minute,' says Jane Austen, 'conducted
them through the Pump yard to the archway
opposite Union Passage. Everybody acquainted
with Bath must remember the difficulties of crossing Cheap Street at this point; it is, indeed, a
street of so important a nature'—important is distinctly good—'so unfortunately connected with the
great London and Oxford roads, and the principal
inn of the city, that a day never passes in which
parties of ladies, however important their business,
whether in quest of pastry, millinery, or even of
young men, are not detained on one side or the
other by carriages, horsemen, or carts.'

How agreeably she magnifies; it was all important—'not a day passes.' We should think so.

One may lament the destruction of the old White
Hart which received the Pickwickians—a once-
famous coaching house, like all the White Harts
over the country. It was 'run' in those days by
the Pickwicks. That amiable master, though he

made light of Sam's finding his name upon the
coach door, must have found a real embarrassment
in being a guest there.   Could it be this, and not
the excuse given, that the party was to stay two
months—was the real reason of their so abruptly
quitting the house and goings into lodgings?   I
fancy this was Boz's own case.

The Grand Pump Room Hotel, which has taken
the place of the White Hart, is an imposing structure, and well contrived to produce effect in the fine
situation where it is placed.   The White Hart is
long gone, and now its successor is virtually gone—
shut up.   It is strange that some of those hotel
societies, the Gordon, Fredericks, and others, have
not seized upon and remodelled it, and brought it,
according to the phrase of the time, 'up-to-date.'
Its style of architecture, I repeat, is very happy, and
suits its *vis-à-vis* exactly.

What is delightful in these opening Bath scenes
is the general holiday tone ; everyone seems exhilarated, pleased with the look of the place, and
anxious to enjoy themselves.   It is like Dr. Johnson's first day in Edinburgh, when he was taken
round the lions.   Boz always contrived to spread
over such descriptions of towns and places a
delightful and inspiring tone of hilarity.   We feel
this holiday exhilaration in Boz's account of Bath.
We wish that we had been there at the time.   The

place seemed full to overflowing, and all in good
spirits.

Boz, as we have seen was his custom, must
certainly have paid a second visit to Bath for the
purposes of the story, which must have been in
1837, just about the time of writing the 'Trial.' It
must have been a quaint experience for him, then
in the flush of his popularity. What! he, the author
of the excruciatingly funny 'Pickwick,' whose green-
clad numbers were fluttering in everyone's hand,
after coming down in Pickwick's own coach, to go
and put up at Pickwick's own hotel! The author
of 'Pickwick' under Pickwick's own roof, occupying
Pickwick's room, eating Pickwick's dinners, and all
the while noting, observing, making fun and comic
copy of all that went on under Pickwick's roof!
Would not the host, likely enough, ask him to find
quarters elsewhere? 'I don't want my 'ouse made
ridic'lous by literary gents from London, and have
my bus'ness injured.' It was certainly a comic embarrassment enough. And Boz seemed to figure it
in Sam's discovery of the name of the coach. In
his vehement way, he was fond of assailing innkeepers and caterers, and holding them up to ridicule—a more risky thing now, it would appear, than
it was then. The worthy confectioner who supplied
the Assembly Rooms could not have relished his
tea being maligned, as it was by Dowler. 'Pay

your sixpence,' that gentleman directed his party,
' for your tea—they lay on hot water, and call it tea.'
Boz had ridiculed the White Horse Cellars ; and
only a couple of months before he had described
another inn in a very personal and uncomplimentary
fashion—the now famous Great White Horse at
Ipswich, a model of which was actually transported
to the Chicago Exhibition —of whose wine and
fittings generally he had spoken in 'what was really
a libellous fashion. ' Having ordered a bottle of the
worst possible port wine, at the highest possible
price, for the good of the house, they drank brandy
and water for their own.'   I suppose nothing severer
than this has ever been said of an inn.

There was yet another inn in Bath to which he
contrived to deal a sort of back-handed stroke.   He
is describing how Winkle in his degrading flight
found his way at early morning to another hostelry,
which he calls the Royal, whence he was able to
depart for Bristol by a miserable stage, drawn by
a pair of poor hacks, who, he says, had to make the
journey back and forward several times in the day,
if required.   More libel!   This house, the Royal
York, always appeals to us from its grave antique
air and faded look of having known better, far
better, days.   There must have been many a coach
and four—Palmer's and others—that set forth from
thence, the York, or Royal York, it makes little

difference ; or it may be that it was often called the
Royal, for short.   The popular Duke of the name
had no doubt lent his patronage.   Queen's Square,
once so exclusive, has now hotels and boarding-
houses.

Boz, by the way, never mentions the two Parades.
Yet they must have been in high vogue in his time
(1837), just as they were lively enough years before
in Jane Austen's.   While enumerating the sequence
of fashionable routine, he ignores this part of the
exhibition.   No one of our time has ever seen
North and South Parades to their full advantage.

Mr. Pickwick and his party, with the Dowlers,
remained only a day or two at the White Hart, and
then, we are told, shifted their quarters to private
lodgings in the Crescent.   The reason, Boz tells us,
was that they contemplated a stay of a couple of
months in the gay city.   This seems a fairly good
cause, but I fancy Boz had something else in his
mind, and this was to bring about Winkle's igno-
minious midnight adventure, which would have been
impossible at a hostelry like the White Hart.   There
the exciting chase could not have ' come off' at all.
Nothing could have been more natural, as it turned
out, under the comparative solitude of the Crescent
—the sleeping inhabitants, the long expanse just
suited for flight and pursuit, and, indeed, the general
propriety of the whole scene.

It is odd that Tupman, the stout gallant, the
squire of dames, should have made no show whatever in a scene so eminently suited to his taste and
capacity. We never hear of him except during the
morning call of Dowler and the M.C., when he was
introduced formally to the latter. Yet he does
nothing, cuts no figure whatever, is never heard of.
We must suppose the man was crushed by his late
adventure with the spinster aunt.

When describing Bantam's costume, Boz speaks
of his carrying ' a pliant ebony cane with a gold top.'
But ebony canes are not pliant. Oddly, too, at the
ball he again appears with this ' pliant ebony cane,'
which seems an unusual sort of accompaniment.
He could not say ' Bath,' but it was always ' Ba-ath '
—long drawn out and oft repeated, ' Welcome to
Ba-ath.' Unlike the Scotch prelate to whom James I.
offered the choice of the two sees, Bath or Wells,
and who replied ' Both,' meaning Bath. But the
King, taking him literally, actually gave him both
sees.

Queen's Square, to which Sam later was despatched with Mr. Pickwick's letter, is a noble
quadrangle, stately and architectural. We can see
the faithful Sam standing at the door, the letter in
his hand. The walls are now well blackened, but
in those days, nigh eighty years ago, they were
fairly clean, having been built only some sixty or

seventy years. This we learn from an allusion in
Jane Austen's novel ' Persuasion,' where she speaks
of ' the white glare of Bath' in 1810. It was no
doubt Boz himself that went to call on the M.C.
for the tickets, and this stamped the address on his
memory. How curious that the M.C. of that time
did actually live in Queen's Square, at the corner of
the most imposing of the sides!

Nothing is more delightful, or a truer piece of
comedy, than the first morning call of Bantam, the
M.C., on Mr. Pickwick at the White Hart. Dowler
brought him.

'Welcome to Ba-ath, sir. This is indeed an acquisition.
Most welcome to Ba-ath, sir. It is long, very long, Mr. Pickwick,
since you drank the waters. It appears an age, Mr. Pickwick.
Re-markable !'

'It is a very long time since I drank the waters, certainly,
replied Mr. Pickwick ; ' for to the best of my knowledge, I was
never here before.'

'Never in Ba-ath, Mr. Pickwick !' exclaimed the Grand Master,
letting the hand fall in astonishment. ' Never in Ba-ath ! He !
he ! Mr. Pickwick, you are a wag. Not bad, not bad. Good,
good. He ! he ! he ! Re-markable !'

'To my shame, I must say that I am perfectly serious,' rejoined
Mr. Pickwick. ' I really never was here before.'

'Oh, see,' exclaimed the Grand Master, looking extremely
pleased ; ' Yes, yes—good, good—better and better. You are
the gentleman of whom we have heard. Yes ; we know you,
Mr. Pickwick ; we know you.'

'The reports of the trial in those confounded papers,' thought
Mr. Pickwick. ' They have heard all about me.'

'You are the gentleman residing on Clapham Green,' resumed
Bantam, ' who lost the use of his limbs from imprudently taking

cold after port wine ; who could not be moved in consequence of acute suffering, and who had the water from the King's Bath bottled at one hundred and three degrees, and sent by waggon to his bedroom in town, where he bathed, sneezed, and same day recovered. Very re-markable !'

Mr. Pickwick acknowledged the compliment which the supposition implied, but had the self-denial to repudiate it, notwithstanding.

Excellent is this complacent assumption that Mr. Pickwick *must* have drunk the waters : as it was impossible for any man of position and culture not to have stayed at Bath, and that therefore there was a mistake somewhere.

How good is Bantam's contemptuous reference to the shopkeepers' assemblies !—'A paradise redeemed,' he said, 'by the absence of tradespeople, who are quite inconsistent with paradise, and who have an amalgamation of themselves at the Guildhall every fortnight, which is, to say the least, remarkable '—a grotesque sentence indeed, most original and 'remarkable, wonderful !' The 'amalgamation of themselves,' as a description of a dance, is truly amusing. Here Boz was most accurate, for I found in an old guide that such meetings did actually take place in the Guildhall.

I am always certain that Boz had turned over Warner's quarto on the City of Bath, for he mentions things that are not found elsewhere. His eye, no doubt, had fallen on this passage : Dr. Oliver

(of biscuit fame) had suggested in a tract on the
Bath waters that 'taking cold after drinking them
might be attended with the most fatal effects.
Therefore in bad weather the drinkers were obliged
either to forego that exercise which is absolutely
necessary after taking them internally, or to run the
risk of dangerous disorders.'

Boz's humorous dialogue is so thoroughly fresh
and natural that we always seem to be listening to
a couple of cheerful persons in exuberant spirits.
To write such, Boz himself must have been in a
similar buoyant mood, and have visualized the scene,
as it is called. No novelist of real talent and
inspiration can work otherwise than by this visuali-
zation. It is a most curious thing, and seems as
though the writer were thrown into a trance or saw
visions. In Dickens's case, George Henry Lewes
called this state hallucinations—that is, he wrote
what he saw. The truth is, no well-practised writer,
when about writing, say, a dialogue, knows a word
of what that dialogue will be ; it is all suggested, or
even dictated, to him as he goes along.

Inhabitants of Bath—Bathonians, should we say ?
—gifted with feeling, charitable hearts, will ever
think gratefully of Boz's tender sympathy for one
of their most useful insticutions. Boz had indeed
a heart that bled for the sorrows of the poor and
the suffering. He seemed almost to have written

mainly with that object, and actually set aside
without scruple the ordinary devices and obligations
of the story. I look upon this feature as an almost
unique thing in literature, for no other novel-writer
has shown this charity. 'Pickwick,' the immortal,
has done much for Bath, nearly as much as its
gifted architect known as 'Wood of Bath.' But
the very jewel of 'Pickwick' is the short pleading
for the Royal Free Hospital. He is describing in
his raciest way the humours of the Pump Room,
taking note of the statue of Nash, the Tompion
clock, the water-drinking, the Bladud inscription
which he missed, and perhaps thought ought to have
been there, when his eye falls on the inscription as
to the Royal Free Hospital. Here is the passage :

'*A golden inscription, to which all water-drinkers
should attend, for it appeals to them in the cause of a
deserving charity.*'

Here Boz alludes to the golden letters, but his
own words deserve to be written in letters of gold,
and proudly pointed out.*

Boz did not take note of a limitation to this great
charity, and which seems to us now a little harsh
or illiberal. It was set forth that no resident of

---

* I have often dwelt publicly on this unusual appeal, which is
so highly significant of Boz's amiable heart, notably at our
Fellowship meetings, at lectures on Boz at the London Institution, and, above all, at one romantic night at the Assembly
Rooms.

Bath was to have admission to the hospital.   Anyone, stranger or foreigner, from far or near, would
be welcomed and treated, but no one of Bath.   The
reason of the exclusion, however, is intelligible.   It
was felt that natives might readily procure the
waters in other ways, and could attend at the baths,
where no doubt facilities were offered.   They could
not, however, like Mr. Pickwick's double, have the
water 'bottled at the spring at a temperature of one
hundred and three degrees and forwarded by waggon
to their residences.'   This prohibition was in force up
to the year 1830, when it was abolished.   Boz, therefore, who came later, knew nothing of it, else, we
fancy, he would have indulged in some scathing
language.

I often stop to look at this Free Hospital.   As
I gaze on the darkened grim walls—Wood's work—
and the inscription,

ROYAL MINERAL WATER HOSPITAL,

I look on it 'with veneration,' as Dr. Johnson
would say.   Those letters, like those in the Pump
Room, are also 'golden.'

In his account of the Bladud legend he again
indulges in the same charitable regrets :

'Less than two hundred years ago on one of the
public baths in this city there appeared an inscription
in honour of its mighty founder, Prince Bladud.
That inscription is now erased.'

And Mr. Anstey, says Warner, 'whose magic
pen, etc., has paid a tribute to the virtues of the
Bath waters in the following inscription, deservedly
painted on a panel in letters of gold, and placed
behind the vase in the Pump Room :

THE HOSPITAL IN THIS CITY,

OPEN TO THE SICK POOR OF EVERY PART OF THE WORLD,
TO WHOSE CASES THESE WATERS ARE APPLICABLE
(THE POOR OF BATH ALONE EXCEPTED),
WAS FIRST ESTABLISHED, AND IS STILL SUPPORTED,
BY THE CHARITABLE CONTRIBUTIONS OF
THE LIBERAL AND HUMANE.

" O pause awhile, whoe'er thou art
    That drinkest this healing stream.
If e'er compassion o'er thy heart
    Diffused its heav'nly beam,
Think on the wretch whose distant lot
    This friendly aid denies ;
Think how in some poor lonely cot
    He unregarded lies.

" Hither the helpless stranger bring,
    Relieve his heartfelt woe,
And let thy bounty, like the Spring,
    In genial currents flow.
So may thy years from grief and pain
    And pining want be free,
And thus from Heaven that mercy gain
    The poor received from thee." '

These lines evidently made a deep impression on
Boz's tender heart ; and no wonder, for they are
very touching, and suggest Dr. Johnson's verses on

Levett. So much did they strike him—at least, did the inscription before its removal—that, as we have seen, he interrupts his rollicking account of the Pump Room and the drinkers to call his many thousand readers' attention to this noble charity!

There used to be a set of antique verses by Dr. Harrington, in imitation of Spenser, also hung up beside the golden inscription. Would it not be a graceful thing if it were decreed that this passage from the immortal ' Pickwick ' should also be ' hung up ' near the other verses ? It would be a tribute to Boz ; it would link his great and universally read work.

It is wonderful how accurately Boz followed the ceremonial of the Bath Rooms, and how much he knew about it. We find from the M.C.'s regulations that the official list was kept at the Pump Room, where the visitors were invited to repair and write down their names and quality. He shows us the obsequious M.C. pressing this important point on his new friends. But Boz seems to have tripped a little here, for he unaccountably transfers the official register to the Assembly Rooms, whither Mr. Pickwick had to follow it.

Bantam, it is known, was drawn from a certain Major Jervoise, or Jervas, who was M.C. at the time of the Pickwickian visit—rather, of Boz's own visit. This gentleman later became Governor of

some far-off island, and a Knight. Now, if Angelo
Cyrus Bantam, with his oddities, were intended as
an actual sketch of this personage, we may wonder
at Boz's courage. True, he was little more than
a youth, who ever 'fears nothin', 'cos he knows
nothin'.' At this time he was unsparing in his
censure of anything that he disapproved ; and,
indeed, it is curious that at the last even he could
not spare his friends when he required them for
literary purposes. Jervoise's best vindication is
that a person so ridiculous as Bantam would
never have been appointed a Governor of an
island—unless that of Barataria. If, then, the portrait was unlike, a serious injustice was done to
the official, for the sketch, like or unlike, was
certain to be applied to him in the locality. All
the same, we can imagine the confusion and talk
in Bath when the number or part appeared.

Boz was very near giving us the actual number
of Bantam's house, for he tells us cautiously of
Sam's 'arriving at the number in Queen's Square
to which he had been directed.'

How Boz has kindled the old Pump Room into
life! We seem to be promenading it there and
looking at the gay company.

'The great pump-room is a spacious saloon,
ornamented with Corinthian pillars, and a music-
gallery, and a Tompion clock, and a statue of Nash,

and a golden inscription, to which all the water-
drinkers should attend, for it appeals to them in
the cause of a deserving charity.   There is a large
bar with a marble vase, out of which the pumper
gets the water ; and there are a number of yellow-
looking tumblers, out of which the company get it ;
and it is a most edifying and satisfactory sight to
behold the perseverance and gravity with which
they swallow it.   There are baths near at hand,
in which a part of the company wash themselves ;
and a band plays afterwards, to congratulate the
remainder on their having done so.   There is
another pump-room, into which infirm ladies and
gentlemen are wheeled, in such an astonishing
variety of chairs and chaises, that any adventurous
individual who goes in with the regular number
of toes, is in imminent danger of coming out
without them ; and there is a third, into which
the quiet people go, for it is less noisy than
either.   There is an immensity of promenading,
on crutches and off, with sticks and without, and
a great deal of conversation, and liveliness, and
pleasantry.

    ' Every morning, the regular water-drinkers, Mr.
Pickwick among the number, met each other in the
pump-room, took their quarter of a pint, and walked
constitutionally.   At the afternoon's promenade,
Lord Mutanhed, and the Honourable Mr. Crushton,

the Dowager Lady Snuphanuph, Mrs. Colonel
Wugsby, and all the company attended.'*

It is extraordinary how the old system of the gay
promenade has disappeared in England, though it
still prevails at the foreign watering-places. In Jane
Austen's stories we see the area before the Pump
Room, and, above all, the Parade, thickly crowded
with gaily-dressed, chatting promenaders. And
she also insists on the curious necessity of showing
yourself at the Pump Room or Assembly or theatre,
at the fitting hours, so that you should meet your
fashionable friends.

We must always lament that Boz never thought
of relating his life and adventures during these
early days, which must have been full of excitement and droll incidents, especially had they been
set forth in his own lively style. This we can
see from the few fragments that he has given us.
On the other hand, as compensation, we have to

---

* In the Pump Room—or, indeed, in any pump room—who
will not think of Sam's talk with Smauker on the waters :

'Have you drunk the waters, Mr. Weller?' inquired his
companion.

'Once,' said Sam.

'What did you think of 'em?'

'I thought they was particlery unpleasant,' replied Sam.

'Ah,' said Mr. John Smauker; 'you disliked the kilibeate
taste, perhaps.'

'I don't know much about that 'ere,' said Sam; 'I thought
they'd a wery strong flavour o' warm flatirons.'

'That is the kilibeate,' said Mr. John Smauker.

look for 'Boz in his Books,' where he tells us
everything about himself—a notable instance of the
literal way in which he has transferred his life and
recollections into his stories.

Every Pickwickian, I am certain, feels the magic
power—the charms of his descriptions which call
up the most picturesque and suggestive images.
The name of a clock—or the name of its maker—
is a barren thing enough, yet I am convinced every
enthusiastic Pickwickian *must* have a curious feeling
of interest as he reads the words 'and a Tompion
clock.' What is Tompion to him or he to Tompion?
A clock by Dent or Benson may be a common or
necessary thing in any large public room. But
Tompion? It was a grotesque family name, and
no doubt attracted Boz—else why name it? why
not say 'a large clock'? But he found it, in his
Warner, who mentions it as if a thing of importance. It is also named in the guide-books. The
'Tompion clock' has an old-fashioned, venerable air,
like some survivor of the past who wears old clothes
of antique cut. Its face is faded. It seems to blink.
It is solidly built, too, made to stand for ages, as it
has done already. Somehow it has a sort of fascination. Boz calls attention to the statue of Nash,
but I confess Nash does not much interest us, as
does Tompion. How well and efficiently does Boz
take stock of the whole, noting even the Corinthian

pillars, which are rich pieces of decoration, as well
as the music-gallery, which he could not call 'an
elevated den,' as he did the little box in the ballroom of the Bull.

Not many know about Tompion, who was 'the
father of English clock-making' and a great in-
ventor. Born so far back as 1639, his was a most
interesting life—at least, for his mechanism, for we
are told that he began life as a common farrier, and
acquired his knowledge by experimenting on the
'equation' of a smoke-jack. When the Royal
Observatory was established, he was selected to
make its chronometers. Thomas Tompion was his
name. I should imagine he was of French extrac-
tion, as the name does not sound like an English
one. He was the first to make an English watch
with a balance spring. As one witness testifies, his
skill was such that, by adopting various inventions
and by a skilful proportion of parts, he left English
watches and clocks the finest in the world and the
admiration of his brother artists. His business
establishment was in Fleet Street, at No. 67.
He made barometers; a 'Tompion barometer' is
to be seen to this day at Hampton Court. He
patented 'the cylinder escapement.' There was at
one time a report that he was being employed to
make a grand clock for St. Paul's, which was to go
for one hundred years without winding, and was to

cost from £3,000 to £4,000; but this scheme did not go further. Tompion died in 1713, and was buried in Westminster Abbey. His portrait was painted by Kneller. 'He is represented in a plain coat and cravat, with a watch movement in his hand.'

But there is something more to be said as to the history of the 'Tompion clock.' Its maker, when in his old age, was ordered to Bath by physicians to drink the waters. It is certain that he must have benefited, and eventually have been cured. For 'the Tompion clock' is actually his gift, and the inference is irresistible that his motive was gratitude and perhaps pleasure at the recollection of the time he spent there. On it is an inscription :

THE WATCH AND SUNDIAL
WAS GIVEN BY MR. THOMAS TOMPION,
OF LONDON, CLOCKMAKER,
ANNO DOM. 1709.

He was therefore about seventy at the time. The clock is described as 'the fine long-case clock in the Pump Room.' A weighty and important thing always asserts itself. 'Sooner or later,' as Mr. Whiffers said, 'a showy servant's uniform must tell on the ladies.' And all these details seem to present themselves in the magic words—'Tompion clock.' Miss Austen also mentions the Tompion clock.

Turning out of Gay Street, as I often do on my

visits, I never come upon the old Assembly Rooms
without a sort of emotion. The very name affects one
—The Assembly Rooms. I think of the time, some
seventy years ago, when the lively party of Pickwickians walked down there from the White Hart.
I have a sort of solemn veneration for the building.
What festivals has it not seen ! What faded glories
within ! Alas ! now its case is bad indeed. It
looks as though it were to be a sort of permanent
sale-room ; the grand old chambers seem to be
always in possession of ancient, shabby furniture,
auctioneers' bills, and the like. Sometimes there is
a bazaar or sale of old pictures.

Boz himself must have been at the Assembly ball
he describes so pleasantly. We can imagine the
gay young man there in his full bloom—about five-
and-twenty—promenading it through the rooms.
' What a handsome young man !' we can hear some
Bath belle exclaim as he passes by—as indeed he was
then, his full auburn locks tumbling about his forehead, with his clear, blue eyes, and showy dress.
There he would wander, round and round, noting
warily and mightily amused. I could all but swear
that he ' saw ' everything that is described in the book.
There must have been, surely, some bewildered old
gentleman captured like Mr. Pickwick, and set down
to play whist with those determined, ' hard-bitten '
old ladies. He may have heard Lord Mutanhed

tell of the mail-cart ; he may have followed the
M.C. and listened to his chatter and compliments.
That obsequious functionary was not likely to over-
look the brilliant young author, and would have
overflowed with praise—'Quite re-markable, Mr.
Dickens! Everyone in Ba-ath knows your "Pickwick" by heart. Re-markable work—quite remarkable! It's long since you drank the waters ?'
And so with the night of last year's festival. A
dream, also. I see the long room, the set-out tables,
the lights, the floors, exactly as depicted by Phiz.

How amusing are the scenes at the Assembly
Rooms! What gay and lively characters flit before
us ! As we wander through them now, and lift our
eyes to their faded glories, we call them all up—the
Mutanheds, Crushers, Dowlers, Matinters, and the
rest. The very girandoles and mirrors that cast
their light down on Mr. Pickwick are still hanging
there—'the wery identical ones,' as Sam would put
it. Lately an intelligent fellow, showing me over
the place, pointed this out to me. 'Those shandy-
liers, sir, are th' identical same as is in the picturs
in the book.'

How vivacious and amusing is Boz's account of
the scene of the Assembly ball, at which he certainly
was present !—

At precisely twenty minutes before eight o'clock that night,
Angelo Cyrus Bantam, Esq., the Master of the Ceremonies,

emerged from his chariot at the door of the Assembly Rooms in
the same wig, the same teeth, the same eye-glass, the same watch
and seals, the same rings, the same shirt-pin, and the same cane.
The only observable alterations in his appearance were, that he
wore a brighter blue coat, with a white silk lining ; black tights,
black silk stockings and pumps, and a white waistcoat, and was, if
possible, just a thought more scented.

Bath being full, the company and the sixpences for tea poured
in in shoals. In the ball-room, the long card-room, the octagonal
card-room, the staircases, and the passages, the hum of many
voices, and the sound of many feet, were perfectly bewildering.
Dresses rustled, feathers waved, lights shone, and jewels sparkled.
There was the music—not of the quadrille band, for it had not
yet commenced ; but the music of soft tiny footsteps, with now
and then a clear merry laugh—low and gentle, but very pleasant
to hear in a female voice, whether in Bath or elsewhere. Brilliant
eyes, lighted up with pleasurable expectation, gleamed from every
side ; and look where you would, some exquisite form glided
gracefully through the throng, and was no sooner lost than it was
replaced by another as dainty and bewitching.

In the tea-room, and hovering round the card-tables, were a
vast number of queer old ladies and decrepit old gentlemen,
discussing all the small talk and scandal of the day, with a relish
and gusto which sufficiently bespoke the intensity of the pleasure
they derived from the occupation. Mingled with these groups,
were three or four match-making mammas, appearing to be wholly
absorbed by the conversation in which they were taking part, but
failing not from time to time to cast an anxious sidelong glance
upon their daughters, who, remembering the maternal injunction
to make the best of their youth, had already commenced incipient
flirtations in the mislaying of scarves, putting on gloves, setting
down cups, and so forth ; slight matters apparently, but which
may be turned to surprisingly good account by expert prac-
titioners.

Lounging near the doors, and in remote corners, were various
knots of silly young men, displaying various varieties of puppyism
and stupidity ; amusing all sensible people near them with their
folly and conceit ; and happily thinking themselves the objects of

general admiration. A wise and merciful dispensation which no good man will quarrel with.

And lastly, seated on some of the back benches, where they had already taken up their positions for the evening, were divers unmarried ladies past their grand climacteric, who, not dancing because there were no partners for them, and not playing cards lest they should be set down as irretrievably single, were in the favourable situation of being able to abuse everybody without reflecting on themselves. In short, they could abuse everybody, because everybody was there. It was a scene of gaiety, glitter, and show ; of richly-dressed people, handsome mirrors, chalked floors, girandoles, and wax-candles.

It will be seen from this that young Boz had romantic feelings, and that he was infinitely struck by the Bath beauties, their exquisite forms and soft, ' tiny footsteps,' though we may wonder how a footstep could be tiny. How he loathed, too, the young and vapid exquisites ! Boz could also be sarcastic on the elderly Bath frequenters.

I always look on Bantam's dialogue, on being introduced to Mr. Pickwick, as one of the happiest specimen of nonsensical chatter, with an air of wisdom. It puts one in spirits to read it. He is a delightful creature, and belongs to high comedy. The most amusing portion of his greeting is when he put his question to Mr. Pickwick as his being 'the gentleman at Clapham Green.' So with his supercilious description of the shopkeepers' entertainment—the tradesmen who have 'an amalgamation' of their own every Monday at the Guildhall. We may wonder how Boz picked up these details, but he no

Gad's Hill Place.
Higham by Rochester, Kent.

Friday Second February 1866

My dear FitzGerald

I ought to have written to you
days on days ago, to thank you for your
charming book on Charles Lamb — to tell
you with what interest and pleasure I read
it as soon as it came here — and to add
that I was hourly affected (far more so
than your modesty will readily believe)
by your intimate knowledge of those
touches of mine concerning childhood.

Let me tell you now that I have
not in the least cooled, after all, either
as to the graceful sympathetic book, or
as to the part in it with which I am
honored. It has become a matter of
real feeling with me, and I postponed its
expression because I couldn't satisfactorily
get it out of myself, and at last I came
to the conclusion that it must be left in.

My dear FitzGerald

Faithfully yours always
Charles Dickens

Percy FitzGerald Esquire

doubt had it from the M.C. himself. It is extraordinary to find Boz so accurate in his local information as to give the actual address of the M.C.
Sam, it will be recalled, was sent for the ball tickets
up to the M.C.'s house, who is described as living
in that fine and stately square, a monument of Wood
of Bath's taste, Queen's Square. It is the house
at the corner. It was Jervoise's residence, and in
later times was occupied till his death by my old
friend, Mr. Austin King. The houses are now
rather darkened in colour, by no means a blemish,
as it throws the details into fine relief, but seventy
years ago it was all bright.

END OF VOL. I